HARTMUT MICHAEL MÖLTGEN

SUPER FACTOR MONEY

Growth in times of
a new economic order

novum pro

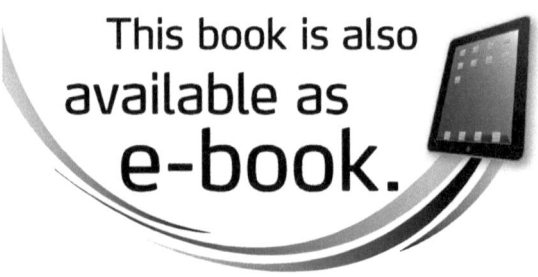

www.novumpublishing.com

All rights of distribution, including via film, radio, and television, photomechanical reproduction, audio storage media, electronic data storage media, and the reprinting of portions of text, are reserved.

© 2022 novum publishing

ISBN 978-3-99131-530-8
Cover photos: Anastasiya Mironova, Perfectvectors | Dreamstime.com
Cover design, layout & typesetting: novum publishing

Translated by Tim Wallbrecht 2021; original Superfaktor Geld
novum Verlag 2021,
Hartmut Michael Möltgen

www.novumpublishing.com

CONTENTS

Prolog 9
Introduction 14

A. NEW VERSUS OLD MONETARY SYSTEMS 19

I. Money and monetary systems 19
II. A new classification 22
   1. Asset and liability order 25
   1.1 The Asset "active" Money Order 26
   1.2 The liability "passive" Money Order 27
III. Money creation, in the now and yesterday! ... 29
IV. Modern Money Creation 31
   1. Asset money 33
   2. Passive money 39
   3. Cryptocurrency, an alternative? 42
V. The role of central banks 44
VI. Safe money, is that possible? 49
   1. Credit and savings accounts without interest? 54
   2. A financial control system
      that provides security 60
VII. Safe Money and the Banks 63
   1. The free bank as a target project 67
   2. How will the new currency be used? 71
   3. Concretely, the new Safe Currency 76
   4. Savings agreement (Ansparkreditvertrag)
      and overdraft more exactly regarded! 81
   5. Credit as the basis and promise 83
VIII. Currency and Financial Capital 84
   1. Capital and assets 86
   2. Capital and Money 89
   3. Capital and investment 90

B. MANAGEMENT AND CONTROL OF MARKETS 93

IX. The Control of Markets and Finance 93
   1. Financial control over the means of production ... 98
   2. The tool in the hands of the workers 100
   3. Are payments processed efficiently
      and in a controlled manner? 101
   4. Interest rates, price formation and
      the labour market 101
   5. Making a welfare society with the
      consciousness to respect human right- 103
   6. How are services to society
      rightfully remunerated? 109
   7. Common currency and national currencies 109
   8. Is performance-related pay being paid? 112
   9. Can the financial market be controlled at all? 113
X. Social control 117
   1. Inequalities and imbalances! 121
   2. Monetary policy, control or enrichment? 126
   3. Welfare state and basic income 135
   4. Prosperity in old age for all citizens 138
   5. Socialisation and state planning 140
   6. Monetary and sovereign communities 144
   7. Global Markets and Regional Interests
      (The Globally Acting Corporation) 145
   8. Communities and their assets 147
   9. Tax assessment: substantial or functional? 152
XI. Community control 160
   1. Legal forms of communitarisation 162
   2. Sports club and religious community 164
   3. Local markets and the new money economy 165
   4. Employment for all citizens? 168
XII. Private control 171
   1. Private capital and tax justice 175
   2. Basic income for all citizens! 179
   3. Money in private hands 183
XIII. Investments with and without capital! 185

C. LEGAL CERTAINTY – MAINSTAY OF THE SYSTEM 187

XIV. Security and equitable distribution 187
   1. Growth in freedom and security 190
   2. Gamblers, gamblers, fraudsters and the grey money market 192

XV. Money Creation, Distribution and Safekeeping! 196
   1. Private money creation versus central bank money 196
   2. The fair distribution of the proceeds! 198
   3. Tax justice and tax simplification 200

XVI. Identity and money, activators in the space of action 204
   1. The rational (physical) time space 206
   2. The relational time space 208
   3. The emotional time space 212
   4. The space of action in the structure of time 214

D. THE GROWTH-PROMOTING INTERRELATIONSHIPS 219

XVII. The Interaction of the Factors 219
   1. Regulated growth, with and without money 220
   2. Decay – Destruction – Growth 222
   3. Disturbances in the concert of factors 226
   4. Profit tax, a tax that does not prevent growth 230
   5. Growth at the different levels 234
   6. Models of economic management 238

XVIII. The digital future? 244
   1. Full employment as a goal! 247
   2. Investment today and tomorrow 250
   3. Growth factors in the digital age! 253
   4. Statistics as a planning aid? 256
   5. AI research and Industry 4! 259

    6. Model and paradigm 260
XIX. Sustainability in Finance 262
    1. Financial cycle and humanity 265
    2. The cycle, the basis for sustainable
       economic activity 267
    3. Disruptive influences on sustainable
       financial cycles 272
    4. Sustainability and justice! 275

Summary 279
Epilogue 282
Bibliography 295

PROLOG

"Money must be something divine. Or is it rather something demonic?"
(Oberhuber 2018)

For the Romans it must have been something divine, otherwise they would not have minted their money in the temple, in the temple of Juno, also called Moneta. The newly emerging monotheistic religions at the time of the Romans were more reserved about money. Nevertheless, the trade with money in as well as with these religions has spread more and more and determines meanwhile all large national economy.

The managers in the large and small companies strive for growth, the company has to come up each year with a higher profit than in the previous year, the balance sheets are to expand, the funds that flow reflect ever higher totals.

Regarding growth, the question is not only what percentage of growth, expressed in monetary terms, we can expect, strive for or describe as real. We must also ask ourselves how growth is measured if we want to scale it quantitatively so that the results can be used for valid forecasts and planning.

In my book "Sustained Growth," I have already pointed out that the general indication as an increase in GDP expressed in percent is not sufficient and, moreover, can lead to false associations. Proposed for my part therefore in the alternative to it a reference to the work performance!

Growth as productivity increase generated by money, work and knowledge can lead with a certain work performance to definable measurement numbers, which can also help to understand the problems arising again and again with the distribution of the economically brought in profits of an economy and to distribute the profit fairly. Those who continue to search for new measures can also refer, for example, to the work of Samans. Samans contrasts GDP with the alternative measure IDI.

The IDI (Inclusive Development Index) does not only include pecuniary data in the index, which makes it a better representation of reality, but it is also not as easy to determine.

Apart from the problem of how to measure growth, we must also keep in mind the problem of relative growth. When growth mania and even growth in principle are attacked by various authors, this usually refers to growth measured in GDP, not to growth through increased productivity.

If productivity per person is increased, this may well lead to a sensitive loss in GDP if there is a simultaneous decline in population growth, even though everyone has to work less to fulfill their desires. In addition, growth is generally to be regarded as punctual, since growth and decay always take place next to each other punctually assigned in certain limitable areas.

Money and financial capital, that can help to generate and secure economic growth. Money is for example in the field area of the finance capital as growth factor in the position to finance the energy necessary for a project and to build up with it ordered structures, order capital. One could also see in this the transformation of the factor of money into that of energy, and thus the possession of energy reserves obtained through money. How this happens, could happen, or should happen, is to be discussed here and in the planned subsequent volumes with the correspondingly assigned factors, in the present 1st volume with money and financial capital, in the 2nd volume with knowledge and educational capital, in the 3rd volume with labor and human capital, in the 4th volume with the always necessary resources and the corresponding physical capital, as well as in the 5th volume with energy and order capital, also representable as negative enthalpy. In the 6th volume then the growth is to be regarded in the interaction of the different factors as in the tension field of the relational cycles developing, reflecting itself in the economic cycles.

Regarding the concept clarification still a few words to the growth! We know growth first of all also from the biology, even though growth phenomena can be observed in crystallography. For growth processes in biology, it is also typical that different substances can initiate and promote growth, the so-called growth hormones. Here, of course, the economic growth phenomena should be the topic. Nevertheless, the question should be allowed what growth is from the basic point of view in the different scientific disciplines and by what it is stimulated. Growth is not simply multiplication, which we indeed also observe in growth, it is always also information-controlled, moreover we need energy and resources, whereby this all takes place in a temporal development process, which builds up new order structures. The information control also requires the possibility that external factors can have an influence on it. This is only possible if sensors and mediators like receptors intervene in a mediating and interpreting way. In this context, money is something like a mediator that is almost indispensable in our economic systems today, even if it is not the sole factor for growth and prosperity in our society and even not a necessary factor. Even if money is neither necessary nor sufficient for lasting growth, it is extremely useful and helpful in maintaining our current economic systems and it is hard to imagine life without it. In contrast, knowledge and information are to be classified as essentially necessary, since without knowledge content and information no growth is possible. Growth in economy is generally determined by 5 factors, of which money is only one. Information, energy, resources and the input of a work performance must be necessarily present. If we consider for the explanation of economic growth first the factor money more near, then the other factors are to be assumed as in sufficient measure present. This volume is the first volume of a planned series, so one or two important pieces of background knowledge are touched on but not elaborated in detail. Much can only be adequately presented in subsequent volumes, the interrelationships only in the last volume, in which the emergence of cycles is also to be discussed. What part the 5 factors of growth have in the observable cycles, to know, becomes perhaps important to arrive at a new model for economic growth. Each factor forms a basic approach for causal and correlative considerations and, moreover, for the study of interconnected relations such as the feedback loop (also known as the control loop). In each case, new equilibrium platforms are to be considered in macroeconomic terms. The equilibria are stabilized by accumulated factorial forces. In the 1st volume now the factor money with the associated finance capital is to be taken into the focus, even if this is exactly the factor which is not essentially necessary and in certain respects even arbitrary! Money can compensate the absence of other factorial forces to a limited extent, nevertheless, it is to be assumed with the consideration of the individual factors that the remaining 4 factors can act in sufficient measure! The interfactorial interactions, always also considered, are to be worked off only later sufficiently justifiable. Thereby only the temporal course can be considered fully in its own dynamics, evident in the upswing and in the downswing, they are thereby the counterparts to the growth and the decay of a special form of construction and destruction of ordered structures. Due to which conditions the cycles in the temporal sequence and in the deflections change, must change, this cannot be discussed here.

Just as the downturn with decay and destruction increases the entropy, so an upturn with growth and building of new orders decreases the entropy. In all of this, information is of central importance, as innovation, in the construction plan, in the business plan and, in the tendency, also in random patterns, which in ordered structures can be built in. In the last volume, there will also be space to examine growth as an all-encompassing phenomenon, starting from the growth phenomena in nature up to the economic growth phenomena, for comparability, perhaps also to take nature as a model in individual cases, as this is generally the goal of bionics, so far unfortunately only used as an application in technology.

Money is the factor that plays only a marginal role in natural growth processes, if at all, because it itself owes its existence only to social agreement. In addition, the commercialization of the economy through the factor of money entails a shift from life-value to money-value interactions, and in this respect, it cannot be equated with the tendency towards higher qualities of life. Higher prosperity may be due to higher diversification and the support of this by the accelerator money in the exchange of goods or in the provision of services. In this respect, one can say that if money did not yet exist, it would have to be invented as soon as possible, would then also have the chance to exclude from the beginning all the mistakes in the construction of money which still burden it.

Since money is versatile and variable, even if not by itself, but because of convention, it can easily be accumulated in hoarded form. Accumulated money is also known as capital, more specifically here as financial capital.

Capital can take very different forms of existence as assets, which is why we don't just talk about the capital, it can be transformed, comparable to the different forms of energy, which can, after all, be transformed into each other. Just as one can transform electrical energy into kinetic energy, one can also transform financial capital into real capital, educational capital, human capital or order capital, if suitable interactable structures and energies meet. Interactable structures like hormones in organic systems may not only exist in biology. In the economic contexts to be addressed here, the corresponding controllable development process is co-determined above all by labor and money. Whether in the economic contexts to be dealt with here interacting structures are to be found which are comparable with those in biology, this may be put here only as a question. The focus should first be on the interaction between the single factor in our economies, in this case money, and growth in a definable economic structure. First of all it is important to distinguish clearly between natural factors and arbitrary factors. Money, as said, is not a natural factor because, unlike other factors, it plays no role in growth phenomena in nature not controlled by humans, phenomena over which humans exert no influence. This is precisely why it is the first factor to be examined for its importance in economic growth phenomena!

INTRODUCTION

"Permanently it is about money: in such trivial processes as paying at the supermarket checkout, looking at the bank account or planning."

(Kremer, 2018)

Money, as we know it today, has 3 fundamentally different functions according to M. Miller:

1. the value storage function
2. the value measurement function and
3. the means of payment function.

In the discussion, these functions are already in the focus of economists of the Austrian school. Miller now also points out that the store-of-value function is probably the most important function and is in acute danger. He is correct in also noting that it does not matter whether money is stored and held as cash or in bits. At the same time, capital created by the accumulation of money is nothing other than accumulated cash and digitally stored money, i.e. money collected and then stored. Therefore, credit cards and debit cards that draw on stored money can also be used like money. The storage of money in banks suffers, of course, when interest and expense accounts devalue the money and thus the money itself loses value faster than rust destroys iron. The storage function is now also a kind of exchange insofar as it is not the current exchange of value that plays a role, but the time-delayed exchange of values. The value measurement function, on the other hand, represents an exchange value in non-real space, which, however, can become a real exchange value in the exchange between real and unreal world. The unreal world is also, on closer examination, not quite as unreal as at first sight. As unreal we would like to list here all those phenomena which influence the physical time space but are superficially not real scalable in it.

Now capital as a real usable medium of exchange seems to exert a special attraction not only for the actors at the market places especially the financial market places, but also for economists and social philosophers like Marx and Piketty. Without money, however, the financial capital addressed here would not exist at all, which is why money must be addressed first after all. Is it possible to explain capital and even to work out the laws of capitalism without knowing and understanding the origin and function of money? Probably not! Therefore, here the attempt to work up this as compactly as possible!

If the *german* economist Thomas Mayer in his book "The new order of the money" in the introduction assumes that in panel discussions, in which he participated, among so-called experts … "hopeless confusion about the simplest terms prevailed", then it is truly necessary to consider these terms here more exactly, particularly since this book addresses itself not so much to the experts as rather to the normal citizen. The latter finally wants to know how money and capital can be used to stimulate growth processes in the economy in order to increase prosperity.

What is money? That would be the first question to be answered. According to Mayer, the two sources from which the answer can be derived are manifested in the following views: For some, money is a special commodity that has become a means of exchanging economic goods through social convention. For others, money is merely a measure of the debt we owe to fellow human beings who have left us an economic good. Perhaps, in sacred-legal terms, the compensation of a debt is even the origin of money in the first place. Money as a commodity or money as a debt, this puts two contrary views in mind to what money usually seems to be for people. I would like to counter this with a third, a mediating definition: Money has become an equivalent for work performed in the form of goods or services. This expresses the appreciation for these labor services, so that this money itself can pay off debts. This always creates a creditor-debtor relationship, even when goods and money are exchanged at the same time. If the seller gives a good, for example a box of chocolates, to the buyer, he expects money from the buyer in return. The seller is the creditor and the buyer the debtor. The settlement is achieved with money, in any case a kind of promissory bill, which is then passed on as money, for example to buy cocoa powder or even a newspaper. As a transferable promissory bill, this bill can in principle remain in circulation forever, unless it contains an imprinted mark for cancellation. This can be a fixed date or just the registration code, to which a corresponding date has been added, on which the bill becomes invalid as a promissory bill, perhaps because the loan then becomes due, or the debt that still exists has to be readjusted. With the nowadays very widespread creation of money by means of a loan, the date for invalidation is also fixed, whereby as a rule not exactly the bill is returned which was paid out when the loan was granted. Generalizing, therefore, only money not tied to a loan can remain in circulation forever, so to speak, without an official expiration date.

Subsequently, the question arises as to what capital is and, connected with this, what the interest is that one may expect for money and capital.

If we first assume that capital is created by the accumulation of money, the idea that saving is the basis for capital formation and lending is obvious. In many cases, the interest on capital made available has now been as a reward for the associated renunciation of consumption. But this interest can only be measured by the scarcity of the capital available, as Keynes already points out. "The owner of capital can receive interest because capital is scarce, just as the owner of land can receive rent because land is scarce" (Keynes, 1974).

Here, artificially created scarcity by producers and traders must be distinguished from the natural scarcity of resources and all other commodities, which derive their value not from the scarcity of a labor input but from a scarcity beyond labor inputs. Keynes does not address this essential distinction, which was not really an issue at the time of the 1st Industrial Revolution and before, and this was because natural scarcity was not general, but rather marginal in limited areas. This has already changed in the course of the 2nd Industrial Revolution and will only change fundamentally in the age of the Internet of Things. The more capital-intensive production becomes and the more this capital also yields corresponding returns, the more capital will accumulate, and the scarcity will dissolve.

We can now also regard capital as an accumulation of promissory bills, promissory bills that have not yet been redeemed, or as a promissory bill that has been created by the owner of capital via a loan at his expense by receiving money from a loan contract. Accordingly, capital does not have to arise from a savings behaviour, with which an essential obstacle in the form of scarcity is not fundamentally eliminated but is nevertheless no longer present in the exclusivity assumed so far. The loss of the previous scarcity in the "safe money system", which will be explained in more detail, means that capital can be made available more easily and growth can thus be triggered more readily by the factor money.

Both high savings and cheap loans can reduce the scarcity of capital. If capital is no longer scarce, the willingness to pay high interest rates for it decreases to the point where loans can only be accommodated with zero interest rates. However, the willingness to give away capital without interest income can only be encouraged with appropriate hedges. A lack of inflation, for example, is an indication of the secure return of funds provided over the long term. Likewise, deposit insurance can help create confidence, confidence that the money borrowed will be repaid. But trust and security are also created by private-law protection through contracts that secure a work performance, as in the case of "safe money," which will be discussed in more detail later.

As a rule, there should be no money stored and kept anywhere in a money system based on credit, since money in circulation always represents a debt relationship. Stored money that is in the piggy bank is comparable to the promissory bill in the chest of drawers that has not been redeemed. There is always, even if only virtually, a creditor and a debtor. If I receive 100 euros as payment for a good in a business transaction, I am the creditor of the good and my counterpart, who gave me money for it, acts as debtor until the exchange of the good for the money received dissolves this debt relationship. The money stands for a promissory bill that is triggered with labor services or goods. If money is withdrawn from circulation, the debt relationship nevertheless continues to exist unless the debt value shown on a banknote is declared void by declaration or by law. It is precisely this invalidation of money by declaration or law that should be ruled out in the case of secured money.

A. NEW VERSUS OLD MONETARY SYSTEMS

I. Money and monetary systems

"It is an old and tempting trap the believe that only the strong arm and single mind of '"Despotic Power"' can really generate loyalty in politics and credibility in finance."'
(Felix Martin: Money, p. 182, 2015)

Whether we conceive of money as a pure medium of exchange or as credit money, a monetary system always emerges that is to be characterised by the use and creation of money. Eucken differentiates the classical view that money is either pure medium of exchange or credit money by taking the money paid for a commodity as a promissory bill with the delivery of the commodity and contrasting this with the exchange, whereby money becomes a commodity or also the money created by credit. Accordingly, Mayer summarises Eucken's monetary order into three points: 1. money becomes a commodity upon exchange, 2. money is created as a promissory bill upon delivery, and 3. money is created by the lender. This points out essentials of a monetary system: 1. there must be a defined process of creation for money, and 2. there must be a generally accepted use of money.

Regardless of this systematic division, one can ask how money came into being, whether as a medium of exchange or as an acknowledgment of debt.

This does not yet capture the poles of power from which the system-determining forces radiate. One of the centres of power that form a pole of force is state power, which can put appropriate money into circulation. Other centres of power are formed by private economic forces, which were initially reluctant to enter the market, but are now increasingly doing so with their own money creations. The question arises whether the citizen can thus take back his money, a money which, after all, ultimately represents his labor power.

Let us return to the question of what money is: According to Eucken, from whom Mayer derives his classification, all existing money systems are mixed systems of commodity money, state debt money and some kind of private credit money.

Mayer simplifies the whole thing even further by distinguishing only between systems of asset money and systems of liability money, following the accounting rules. According to this, one can then distinguish between asset money systems and liability money systems in the different money systems.

Historically, money first saw the light of day as asset money. Just as lands were given as fiefs for merits earned in previous campaigns, money was given for services rendered at court and also for goods delivered by citizens, thus creating active money for the citizen's hand. Passive money, on the other hand, entered the scene mainly with the creation of exchange offices and banks, especially central banks. Thereby, in the last historical phase, money is issued by the central banks to the licensed commercial banks as credit. Thus, we have also already highlighted 2 of the 4 positions in the asset-liability money system. In addition to asset money and central bank money, Mayer's table also shows commodity money and giro money.

Commodity money is clearly of a private nature, and a closer look will show that giro money is also of a private nature. Pure asset money and central bank money, on the other hand, are government money. If we now view the historical development in the money market systems as an evolutionary development, we can record a sequence which begins with commodity money in simple barter societies and, in the second stage, via the active money of the rulers as a means of payment, then sees the light of day in the following third stage as central bank money, in order to arrive in the fourth stage at the conclusion as Giralgeld, a privately created money, to dominate the market. Even if the trade with money was once such with commodity money, this is not a proof that the barter trade is the beginning of the trade and the money in itself. Money can also be an offering as a substitute for goods and be used to pay off a debt, and was used in exactly the same way, among other things.

If Thomas Mayer now demands a pure asset money system as the New Money System, this is a step backwards from the point of view of evolution, even if the analyses of Mayer himself are very brilliant and bring to light new findings in detail which make his preference for the asset money system quite understandable. The current state of affairs, with a mixed system of primarily state and private passive orders, is certainly not the best of all conceivable orders, but neither is the regression to the active money order; rather, we should follow evolution all the way to the last step and provide the assistance needed to reach the final stage of a pure private passive money order. To avoid misunderstandings, it should be noted that even if the private passive money system is at the end of an evolutionary development, other systems will still persist alongside it. Private credit certainly existed in Babylonian times, but there was no banking system in the modern sense. Even the exchange offices, which existed up to the time of the Roman empire partly only as table in the temple district, were not yet banks in the today's sense, although as precursors to be classified. The foundation of the Bank of England in the 17th century represents a quantum leap with regard to the conception of money, in which John Locke, according to Martin, played a considerable role. The next step to be hoped for in the 21st and in the 22nd century could be a kind of paradigm shift towards a denationalisation of the previous money creation by the new money creation of free banks and private financial institutions as private internationally operating financial institutions with contractual security of the customers money!

II. A new classification

"Asset money is endowed with the confidence of users that it will be accepted by other users as a medium of exchange. Passive money, on the other hand, is a financial instrument that can take on the character of a debt or equity instrument."

(Thomas Mayer: The New Order of Money, pp. 25-26, 2014)

As already mentioned, Thomas Mayer distinguishes between the asset money order and the liability money order. Here, the asset money order (active money order) includes commodity money and asset money. In contrast, under the liability money order (passive money order), Mayer lists giro money and government central bank money.

Let us take the table drawn up by Mayer and look at the whole thing in terms of the four fields listed in it: He assigns two fields to the asset money order in the first column: 1. commodity money and 2. asset money. In the 2nd column, he assigns 2 further fields under the liability money order: 3. the giro money and 4. the government central bank money. Thus, position 1. and 3. are in one row, i.e. commodity money and giro money. Asset money and central bank money are in the row below. Commodity money and scriptural money emphasize the private origin of money creation, while asset money (2) and central bank money (4) emphasise the government's role in money creation. As already mentioned, the following sequence can be used to describe the phylogenetic stages in the development towards a modern monetary economy:

A: Goods were exchanged even before money existed, with which, however, exchange then became easier. Before the introduction of money, gold, among other things, was used as an exchange equivalent, Gold as weighable precious metal, and then derived from is money introduced as intermediate step in the barter trade and/or replacement for the commodity for the redemption of debt and expiation.

B: Afterwards we come to the asset money, in that a ruler formed countable coins from the medium of exchange gold, which was still traded as commodity, by means of a coinage and thus the asset money was created.

C: It was not until much later, that central banks were founded, which initiated the transition from asset money to state central bank money as credit money. In the course of the 17th century, the Bank of England felt compelled to introduce paper money in order to prevent the melting down of coins, because many times the metal value was higher than the coin value.

D: Only in the last century the detachment of the credit money from the state institutions developed, without ever having fully detached itself from it until today, the Giralgeld developed.

E: Therefore, the last step the total detachment of the private credit money creation from state defaults within a legally regulated money system should be implemented as immediately as possible, with which the four fields are dissolved then lastingly, by dipping into a growth spiral. The optical clarification is to be represented here by a tabular listing of the development series as a graphic substitute. The fields follow each other in a spiral, beginning with field 1 in the primeval time and ending with field 4 in the present time.

Field 1: The commodity for the settlement of debts!
Field 2: The coin to the settlement of the debt!
Field 3: Paper money for the dissolution of debt!
Field 4: The credit card (the cell phone) to the settlement of debts!

In the today's system the 4 fields still exist side by side, the commodity as exchange object and object for the settlement of debts, the coin as part of an outdated asset money system and the paper money as part of an asset money system and as convertible credit bill in the passive money system, as well as credit card and cell phone in the transition to the purely credit-oriented passive money system!

If one follows the historical expiry in the way explained before, then at the end of the historical development the legally secured passive money system in private administration should stand. Now it is not to be assumed that the other money systems disappear, it concerns only an evolutionary final state, which does not exist without the predecessors, these also does not have to eliminate completely. The very fact that a commodity money still exists, starting from the "primitive culture" to the most sophisticated forms of modern civilization in the private exchange among friends. Nor is the emergence of passive money to be equated with the emergence of debt. The debt in the civil-legal sense and before also already in the sacral sense probably exists, since Homo sapiens entered the world stage. The passive money system arises only with the banks and the central bank credit, which holds the commercial banks in the harness of the regulated money creation at the reins. The reins, which were initially held tightly with the money reserves, were loosened considerably with the withdrawal of a gold backing. For the complete unblocking of money creation by commercial banks, there is still a lack of rules that can prevent the limitless creation of new money. Only appropriate rules can guarantee the necessary limitation of borrowing. If, in the absence of interest rates, hedging requirements are also inadequate, it will be difficult to limit borrowing.

1. Asset and liability order

If we take the barter trade in gold, this is an asset-liability exchange, since one commodity is exchanged for another on the asset side. commodity exchanged from the assets. This is still true after the minting of coins turned the weighable commodity "gold" into a countable commodity "money". Even in the purely gold-backed paper currency, one could still speak of a commodity currency insofar as one could exchange these banknotes for gold at any time. How the currencies are to be classified in the times of the partial cover, that becomes then already somewhat more complex and thus more difficult in the right classification.

In any case, the asset money system is based on existing values and not on the creation of these values. In addition to existing tangible assets, however, money that is not based on tangible assets but purely on conventions and secured by commitments can also be booked as an asset. If money is provided by a state institution without securing this with a credit agreement, this can work if every citizen is granted the same amount of money or if services for the state are remunerated with money created for this purpose without a credit agreement. But attention, even if everyone receives the same money quantity with a money reform, the starting conditions are nevertheless by far not the same for all, rather already with same payment for comparable achievement. Existing tangible assets and generally non-pecuniary capital can easily be converted into financial capital, so that the equilibriums can already shift considerably within a few days in the case of a monetary reform and the new millionaires can also be quickly identified in the new currencies. Asset money is also the gold or generally precious metal, if it is used as means of payment and for the storage of claims from any kind of legal transactions.

All money created by means of credit, on the other hand, is passive money and gives rise to the passive money order, but let us first take a closer look at the asset money order in general.

1.1 The Asset "active" Money Order

If we go back in history to the beginnings of monetary systems, to the first money creations, we dive into a cosmos of barter transactions and commodity currencies. The simple barter trade moved at first certainly fully in the private responsibility of private persons, this also still, after it became naturalised to exchange the goods no longer directly, but to use valuable precious metals as intermediate stage with the exchange. The commodity gold was finally transformed into easily countable gold pieces with coinage for better handling. Money, however, is not in itself a commodity, but a social convention, and thus a social achievement.

The social convention can be enforced by a ruler for his sphere of influence, but it can also be enforced on a smaller scale by active groups, as in the case of free money in the "Wörgl" model experiment. A brief but essential description is given by Kennedy, who also describes other comparable experiments and approaches.

Kennedy's different approaches to a new monetary order can all be attributed to an asset-based money order, which is also where the historical tragedy is hidden. Kennedy probably considered the credit-based passive money order to be indefensible only because it was irrevocably associated with interest and compound interest. However, if it were possible to keep interest transactions out of the liability money order, I could well imagine a change of mind in Kennedy as well, so that she might welcome a liability money order based on interest-free credit. The First Experiments cited by Kennedy, however, clearly fit into the asset money order. Nevertheless, the possible turn to a passive money order should not be ruled out here in these approaches.

1.2 The liability "passive" Money Order

Active money always involves institutions which, according to their position of power, are able to put into circulation a kind of free money in the language of Gesell, or in the diction of the 21st century a helicopter money, or to supply a bureaucratic apparatus with the necessary money. Only because of the special position of power of the financiers can this money be sure of acceptance by the citizens in their region. Passive money, on the other hand, gains its acceptance primarily through the underlying loan contract and is created today by the commercial banks, in private loans without or with the most diverse hedges contractually create a money that is given a limited life by the term of the loans. However, the partial linkage back to the central banks and the fractional reserve holding in the conclusion of private loans disrupts and dilutes the purely private character of this private lending business. On the one hand, private character is diluted via the central bank's hedging, and on the other hand, the splitting off of 1 % of the loan amount causes the money thus generated to lose value with each round of lending. This loss must be added to the loss due to inflation, so that a loss of at least 2.5 % per year must be expected, assuming inflation of up to 2 %. If we want a stable monetary system, these losses should be excluded. But how can these losses be minimized or eliminated? Fractional reserves can be prohibited by law, as was the case under Roman law. Inflation, on the other hand, cannot be prevented in principle neither by law nor by the activities of the central bank. However, it is possible to think of price formation limits in relation to the actual labor time spent or to use the labor time spent as an equivalent for the value of money.

One problem with passive money is correctly worked out by Mayer. Passive money always requires collateral or guarantors, with the state often being brought into play as the ultimate guarantor. This puts forward and reinforces the view that a passive money system can only work if it relies on state guarantees. Thomas Mayer, however, rightly rejects this state guarantee. If we now replace state protection by equivalent private protection, the passive money system appears in a different light. In this way, too, only total decoupling from the state system is possible. A private institution can indeed bring money onto the market, but as asset money always only in a limited range of validity or in dependence on other currencies, to the extent that these are not freely convertible currencies or so-called cryptocurrencies. If, on the other hand, the asset money is issued by state institutions, this leads to a clear dependence on these institutions; after all, gifts can also create undesirable dependencies.

In a nutshell, helicopter money from the state side can satisfy the money needs of an economic region, but never the money needs of the world economy as a whole, it will always remain linked to a specific region and its power structure of a state nature. Thus, the money is not really safe, currency reforms due to value losses are already pre-programmed and thus the money is by no means stable and sustainably secured.

III. Money creation, in the now and yesterday!

"For in every country of the world, I believe, the avarice and injustice of princes and sovereign states, abusing the confidence of their subjects, have gradually diminished the actual quantity of metal originally contained in their coins."

(Adam Smith, 1776)

Money exists today as cashless money in bank computers, but also as coinage and as paper money. Predecessors were sometimes giant stones, shells and other rare and less rare natural products.

From history, coins are known from almost every era of recorded history. Not in all cultures were precious metals used as a means of payment; ethnological studies show that even stones and shells were used like our money today. This shows that it is not the value of the medium of exchange that is decisive, but the exchange value attributed to it. Whether stone, precious metal, shell, or specially prepared paper with an official imprint, there must always be a social agreement that assigns a value to the medium of exchange. Croesus was the first to mint gold coins, thus establishing his immense wealth. With the gold coin one had an exchange value in the hand, which could be used fast by counting for the acquisition of the different goods with different value measurements. This money was created virtually out of nothing, even if the content of precious metal carried a certain material value. Simplified one could say that here active money, out of the nothing was created, quasi due to the authority of the ruler. Only due to a trust basis between the creator of the money and the customer, who uses the money, this money receives its value. A second strand from which money emerges is the debt, which had to be recorded in history so that repayment could be guaranteed. Money in this context is rather an object that is there to keep the memory alive, a mark in the accounting. Since this money is not actively presented, but stands only in the books, thus passively only present, and as not activated book money, one speaks here also of passive money.

Passive money gets its value from the confidence in the enforceable contractual text of a loan. Money does not grow and is not found in the ground; it is the product of a social convention. The corresponding conventions are primarily handed down and are usually renegotiated from time to time behind closed doors. Even in our Western democracies, the financial industry is reluctant to show its cards, and the responsible protagonists can at best show good academic degrees, but no democratic legitimacy. This is the central problem of our current monetary economy, which is neither a pure asset money system nor a pure liability money system, nor does it have any legitimacy. Since money creation has to reckon with both state and private influences and, moreover, bears the features of both an active money order and a passive money order, the complexly interwoven strands are difficult to distinguish. Both a clear active money system and a clear passive money system would be preferable to the current system in terms of transparency close to the citizen.

IV. Modern Money Creation

"The growing unease about the state of the existing monetary order is reflected in fundamental criticism. It is directed not only against the monetary policy of the European Central Bank, which is accused of self-empowerment with covert government financing and the creeping expansion of its competence, but also in general against money and our current financial system!"

(Kowalski, 2018)

We live in the 21st century in a time in which money, rightly or wrongly, threatens to lose all reference to substance values. Digitization has already largely displaced cash, but how is money created in the first place and is purely digital currency the future? Perhaps the purely digital currency is only the future because it is easier to produce, since there is no longer any need for money presses or mints. Regardless of the new possibilities of digitization, we should first take a closer look at the money creation processes inherited from the era of gold-backed currencies. For many years, the student book "Geld und Geldpolitik" (Money and Monetary Policy) published by the Bundesbank conveyed the image of controlled money creation by means of a multiplier, which can limit it and thus ensure a stable currency! The reserve maintenance of 2% was to control according to it with the multiplier 50 the credit creation by the commercial banks and to limit it to the 50-fold of the reserve maintenance. In the meantime, experience has led to the realization that this is no guarantee of limiting lending. Even the current minus 4% interest rate on central bank deposits has no real restraining effect on lending. The lifetime working time available to everyone is more of a serious limitation on borrowing in the case of the safe money NIM or Moneta envisaged here. The granting of credit in the current traditional lending business is more likely to be restricted by ever-increasing requirements for the banks' equity capitalisation, although the sense of such measures is only superficially apparent. If one takes a look at the high stakes of borrowed capital at the banks, the level of equity capitalisation will only be of marginal relevance. In this respect, a multiplier is of no help at all. Braun now writes about the new edition of the Schülerbuch after the last financial crisis in 2008: "Under the new monetary policy regime of quantitative easing, the multiplier myth of the old Schülerbuch had had its day." It is interesting that this new independence of central banks from the myth has now been celebrated by one of the representatives, indeed by the "Bank of England", with a photo in the basement of the bank, with a photo in which the picture sideways depicts the storage of gold reserves. Does this perhaps mean that one would prefer to return to the old gold currency? Moreover, the Bundesbank's new Money Museum even provides a gold bar to touch, perhaps so that the value of money can also be tactilely grasped by touching the gold bar. Of course, the process of today's money creation is also explained in the student book and in the museum, but whether it is comprehensible for students, where it is used and at what place in the school canon the museum and student book find their place, that is just a question. Whether the desire for a new edition of a gold-backed currency was buried with the retrieval of gold reserves from abroad is also a question that cannot be answered.

Since the money supply is now largely determined by commercial bank loans, the central bank is also increasingly losing control over the money creation process as a whole. In addition, cryptocurrencies, which are springing up like mushrooms, are taking over more and more shares of the banking business without thus becoming fully valid currencies. Since cryptocurrencies can only take over partial tasks of a currency, they do not endanger national currencies in principle, unless they are granted the status of a fully recognized and accepted currency by the state, in which case the question of value stability must be raised anew in any case.

Central bank money, which does not originate from reserve holdings, will recently contribute to long-term devaluations by means of inflation, for example, through actions such as QE. One could now understand the devaluation of money, regardless of how it comes about, as a counterpart to the wear and tear of commodities. In the case of money, however, this is by no means a natural process and, moreover the regulated devaluation, which is actually to be expected is then missing. Since the regulated devaluation would be attainable only with a pure central bank currency, which could guarantee a hundred percent active currency, a possible alternative is the full currency. In a fully valid and solely authorised full currency, the asset money can be controlled by the national central bank without any problems; the only question is whether one wants it that way?

1. Asset money

If the central bank prints money and makes it available to the government in office, for example through the treasury, all civil servants and employees in government service could be paid with it. In this way, money can be put into circulation for everyday payment transactions in a very simple way. The general use is then guaranteed by the fact that this money put into circulation and only this money is accepted to pay the debts of the citizens to the state. Whether the money thus created by the state is sufficient to cover the money needs for all the transactions of the citizens may not be so easy to grasp and to control. In such an asset-based money system, central banks and governments would be called upon to monitor money flows and to maintain a balanced money supply with sufficient replenishment, if necessary, by expanding the bureaucratic apparatus. Such an asset-based money system thus presupposes an extensive state apparatus and runs counter to the demand for a lean state. In principle, a currency fully backed by gold can also be regarded as a currency with asset money, since money is issued 1 : 1 against gold without, ideally, creating money via loans. Since the creation of money in Bitcoin is comparable in process terms with the fully backed gold currency, the money is ultimately created via an exchange process, albeit not based on tangible assets, but directed by algorithms, the "mining", comparable vocabulary is used here in reference to the gold mining in the gold mine. In this mining, however, no tangible assets are created, not even real debt instruments. A major disadvantage of "mining" is the high energy consumption and the fact that with the expansion of the decentralised Bitcoin network ever higher computer capacities are required, in this respect hardly suitable for building sustainable financial systems.

Another of many ways to establish money as asset money in an economy could be to give money away as paper money, coin money or letter money. Such a procedure then makes money available to every citizen without imposing credit on him, a kind of helicopter money that is not credit-based.

Now, if this is a certain pre-determined amount of money that is made available to each citizen, it is quite possible, with the right calculation, to put enough money into circulation so that there is sufficient liquidity for the various activities. In order not to pump too much money into circulation, there must be rules on how the money issued can flow back again. If the amount of money per capita is to be kept equal, then the money issued must be retrieved at the latest after death.

One possibility that suggests itself is to retrieve this from the inheritance. Realistically, however, one will have to assume that not everyone will still have so much money on hand at the end of their lives, that it will still be possible to repay the sums of money received in the course of their lifetimes, even partial sums. Of course, inheritance tax can recoup some of the money assessed per capita. In principle, the state will have to recoup the active money put into circulation through other taxes, and inheritance taxes offer only one of these possibilities. If the bulk of the taxes is melted down in favour of a profit tax, an accounting can also be made with acquired licenses as well as lease and rental income. This makes the calculation more transparent, fairer and easier to perform. If we now assume for the sake of better calculability that there is only one profit tax and that all asset money that has been issued is to be recouped via it, then we only have to calculate how much money has to be regularly siphoned off by taxes so that the money pumped into the market comes back again. If we simplify our basic conditions to the effect that every citizen receives 600,000 euros from the state over the course of his or her lifetime free of charge for free disposal and must likewise pay off 600,000 euros via taxes, then this could close the money cycle. We could go on calculating here and certainly get a reasonably satisfactory result, but who controls all this? Even for a self-regulating control loop, it seems to me that there is still not enough controlling here. Banking supervision and the ECB are already assuming more and more control functions within the European framework in the euro zone, but unfortunately not to the extent and with the objectives that would be desirable and necessary in a pure asset money system. Moreover, democratic feedback is lacking; mandatory reporting to parliament would be a good first approach.

Another option is to rely more on self-regulation but appeals alone are certainly not enough. It would also be possible to use all recognised tangible assets as the basis for a currency, which would at least provide a hedge that would already offer more security than is currently the case. Gold, for example, in a custody account can also be this security. Payment cards on credit basis can appear then likewise as part of an asset money order.

The methods presented here are only some suggestions to bring money into circulation among the many possibilities that present themselves.

However, this can work well in the asset money system only at the national level, and even there, problems will arise because such a system, even in variations, is not flexible enough to be able to react quickly to all eventualities. However, in this way or by other methods, it is possible to create a pure full money of the central bank, which is not created by a loan, that is for sure, but not much more.

In the same way as before the free money, a suggestion of Gesell is bound to a socially legitimated institution, and can therefore hardly lead to a free financial economy, fits rather to a state-directed economy, but not to a market economy. This probably also led to the misunderstanding according to which many of the contemporary economists assumed that a socialist theory was presented here, which shows only marginal deviations from the Marxist doctrine. In fact, there is no socialist-communist theory here. For example, another of Gesell's proposals, that the land be understood as a kind of commons, a "free land," is not conceived as the socialisation of a means of production, as in Marxism, but as a common good of the local community and necessary to keep the market functioning. Gesell already recognized that commodities and goods that cannot be multiplied and cannot be worn out cannot achieve a fair market price. Accordingly, land as a commodity does not have the quality of a normal commodity; just as air and water it is not really a depreciable commodity, and neither is money itself.

The last of the suggested possibilities to generate active money seems to be established just in a small scale, so far still hardly noticed, over precious metal and special metal funds. Gold-Money offers a credit card as a Master Card with coverage via a precious metal deposit. By the fact that with this card completely normal purchases, even cash withdrawals are possible, the precious metal in the depot becomes quasi an everyday usable money. Withdrawals and deposits are possible in euros or U.S. dollars via a bank account, and within future times it should also be possible to process them via a Bitcoin account, as well as via other credit cards. Settlement takes place in euros or dollars, in the future perhaps also in bitcoin, which should have purely pragmatic reasons. The direct exchange of gold is also possible, which underlines the active money status. It is therefore possible to pay directly with gold here and settle any invoice in the future, although a conversion then becomes unavoidable depending on the currency in which the payment is to be made, insofar as no gold quantities are specified. The basis is the amount of stored precious metal in the respective account. Since the credit card allows subordinate settlement, it is also possible to transfer precious metals from one account to another without transporting the physical values. The computer makes it possible to trade and purchase here without weighing or transport even a gram of gold, yet in a pure gold currency. This has solved the problems of the past with gold backing of banknotes, in that the physically available precious metal stored in Zurich or Singapore is no longer weighed out immediately in each individual case but is first recorded as a claim in the IT system and then the total gold holdings are either expanded or also reduced, depending on how much gold has been ordered or sold by the customers.

The advantages of gold money are obvious, each partial amount is fully covered by the metal value, as is the total amount. The algorithm of cryptocurrencies such as Bitcoin does not provide this full coverage. A disadvantage of precious metal-backed currencies is the necessary physical storage of the precious metals registered in the deposit. Since the deposits must also be protected, this currency can become expensive due to storage and be quite specifically dangerous. Besides it could become scarce with the precious metals, wanted everyone to open such a depot and to deposit the necessary money need there in deposited precious metal. Exactly this scarcity of gold was the reason, why in the 80's of the last century the gold cover of the western currencies was abolished, whereby it was in the end anyway only a partial cover. In the meantime, of course, the question arises as to why a currency that is not backed by physical assets should be trusted at all. This would be the time when many would not only long for a secure full coverage for their means of payment, but also revive it with a new currency, and thanks to credit cards, this is also possible. But how secure will the new card currency backed by physical assets really be? In an environment with only weak legal structuring, as was the case in almost all countries outside Roman law until the Middle Ages and is still the case today in some areas on the fringes of global markets, the gold in one's hand is worth more than the contractual promise of the trading partner. With well-developed legal structures and enforceable contracts, the contractual security is sometimes worth more; in any case, even all else being equal, it carries the greater security. Whether gold, silver or any other precious metal, it can be stolen and therefore must be kept separately well secured. Purely only contractually on the person secured values are safer than the best physical values. In the case of physical values, the permanent loss of value must also be taken into account; iron, for example, loses its original value very quickly due to corrosion and is therefore not a precious metal; but even precious metals can lose their value, albeit to a lesser extent, corrode, are also subject to changes with the spirit of the times in general appreciation.

Active money will always require a closed, centrally controlled and managed user community. Money is produced and made available before the user requests or uses it.

An active money system is also conceivable within a user community on a communal level or on a purely private level, if a contractual relationship is established through membership. In the simplest case, this is the neighbourhood help association, but also the experiment of Wörgl. Moreover, the contractual commitment that usually has to be assumed in the private sector can be replaced by trust, for example trust in an algorithm. Bitcoin, as one of the best-known cryptocurrencies, can in this respect be understood as money belonging in principle to the asset money order, despite its dependence on other currencies. If the entry into the exponential phase of value growth fuels doubts that Bitcoin has no future because it is just a snowball system after all, then this should not be used as an argument for considering private currencies in general to be unsurvivable.

Confidence in a currency that is fully backed by state guarantees still seems to be more likely to the citizen nowadays, which is why the initiative for a full money in Switzerland in 2018 should be analysed with attention, even if it has failed for the time being. Book money as legal tender could solve some of the problems of current monetary policy at the national level, but probably not on a global scale.

If we now look at the history of the creation of money, we very soon come across the monopoly of money creation by the regent, the ruler and subsequently the respective government, nowadays represented by the central banks, still with the sole right to create money without cutbacks as full money, this with the full state acceptance. The government and the central bank generally determine the value of the money and the amount of money put into circulation. A fundamental change has not occurred even with the transfer of the monetary monopoly to the European Central Bank within the scope of the euro. Here, what Hayek states about the money monopoly of governments still applies: "Present policy relies in many respects on the assumption that the government has the power to create any amount of additional money it wishes and to force people to accept it. For this reason, governments will defend their rights fiercely. But for the same reason, it is also important that it be taken away from them." One way to break this monopoly is to establish private passive money.

2. Passive money

In the pure passive money system, money can only be created anew via a credit contract. While money creation by credit contract is not new, it is still not done purely in the private passive money system. The money lent should either come 100% from deposits of other customers or be 100% newly created against collateral provided by customers, i.e. newly created. Only in the case of a newly created purely private credit contract with 100% collateral is money created as safe money, and if this is a private credit contract, as assumed, one can speak of private money creation. If, on the other hand, loan money is taken from the deposits of other customers, this is not money creation and should be viewed strictly separately. All contracts with a saving phase, typical of the classic home savings contract, should be interpreted in such a way that no new money is created in the process, which is why these contracts should not be addressed here for the time being. Credit contracts without a savings phase require more collateral than contracts with a savings phase, especially since they simply create new money. This new money must be secured by contractually guaranteed work in the future or in the past if the newly created money is to be considered secure. These credit contracts should be granted without interest, which will be discussed in more detail elsewhere, but they should be secured to a limited extent by the available lifetime work performance and also be subject to fees. To avoid being enslaved by such contracts, only half of the potential working life should be allowed to be used as collateral for loans. The contracts should also be designed in such a way that, with monthly repayment in manageable instalments, these funds are accumulated and can only be used to cancel the loan at the end when the entire loan is redeemed. If the processing fees and the fee for account management are related to the amount of money to be managed, this can also be done in such a way that the fees on the credit account are calculated as a percentage of the amount of money to be managed, this way they would decrease with the reduced credit debt over the years. Without fractional retention on deposits, central bank deposits and loans could be treated with parity. The commercial bank acts only as an intermediary here, as it does in the case of savings contracts, which is why it does not have to hold cash reserves in relation to this area.

In any case, we need a move away from the partially covered banking system and fractional reserve holding, as Mayer also calls for. This can be achieved by switching to an asset money system, but better by fully covered private credit in the liability money system, to use Mayer's terminology here. In the fully covered passive money system, the potential labor output deposited in a directory should be used as reference and collateral for credit contracts. In such a register, the working time account, or better the labor service account, not only the potential future services but also the assets from previous labor services already used as collateral in the classical system should be recorded. If one calculates with potentially 1632 hours in the year (34 hours in the week), then one comes with 50 years in an employment relationship on 81,600 hours, which are available within a life span. A total of 40,800 hours of this could be used for coverage. This then also means that this represents a limit for a maximum possible coverage and thus also for the maximum loan amount. If you multiply the working hours by the value in the new currency, you get the basic credit amount that can be made available in a lifetime. For example, assuming that each hour worked by an unskilled worker is valued at 10 euros, perhaps 10 NIM in the new currency, there is a possible credit amount of 408,000 NIM available in the base version. As a rule, higher amounts are to be expected, since even the unskilled worker will have a certain amount of experience after a period of training. If this money is used to purchase real estate, the new material value can also be included in the calculation when deciding whether or not money should be made available. If the material value at the time of purchase corresponds exactly to the purchase sum made available, the loan is thus also doubly secured. If this mortgage is no longer serviced, the bank can also recover the missing money from the sale of the property. Sale proceeds and repayment contributions already paid should then be offset in such a way that the amount from the sale exceeding the loan amount is credited to the borrower's account. Any shortfall can only be made up by insurance if and when other sources have been exhausted. By requiring the insurance company to step in only as a last resort, insurance premiums should also be bearable.

It is important that the creation of money through credit agreements be secured purely under private law and that no safeguards be provided by state institutions. Private-law safeguards must be verifiable and controllable on the basis of laws enacted by the legislative branch and compliance with which should also be enforced by the executive branch through controls.

3. Cryptocurrency, an alternative?

First, the question arises as to whether cryptocurrency can also be a full currency by nature, moreover, an asset money or a liability money, before we ask about the special money creation of these digital Currencies search. What cryptocurrencies are in no case, they are no kind of full currency, they are characterized by the fact that they cannot exist without the exchange into or from a state-secured currency. Since all digital currencies, which do not originate from credits, also do not originate passive money, so the digital currencies originated up to the year 2000 can be assigned only to the active money, they originate in no way from credits, but from algorithms as with the so-called mining (Bitcoin). However, this is an active money that does not have the character of full money, which should be pointed out separately, since the terms full money and active money are often used synonymously. The first-generation cryptocurrencies are also not backed by reserves, as is discussed for Libra in the planning phase; unlike Libra, they are not stable coins. Before explaining the money creation through mining, which is known primarily from Bitcoin, the question of why and since when cryptocurrencies have existed should be briefly clarified. After the financial crisis of 2008/2009, the so-called cryptocurrencies mushroomed, the best-known example being Bitcoin. Cryptocurrencies are not created by the activities of central banks or commercial banks, but rather by the processing of algorithms, in the creation and control of blockchains in mining. Mining requires with ever longer chains, the Blockchains, also ever larger computers and beside ever more computer capacities also ever more computing time and energy! The blockchain thereby conveys a security that is solely due to the algorithm used, a value reference is missing. However, the reference to values to tangible assets of the most diverse kind was and is an essential aspect in the valuation of money up to modern times. The trust in the algorithm only became possible after the successive replacement of gold with the final detachment from the gold backing was completed in the 1980s. Thus, at the end of the 21st century, only trust in the political system remains. Of course, this raises the question of whether the current privately issued digital currencies could not be followed by digital state currencies, currencies that no longer have the character of a cryptocurrency due to the promise of unlimited state acceptance, but rather that of comparable full currencies. The ultimate safeguard here, as with all central bank money, is the taxpayer. The situation is different when large Internet corporations like Facebook announce that they will launch their own cryptocurrency on the market. Thus, international currencies are established from the beginning, but dependent on the state-backed central bank currencies, thus also secured via the taxpayer as the ultimate guarantor.

In contrast, in the safe money proposed in this book, the ultimate guarantor is not the taxpayer, but the borrower and the insurance policy taken out by the borrower, with the sovereign only having to ensure compliance with the relevant insurance policies and hedges in the last instance, as it were by law.

V. The role of central banks

"The lending rate, which is controlled by the central bank, is the most important factor in determining money creation by banks in our current monetary system"
(Thomas Mayer, p. 46, 2014)

Central banks in the current monetary system, let's get this straight in advance, not only create money, above all they control and steer the money market. The money creation can be considered banally simply by order over the press.

The money will be printed on a printing press and care will be taken to ensure that it is counterfeit-proof. However, the question now arises as to the legitimacy and legal protection with which this money is printed.

The central bank can print money, and it does so on behalf of the respective government, i.e. on behalf of the sovereign. Strangely enough, even in countries that call themselves democratic, there is no question of authorization, of legitimacy, and as a rule there is no explicit mandate from the executive, let alone a decision by a parliament, only a decision by the central bank. Neither the Fed in the U.S. nor the ECB in Europe act on a direct mandate from politicians, even though political influence is quite common when appointments are made. The independence of the central banks can also be seen as a positive factor, as it prevents a monetary policy in the interests of the politicians currently in power and can thus bring about a certain necessary stability in the money market independent of the respective political system. For this reason, central banks should even be explicitly independent of the respective current government and ensure that the money in their sphere of influence remains stable in value and, moreover, does not become scarce, so that the economy can develop and grow. Growth and no recession, that is the central banks' credo. Growth itself is not questioned, nor is the yardstick used to measure national growth. In general, growth is measured by GDP, the gross domestic product. It is not asked how this growth is generated and where the money comes from! These questions should be answered, however, if also here for the time being postponed until is clarified, how money originates at all and gets on the market.

Central banks can produce money without giving a reason for it, except that the economy stagnates without enough money in circulation. Of course, money is necessary to keep a diversified economy going on, but in many cases, this is not the real reason, but rather that the state needs new money to be able to finance expenditures, expenditures that are not always really necessary. So that this would not be too much subject to arbitrariness, at least would not give the appearance of arbitrariness, one established rules in the course of time which arose mostly from certain situations. Let us start with an action that has recently become known, namely that of buying up bonds, also known under the term "quantitative easing". The central bank does not simply print money to distribute it, but buys securities from commercial banks and pays for them with freshly printed money. This puts money into circulation, which does not remain in circulation forever, but returns after a fixed term. If the money is then to remain in circulation, securities (bonds) have to be purchased again. In this way, the central bank intervenes in the financial market, thus also supporting companies looking for sources of money, but indirectly also financing the state when government securities are bought up in addition to corporate bonds during these actions. If the money supply in circulation is to be permanently increased in this way, additional purchases will have to be made again and again, making the intervention in the financial market ever more massive. Normally, the money for such purchases should not come from the central bank, but only from citizens' savings deposits or loans provided by commercial banks. Until the maturity of the purchased securities by the central bank, this money is additionally in the market, and can then be withdrawn from the market again when it is repaid, unless new purchases compensate for this. In this respect, one could speak of a sustainable monetary policy, were there not the side effects on the market already mentioned. It should also be noted that, by selling bonds twice, the banks virtually earn twice, to name just one component in this procedure, which consumes money that does not benefit the citizens but the financial market. It is true that, with the money for securities bought up by the central bank, the banks also receive the means to deposit money with the central bank, a good deal for the central bank and an opportunity for the commercial banks to grant further loans. This system has become outdated, however, as it does not really manage lending in a market-driven way. It is true that the commercial banks have to deposit a share with the central bank for every loan they grant, which can have an inhibiting effect on lending, even if only 1% has to be deposited. Together with the requirement to hold own funds, this could subject lending to precise control, were it not for the ever-increasing potential for uncommitted capital. The question arises as to whether the additional money from the purchase programs is still needed. Nevertheless, it can be assumed that a purchase program such as the one implemented by the ECB will increase rather than reduce bank lending. The effect on the level of interest rates must also be taken into account, as the purchase of bonds by the central bank also pushes down interest rates and thus acts in the same direction as the reduction of the key interest rate and the prime rate. For example, lowering the ECB's key interest rate to 0% means that banks can borrow money from the ECB without having to pay interest. Nevertheless, the bank customer has to pay between 10% and 15% for the overdraft at most banks. Accordingly, the central bank does not directly determine the interest rate level at the bank and in other money transactions on the market, but it can lend money without interest and buy up interest-based securities! With the demand for a prescribed capital formation, it can exercise just as its influence on the commercial banks, as also with the demand with each credit a portion of 1% with the central bank to deposit, as far as this is no longer alone creator of the money. Nowadays, the central bank supplies only the cash in the form of bills and coins. Alone by the fact that with each credit round a small part of the money is diverted, immediately after it was newly created or also taken from savings, it comes to a devaluation of the money already at the source. The central bank does not really care about the value stability of the money, but about a permanent devaluation, with which it plugs the holes in the national budget, evident also at the goal of wanting to level the inflation at 2%. If we now take credit as it was originally organized and then ask again what has become of it, we must assume that in earlier times the central bank deposited all its credit in gold, which meant that you could exchange your money for gold at any time. The practice has moved further and further away from this over the years, initially with partial cover up to zero cover in the last century. Since book money became more and more widespread, a money that is only held in the account as a credit balance, that is no longer held in the form of cash, one also speaks of giral money, since then the central bank has also gradually lost the overview of the totality of the money in circulation. Central banks are increasingly concerned only with the supply of cash, which is also disappearing more and more from the scene with the advent of plastic money. This also explains why central banks in Scandinavian countries are the first to consider issuing their own digital money.

If the central bank replaces cash with its own digital money, this is asset money in the sense of the previous explanations. However, this does not mean that all money becomes asset money, since credit money will continue to dominate the market as book money. Let us therefore take a closer look at credit money. Insofar as in the further past the private banks originally If savings could only be passed on as loans, lending was dependent on the available savings deposits; only if savings rates were high could high lending rates also be achieved. In the same way, gold coverage, to the extent that it was still close to full coverage, could have a limiting effect. Since credit is now covered primarily by a promise to the future, it is important to know something about the bank's capitalization and to trust the sovereign's guarantees, especially since it is the ultimate guarantor. However, a stable-value currency is not promised in any country and certainly not kept. Gold, which was initially included in coins, was then held by central banks as the ultimate collateral to cover paper money, albeit gradually with ever smaller partial cover. In the days of full coverage, it would have been easy to keep the currency stable in value, had it not been for the incentive to devalue the currency by continuously reducing the gold reserves stored as collateral, to the benefit of the state, which was supposed to be the guardian of the currency. This was an opportunity for all commercial banks to increasingly withdraw from the central bank's loans by gaining the right to participate in money creation themselves, while only having to deposit a very small portion with the central bank as collateral, which meant that the newly created money was also immediately subjected to a devaluation process. It should be possible to create new money through credit without devaluing it during the creation process by paying out 100% of the money as stipulated in the credit agreement and repaying 100% of it at the end of the credit phase. This would also give a clearer picture of the current quantity in circulation. Of course, this also applies if the central bank is the source of all loans; after all, it could most easily compensate for losses by simply reissuing missing funds and putting them into circulation as replacements. The commercial bank, on the other hand, must be able to make up for losses with its own funds or else ask the sovereign for help.

However, the security provided by the sovereign dwindles the more the sovereign itself becomes indebted. It is time to think about new banks and central banks, for example, free central banks, which are not dependent on state bodies and follow only private contractual arrangements. In contrast to the present state central banks, the private free central bank should secure money not with state hedges and not with the last liable, the taxpayer, but only over the best of all creditworthiness hedges, the current and the already realized working power of the borrower.

VI. Safe money, is that possible?

"As early as 1921, the American economist Frank Knight, who later researched and taught at the University of Chicago, distinguished between risk and uncertainty, risk we can measure, uncertainty we cannot."

(Thomas Mayer: The New Order of Money, p. 65, 2014)

As we have seen, the central bank can only guarantee the value stability of money to a limited extent, and usually does not want to. The financial mathematician can calculate risks, but also cannot offer collateral. However, anyone who accepts money for work performed wants to be able to use it to purchase adequate other services and goods, and, if possible not only for the next few hours, but also for years to come. Money should therefore be stable in value, if possible, for all eternity. This seemed to be the case with the gold coins since Croesus, since the minted value was secured by the metal value, the value indication on the coin was only intended to facilitate the determination of value in everyday life, one no longer needed to weigh, could determine the value by counting. Therefore, the Johannisthaler, which was minted in silver, was kept equal in weight as a coin to the common gold coin in the 16th century, in order to achieve parity with the gold coin, although the precious metal was a different one. This thaler, invented 500 years ago, was still stable in value, insofar as it carried its value through the metal value in itself, and only additionally also stable in value through the convention reflected in the imprint. Money, which is created only by general conventions, whether by the central bank or the commercial bank, should nevertheless also be able to be secured in accordance with the gold coins in the Middle Ages. In the case of a system of asset money, this can be trust in the institution and its representatives, without valuable tangible assets as a hedge, the only hedge still possible. If money, like a gold coin, consists of intrinsically valuable material, this supports the basis of trust, but still presupposes a fundamental confidence in the institutions.

Precious metals can strengthen the necessary trust, as can government assurances and guarantees, but it still remains a necessary basic trust. The passive money system, on the other hand, offers contractual agreement and assurance at the private level within the framework of civil laws. If the legal certainty for private contracts is given, money can also be contractually secured at this level. Assets and income can be considered as collateral. In the case of assets, the question is, with what certainty can the borrowed money be recovered in the future? If this money is tied back to imperishable tangible assets, as in the case of the fully collateralized gold currency, I can expect with a high degree of certainty to be able to get back the previously agreed amount of gold in the future. This recommitment to gold can be maintained as long as sufficient quantities of gold are available. This clearly raises the question of the amount of money needed and the hedges that can be achieved with it. With an ever faster growing population, the need for hedging also grows, with the gold standard the need for pure gold, with silver as the standard the need for pure silver.

Another hedge can be provided by the central bank by guaranteeing the issuance of any money reclaimed for deposits made. State central banks can give these guarantees, because they create new money if necessary, in order to be able to meet the corresponding liabilities. This money can then be reclaimed from the citizen via taxes. In this way, we get a state-backed money, which, because of the state backing, can also only exist on a national level and moreover, also only offers a kind of pseudo security. The departure from the gold standard in the 80s of the 20th centuries was also the final departure from the idea that the value of money must be covered by material assets. Since at the end only a partial cover was present, the security by the central bank and the state was already for a long time only a pseudo security, since in the case of a financial crisis no timelessly valuable equivalents for the deposits are deposited with the banks, the money itself is sometimes absolutely worthless.

At the private level, money can only be secured by private collateral for loans. These should be able to be claimed anywhere and at any time, on the basis of contractual agreements. These securities, whether tangible assets or contractually guaranteed rights such as access to current income, must be precisely fixed and meticulously recorded in the contracts. Let us first ask ourselves what can secure the general values and make them convertible values. A real estate can serve as a security in case of debtor's insolvency, as it is possible to recover the missing funds by selling it. But how do you determine the sale value of a property, for example, for a date 20 years in the future? If one assumes the current market value of a property, this may exceed or even fall short of the true value. Therefore, it is proposed to take as a reference point the work that has been put into the property. The land is to be excluded here, which is why we want to start from a hereditary building plot. Since the property is subject to wear and tear, it can be assumed that after 20 years the value is lower than at the beginning of the credit period. The reduction in value can now be objectively. The easiest way to determine the current value of a building is to take into account the expenditure required after the loan has expired in order to bring the building up to the current standard compared with the equipment of 20 years ago. If this expenditure is subtracted from the initial value in monetary terms, the final value should be the current value if no maintenance expenditure made in advance is to be offset.

In addition to the maintenance expense, the expense for modernization must also be accounted for, since no one wants to do without the comforts of technical progress in 20 years' time.

If the future construction costs are calculated on the basis of the working hours expended, it will be possible to calculate both the maintenance costs and the modernization costs in 20 years' time.

The working time as the last reference point for value determinations can also be used for security, if one wants to keep the value of money stable for the future, so that in this future the same values can be created with the money as at the time of the acquisition. For this purpose, working time accounts must be kept.

Strict requirements are to be placed on the keeping of working time accounts, which are to be observed as requirements by the institutions keeping the accounts.

1. the registers must be kept in accordance with the same, uniform and comprehensible criteria.
2. working hours must be recorded as accurately as possible, both in terms of paid working hours and in terms of voluntary activities and private activities to maintain the work force.
3. in the case of working hours, in addition to chronological data, the qualification available at the time of performance shall be recorded.
4. loans, including those in other currencies, shall be recorded not only as such but also converted into the unit of labor services.
5. assets, whether real estate or machinery, as well as automobiles and other depreciating goods, shall be listed, with the corresponding converted labor time rates.
6. working hours already used in the working hours account shall be presented in a directly comprehensible manner, with regard to the hours that can still be used.
7. repayment modes and positive as well as negative occurrences are to be noted and highlighted separately.

One can now write these requirements into the preamble of any account-holding institution such as the free central banks. In the end, however, legislation will be required that additionally translates these demands into laws that can also be used to successfully control these banks. The control can be carried out by the banking supervisory authority and the national central bank, whereby it must be assumed that these central banks themselves no longer generate money, but only take over control tasks. To ensure that the free banks do not lose their freedom as a result of the controls, it must be specified exactly how these controls can be carried out without producing the transparent customer. As a matter of principle, the very extensive data records, in particular on work performance accounts, should not be disclosed unless the customer demands this with regard to his data or a court ruling calls for the disclosure of specific data for an upcoming lawsuit. The central bank's controls should initially be limited to monitoring non-credit related activities and, with respect to credit accounts, whether the bank's information obligations to its customers are being met and whether the bank's balance sheets are balanced and not inflated so that there is no threat of insolvency. In the event of a threat of insolvency, it can be assumed that neither the taxpayer nor the bank customer as account holder will be negatively affected. In the case of Safe Money, the money in the accounts, insofar as it is Safe Money, is safe even in the event of the bank's insolvency, since the accounts are taken over directly by other institutions, for example in the association of free banks (according to the agreement between the bank and the customer). Liability can be effective only within the framework of the deposit as a co-owner. Since the accounts are loaded with more or less large credits secured by work performance, there can be only one main account in the association and only one bank that holds the working time accounts with the obligation to provide evidence. In the event of a move, the assigned archives must also move with the main account. During a transition period of 1 to 2 years, it should also be possible to use a sub-account of the old main account at the bank in the new place of residence as a temporary active account.

Main loans or even lifetime loans should generally be secured through working capital accounts. This, of course, requires that all liabilities and performance evaluations, including hours worked, be stored in a work performance record. Unplannable downtimes due to illness and accident should be covered either by the community or by private insurance contracts. In order not to disadvantage the mother of 2 children compared to the sole wage earner, domestic work and time spent raising children must also be taken into account as working time. Thus, one goes the way of the commercialization of the originally not the money subjected areas of life a step further, must however, for the sake of the justice in such a way accomplish. We can recoup the values of life that thus become monetary values by defining the safeguarding of the personal standard of living at a level worthy of a human being as a goal of society, for which the economy owes it a contribution. This can be realized with a sufficient basic salary for every citizen as a solidary benefit from the profits of the local economy and generally the profits on the local market with their market contribution.

If one assumes in addition a right to work up to a safe money based on work performance, then the discussion about the right level of inflation will prove to be irrelevant, the money should be stable in value, i.e. no inflation should take place.

1. Credit and savings accounts without interest?

"If banks receive money without interest as deposits, and if they also have to pay commitment fees if they do not pass the money on, borrowers will also no longer have to pay interest."

(M. Kennedy, p. 54)

M. Miller, under the heading "The Interest-Based Monetary System is Fundamentally Sick," points out that the difference between zero interest rates for commercial banks and the high overdraft rates in the Eurozone of up to 21.8% is no longer normal:

"This is simply sick."

Now this is not a fundamental attack on the interest-based monetary system, but rather on its excesses. Not only those who have grown up in a capitalist society can hardly imagine that the interest rate suddenly no longer exists, since the interest rate obviously has the function, according to classical economic theories and also according to general opinion, of mediating between the will to save and the will to invest. If there is a lack of capital for investment, the interest on savings can, by increasing the interest rate, encourage the saver to save more and thus provide the necessary capital. If there is sufficient capital thereafter, it is also to be expected that interest rates will fall, running toward zero at full employment, since the willingness to save is then at its highest and can no loer be further encouraged by higher interest rates. Keynes states: "We could thus in reality (and there is nothing unattainable in this) aim at an increase in the quantity of capital until it ceases to be scarce, so that the functionless investor will no longer receive a bonus." Now, one could interpret this to mean that when capital ceases to be scarce, the corresponding interest is no longer appropriate, thus removing the basis for the capitalist to "grow" capital via interest. Capital in abundance makes it possible to do this even in return for reimbursement of the debtor. In the 21st century the scarcity of capital will probably only play a role in relation to the creditworthiness of the debtor, and security will become the decisive criterion. Since the banks can produce in principle money as a bond on the future in any amount they are no longer dependent on their customers' deposits so there can be no question of scarcity for this reason alone. As a result, the banks create a pseudo-scarcity in relation to the creditworthiness of the customer in order to justify the interest rate which, on the one hand, as an overdraft facility (overdraft facility) at the beginning of the 21st century is set at 12% and more for private customers, although, on the other hand, with a central bank key interest rate of 0% in Europe, the municipalities and commercial banks are offered money at zero cost. In principle, the public sector can also obtain money for 0%, which is hardly an incentive not to take out a loan. Nevertheless, politicians have managed to popularize public sector savings on the basis of fundamental considerations. In the meantime, however, there is a growing number of voices advocating, now that interest rates are low, new debt should be used to fuel the economy further and that the overall interest burden should be reduced by rescheduling debt. Surprisingly, the insolvency of the over-indebted states in the monetary union is not seriously discussed, although the debt cuts so necessary would hardly affect the normal citizen! The cancellation of all interest on old credits would be sometimes already sufficient, in order to be able to reduce the overindebtedness of the public authorities gradually. In order not to let also the private interest grow into the sky, the credit interest should be capped with 5%, if at all still interest is computed. With interest-free Safe Money, such measures are of course not necessary, but we must reckon with interim and transitional solutions if we realistically want to give the money system with Safe Money a chance. A change of consciousness that sees it as necessary to grant citizens the right to create their own money and to promote this new consciousness should become reality.

If, in this sense, the banks are deprived of the possibility of making profits from the pseudo-scarcity of capital and only grant credit contracts without interest, all costs and the necessary profit for the bank must be covered by membership fees and charges. This may be difficult to communicate at first because of the different habits of dealing with banks, but in the long-term model it should be the better model to communicate to the customer simply because of the transparency it achieves. M. Kennedy proposes a circulation guarantee via commitment fees for this purpose. Kennedy also already points out that the omission of a liquidity premium "interest" allows better control of the amount in circulation than was previously the case.

If the bank finances itself solely through fees and membership dues, the risk for the bank and the customer is also reduced enormously; it is reduced to such an extent that it is possible to dispense with reserve holdings and provisions in monetary transactions, thus creating additional transparency. The interest rate has often raised problems and evoked countermeasures. Debt forgiveness, on the one hand, and the prohibition of taking on debt, on the other, have been the means of restarting an over-indebtedness and the resulting stalled economy, of generating new growth. If everyone can only take on as much debt as he can offer in terms of labor, then in principle there can be no over-indebtedness.

If money is stable in value, and the costs are settled elsewhere, then it is also possible to do without interest. To have to pay no interest to the bank, that can imagine still nobody, sometimes still rather with this thought to befriend, as far as it must pay no interest itself, however rather less, as soon as also absolutely no more interest for saved up money is to be received. Therefore we need a new form of saving. With the Ansparkredit to be presented here it is no problem to imagine that in the credit phase no interest is to be paid, if in the accumulation phase also no interest was paid, the parity of the two phases presupposed. In the case of direct credit, or main credit, lifetime credit, which is associated with money creation, this sometimes becomes a bit more complicated. If the costs of money creation are charged to the customer together with the processing costs charged, there is no problem in waiving interest payments here either, but this credit will understandably be more expensive than a savings credit (Ansparkredit). It is then always assumed that these contracts work with "safe" money, so that no risk premium is necessary either, since the value of the money is fully covered by the hedge on work performed or potential work performed. Start-up loans are now based on the principle of time-shifted money-based reciprocity, so you help me today, I'll help you tomorrow. In the case of main credit, or lifetime credit, money-based reciprocity is replaced by labor-based reciprocity, which will be explained in more detail below, but first to the status of a potential Safe Money with labor-based reciprocity in the environment of an economic order in which other currencies are also used.

If the Safe Money is exchanged for money of another currency, which is necessary in any case in a transitional phase, this is only possible via an account at a Free Bank with Safe Money, which is involved in the money creation of Safe Money, because of the Safe Money's security-generating ties. It is also a prerequisite that foreign currency accounts be maintained alongside the Safe Money accounts (NIM accounts). All customers of such a Free Bank must also set up foreign currency accounts already when opening NIM accounts, so that transfers into the currencies used in parallel in the market are possible at any time, i.e. not only for customers who are primarily interested in storing their cash assets in safe money accounts. Customer A, for example, could deposit 10,000 euros in his foreign currency account and offer it to the bank as an intermediary for exchange. If the bank finds a customer, say customer B, who is eager to exchange his NIM for euros, this can be done with a pre-prepared contract that, when presented to the bank, triggers the following transfer exchange if, for example, exchanged on a 9 for 10 basis: B transfers to the account of customer A exactly 9,000 NIM and receives on his account from customer B 10,000 euros. The bank ensures that the amounts are allocated to the correct currency sub-accounts. Customer B thus has a NIM account with 9,000 NIM and pays for the storage his account fees like any account holder at the bank, plus a fee for the transfer. Although he does not receive any interest as with other banks, and even has to pay fees, he has the guarantee of being able to save his assets secured in his account over the next decades. On a euro account at another bank, he could perhaps earn 0.5% interest, which leads to a loss of 1.5% with an inflation rate of 2%. If one deducts another 0.5% for fees on safe accounts, there is still a gain of 1% compared to the conventional account, and that even though no interest is paid. If this is calculated alternatively using the real interest rate, the picture for the current conventional monetary system becomes even bleaker, because the devaluations due to high interest costs in other areas also have an impact, such as overdraft facilities and the various discounts on money creation by central banks and commercial banks, which tend to remain hidden from the public.

But how are account overdrafts handled if no interest is charged? Without restrictions, the interest-free account could quickly lead to credit amounts that are no longer manageable, and everyone would be in debt over both ears, to use the proverbial metaphor. A bank without interest calculation must build the business model on the principle of reciprocity and the real accounting of working hours. With the overdraft one can assume that this is always possible in the framework, in which one also made the money available to others interest-free. Who would like to have the buffer of 4 weeks for a possible overdraft, which should have made available in advance 4 weeks exactly as much money on his account, as he himself would like to use this later, as an overdraft. In addition, for longer-term needs, loans should be limited to lifetime working time and the possibility of repayment. Anyone who has already set aside 25% of their lifetime for credit should only be able to obtain up to 25% as credit if there is a general restriction on coverage to 50% of lifetime. The second restriction, which should guarantee a smooth and safe repayment, can be based on the cost of living declared to the tax office: If 2,000 Euro for living expenses is deducted from the income when calculating the profit, it is obvious that then only what is available above that can be used for a repayment of loans. In general, it can also be said that a maximum of only 50% of the profit should be available as a resilient repayment. This rules out the possibility, that the interest-free nature of the loans will lead to them being drawn down to an exorbitant extent. Savings credits and especially also overdraft facilities as a special type of savings credit should, if possible, not burden the lifetime credit account; here, the only limitation is the chargeable instalment amount. If there is a lifetime loan with a repayment rate of 500 euros per month, then with an average profit of 2,000 euros per month, the overdraft can only be within the scope of an additional load of 500 euros per month. This, I think, could make the interest-free account socially acceptable.

Lifetime credit and savings credit offer an opportunity to finally arrive at a functionally manageable money system in which the repeatedly demanded turning away from interest-based money transactions may finally succeed.

In the Old Testament an interest remission is demanded for each 7. year, emperor Justinian issued a prohibition of interest and pope Leo I. the Great issued a prohibition of interest in the year 3 B.C. As far as I know, only in Islam there is still the interest-free credit, with the Islamic banks accordingly until today received, and/or revived, and to the information, there is in the meantime also an Islamic bank in Germany.

Nevertheless, in the present monetary system the interest loss of the saver, in times of the zero interest with the leading interest rates of the central banks, is felt as expropriation of the savers not only in such a way, the saver receives actually neither a recompense for its saving behaviour, nor a compensation for the real interest sinking into the negative range. It remains difficult to convey to the citizen that this is the consequence of the interest charges still present on the money, which is accompanied by a devaluation of the money, yet this is exactly how it is. It should be noted that the overdraft in most banks in 2018 stands at 12% and above. Secure money without a pre-planned devaluation procedure, this becomes all the more important because the collateral in the classical monetary system is dwindling away more and more every year.

2. A financial control system that provides security

Safe money, and not only this, should be integrated into a concept of safeguarding any kind of financial transaction, including the safe transaction and investment of funds. It would be desirable if the Bafin would not only formally control any kind of money transactions and financial business as it does now, but also scrutinize the transfer of funds. An obligatory reference to financial transactions subject to approval and those not subject to approval, which is apparent to the customer, should already improve the current situation. Unfortunately, the approval requirement is currently limited to purely formal criteria such as the type of prospectus advertising and not to hard data from the financial companies. Many enterprises evade even still this obligation and the references to the actual risks with these financial investments. In the grey financial market besides almost uncontrolled participation in closed funds is offered, whereby it is not pointed out at all that with unforeseeable money, need the premature sales of the papers is usually absolutely impossible. This grey financial market should also be controlled as best as possible. Only a controlled financial market can and may be allowed to work with Safe Money.

Since with Safe Money, payment is ultimately made with one's own labor, which has already been provided or is still to be provided in the future, the question of valuation must also be raised, since there is a difference between a doctor providing his labor and a shipyard worker. The price paid on the market evaluates the labor hour and takes into account training and experience, but above all the scarcity of corresponding labor. The valuation according to scarcity and that according to quality should not differ too much, but neither should they simply be equalized. For the credit, the quality should be the decisive criterion for profit expectations not only scarcity. An effective financial control should point out these differences and make transparent, naturally also criminal beginnings of an illegal profit maximization.

Since with safe money, in the long run you pay with the own manpower, this in the future furnished, the credit repays, it is important to prevent that at the market prices are demanded, which are to be settled far over the actual work achievement, or also the work achievement not sufficiently considered. This raises the question of the scarcity of the demanded goods and how to ensure a sufficient supply of the demanded goods. If one pursues this line of thought further, one will have to ask whether the necessary training capacities are available and whether goods that cannot be brought to the market in arbitrary quantities should not be withdrawn from the market and distributed in a non-market procedure under state supervision. An example of goods that cannot be supplied at will is the soil on which the houses in which citizens live stand, as well as the soil that is worked and used by the farmer. Everything that cannot be increased arbitrarily with the labor of the people should be managed as common property by the community and made available to individual citizens with a contract in return for compensation for use or rent. Here, too, financial supervision can be involved in order to achieve fair pricing. The goal here should be to curb overpricing and prevent financially induced enslavement. Excessive discrepancies between the market price and the valuation of working hours should be made public, thus ensuring that such discrepancies are contained. Where appropriate, consideration should also be given to upgrading the performance evaluations on which working time accounts are based. It is not only the pseudo-scarcity that must be kept in mind, but also the pseudo-oversupply.

The financial supervisory authority should intervene in cases of both usury and unrealistic value increases of any kind. Short-term increases in value of more than 100% should in any case be taxed. In this context, it is also regrettable that Bitcoin exchanges can be founded in Germany without Bafin approval. It is time that laws are finally drafted that can guarantee sufficient control of all financial transactions. The security that can thus be achieved should not only protect many citizens from losses, but also encourage investment in solid companies and thus promoting equally real growth.

VII. Safe Money and the Banks

> *"Despairing of the hopelessness of stopping a politically practicable problem ... namely, inflation ... I made a somewhat startling suggestion in a lecture about a year ago, the further pursuit of which has quite unexpectedly opened up new horizons...The further pursuit of the suggestion that the government should be deprived of the monopoly of money issue opened up the most fascinating theoretical approach..."*
>
> (Hayek, Monetary Nationalism and International Stability; 2011, [1937])

With the state monopoly of money creation, banks are also locked into a monetary system that, in principle, does not allow them to accept other monetary systems. Nevertheless, more and more non-state money systems have been established in recent times, although they are not completely independent of the state system.

The acceptance of money in a particular currency area is based on the trust that is placed in the issuer, the creator of the money, believed to be able to create money. Money, based on social agreements, is a matter of trust. With low trust in a project, it can sometimes still be persuaded to invest because of the high interest rate. It will therefore only be possible to invest without the high interest rate obtaining interest-free trustworthy institutions offering the necessary security. Precious metals already offer a certain degree of security. Better, however, is the contractually secured promise of a work performance. An institution that keeps and monitors working time accounts and also keeps records of all the debtor's debts and possessions could create the necessary trust for the creditor. The necessary control can be carried out or at least supervised by a state institution or also a legally and morally unencumbered and generally accepted authority. With appropriate legal safeguards, this can certainly be done by a private institution as well. In contrast to cryptocurrency systems, which do not have to record customer data on the possible work performed by their customers, this is absolutely necessary for a secure currency, and in a legally impeccable verifiable form. At this point it also already becomes clear that Safe Money can only be disbursed as credit to private individuals, in legal parlance natural persons and not legal entities. Only private persons can secure the Safe Money with their work performance. Therefore, in the Safe Money system, neither public authorities nor companies and institutions as legal entities can conclude such credit agreements. It is now also important to ensure absolute discretion and secure storage of customer data; for this purpose, not only the secure data safe must be provided, but also the secure legal space in which this data is stored in a legally secure manner. Once the framework conditions have been suitably clarified and fixed in statutes and other regulations and laws, there is nothing standing in the way of banking with secure money. However, this can hardly be compared with the classical banking system in state licensing from the 20th century. Those who want free banks with secure money may well consider the conventional banks in the current classical system to be superfluous, as Jonathan Mc. Millan puts it in his book on the future of finance. According to this book, we indeed will no longer need the classical banks in the future of electronic money. If a monetary authority is set up instead, it could control the money supply via an unconditional basic income and a liquidity premium, according to Mc Millan's view. In Mc Millan's system, it is the state, or the state institution, with which the necessary collateral is generated. In fact, however, this can be guaranteed in the long run only by state regulations and laws, but not by the state itself.

If the necessary rules and regulations are in place, the field is naturally opened up for free banks, meaning banks being independent of state institutions and committed only to their customers. Ideally, the free bank should be owned by its customers, so that both the equity ratio cannot pose a problem and the question of safeguarding and conducting banking business in the interests of the clientele. The free banks addressed here certainly do not have much in common with the free banks that still existed in the USA at the beginning of the 19th century.

In particular, the future free banks should submit to voluntary control without any ifs or buts, a control that could also be carried out by state institutions.

The bank must carefully check the customer data, and keep the data electronically secured and physically secured. If the data is kept securely by the bank issuing the loan agreement, this also means that further loans must also be processed by this bank, where the initial loan was processed, the customer's so-called house bank. If, for example, because of a change of residence, further loans are to be taken out with another bank in the association of independent banks, the entire data must be transferred to this other bank. Of course, a banking association could also set up central databases that all banks in the association can access. For security reasons and because of the proximity to the individual customer, however, decentralized data storage and data backup is preferable. The network should, however, guarantee that all affiliated banks can, if necessary, make a brief request to the issuing bank to view data for verification purposes. Where the credit agreements are issued, there one can also keep track and carry out both paper and electronic data archiving.

The bank must be contractually involved in such a way, that the necessary archiving is ensured, and legal requirements are met without any problems. In this way, the highest possible level of security can be conveyed to the customer. Laws and the verification of compliance with relevant laws should strictly ensure that in the event of insolvency customer funds are not attacked and that even after the bank is closed, the preservation of data and the continuation of accounts by another bank is ensured. In such a system, the bank is also not allowed to purchase securities on its own account but may only act as an intermediary. Deposits may be used as collateral for loans but may have to be additionally secured by insurance.

It is also important to note that the banks in the safe money system, the free banks, receive neither money from the national central bank or the ECB nor from other banks as loans, i.e. they are only involved in a transitory monetary transaction.

In addition to exercising control functions, the national central banks can also help to eliminate general liquidity shortages. To do this, they do not have to grant loans; they can transfer a certain amount of money to all citizens on a specific date, which does not have to be repaid but is only valid for a limited period. It would be possible, for example, to allocate 1,000 euros to every citizen in November, which would be accepted by every tax office and public treasury as money to settle liabilities within 12 months, and in the case of business owners within the following 18 months. Even a 1% increase in profit tax in the following year should not completely reverse the positive effect.

It is also important that no profit tax is levied on separately issued extra money of the national central banks with limited maturity, because the money must come back exactly as it was issued.

Free banks as free central banks can only be called free if there is no connection to the classical banking system as found in the EU. Under no circumstances may free banks assume liability risks for other banks, which is why either a special position in the EU area must be negotiated, they are not regarded as banks in the traditional sense, or bank formations must take place outside the EU area. One may well ask whether Safe Money still needs a bank in the traditional sense at all. Sometimes it is sufficient to create a free financial platform where work is exchanged and purchased, but not where loans are granted in the conventional sense, and which therefore cannot become part of a banking union. Perhaps it is also necessary to break away from the banks with which we are familiar. Banking associations or mutual financial institutions could be seen as an alternative and launch the necessary change in finance. The time is ripe for a new monetary economy with free financial institutions and free banks, a financial system that points to the future.

Safe money can only be issued by banks or associations that are independent of governments of any kind, do not assume liability risks from legal entities, and do not assume liability risks from other banks or companies. A transparent safe money system also requires a general transparency in the remuneration system, comparable to the current situation in the Scandinavian countries. If there were a general obligation to disclose salaries, then the exaggerated salaries repeatedly observed at banks and car companies would not occur.

1. The free bank as a target project

We need Free Banks or banking associations if we want to establish safe money, banks that are free from government influence and dependence. The Free Bank, whether under one umbrella or as a cooperative banking association, federation of banking associations or even just a financial platform, must also maintain its independence vis-à-vis other banks and financial service providers based from the outset on appropriate statutes that cannot be changed. All banks, financial service providers and institutions in the association of free banks should be interconnected via an IT platform so that information and transfers can always be made directly from bank to bank, from customer to customer. Exceptions are activities via foreign currency accounts, if these have been set up. If a customer wants to pay an invoice directly in euros, this can only be done using the classic procedure, even at free banks.

In order to increase general acceptance, it should be possible to use the foreign currency accounts of a free bank in the same way as the old, familiar account at the former house bank, but this does not necessarily have to be offered in this way by all financial institutions in the association of free banks.

What all banks working in the network of free banks should have in common are the working time accounts in which every customer has to enter his data on the existing assets and the debts still to be paid off. The working time accounts must be kept according to uniform rules first of all, the working hours per year must be entered into the register after the end of each year and multiplied by a factor representing the level of education plus the experience gained and the general level of education. As a formula, this might look something like this:

$Ah (Bs + Ag + Be) = Al$. Enter the hours worked (Ah), the level of education (Bs), the level of training (Ag) and the work experience (Be), which should then give the potential work output (Al). Existing assets should be entered as work done, with the original work done minus the wear and tear to be accounted for. In addition, future work output can be calculated and entered as expected value. The task of the Free Bank is thus quite different from that of a conventional bank, which is why it cannot be successfully integrated into the conventional banking system.

To the extent that a banking license in the euro zone is linked to the fact that one simultaneously enters into the cross-guarantee system of the banks which is supposed to make the European banks safer, the foundation of a free bank in this sphere of influence is only possible to a limited extent. In this respect, a free bank is not a bank in the conventional sense.

If legal problems should occur, the establishment of such a bank in Lichtenstein, Switzerland or in Norway, possibly also in Great Britain, offers a way out. However, this can mean moving a long way away from the desired location, which can be just as problematic as setting up a bank in the EU. Fortunately, there are other ways of managing and establishing payment instruments in the financial sector without having to set up a bank.

If one goes the way of e-money institutions, it is possible to make card payments and issue transfers through e-accounts that work with a card without having a general banking license. Permission to offer e-money services can be obtained through Bafin. It is interesting to note that an e-account can also be set up as a garnishment protection account. This means that you do not have an account with credit money, but you can deposit credit money into this account. Loans can also be negotiated between private individuals via corresponding platforms. First, however, as with Bitcoin accounts, one can also deposit money into a card account that is managed in a foreign currency. Thus, one could exchange euros for the Safe Money and then use this simultaneously credited to an account at the Free Central Banks for Safe Money or an assigned e-account.

In preparation, banking associations and financial services associations could be constituted, which could also compete as savings associations, for example, with the aim of saving money for larger purchases and, after reaching a half-savings target, having money made available to them by other savers. In conjunction with a cooperative for the acquisition, maintenance, and marketing of real estate and other assets, bank-like services could be provided without the banking license that would otherwise be required. The cooperative, with or without a banking concession, could well collect money based on work performance evaluations and also issue it in exchange for some kind of employment contract, without doing traditional banking with it.

The first step is to establish an association that sets out in its articles of association how the work performance of individual customers is to be evaluated and then lists this in a catalog. An algorithm with which the hourly performance is to be calculated must not be missing. In the case of a house, for example, it is necessary to calculate the number of hours required to rebuild it if everything has been destroyed by fire. It makes sense to record the hourly performance in a new fictitious currency, for example, the New International Money (NIM), so that conversions into other currencies are also easily possible. If the hourly output of an unskilled worker is defined as one unit in 10 hours, the hourly output of a teacher, a journalist or a salesperson can be determined on this basis. For the determination of the individual hourly benefits one can of course initially also take into account the current wage and salary payments. Securing the new money through work performance also requires coverage for the case of illness and death of the account holder. In this respect, a risk insurance policy must be taken out on the work benefits with the credit agreements for the Safe Money, so that these are secured in the event of illness and after the death of the borrower. Whether external insurers are involved, or an internal insurance company provides this service should be decided by the future bank customers and bank owners when the statutes are to be determined. The goal of a free bank is to create an institution that transfers existing and future labor benefits into a currency that is backed by the reference to labor benefits. In a world with many other currencies, it becomes necessary to plan for a possible exchange into these other currencies from the beginning. Settling exchange rates can sometimes put the special position of the free banks into perspective. In addition, each customer must have a clearing account, a credit account and if possible, likewise a foreign currency account.

In the clearing account the credit should be made available in the new currency, the not up-to-date used funds on the credit account and foreign currency on the foreign currency account. In total, every customer in the Safe Currency System should therefore in principle have three accounts, the clearing account, the credit account and the foreign currency account.

In contrast to the classical banking system, the Safe Money system should charge the same money for the same services, payment should be made according to expenses and not through interest, low construction interest for the rich and high overdraft interest for the less well-off citizens.

2. How will the new currency be used?

With a safe currency not only, the employment should be safe with the purchase, the individual steps up to the repayment of a credit if necessary surely step by step to be able to be traced, finally it concerns the security of the same. If the currency exists only as a virtual currency on the network, each individual step can be traced in a protocol such as the blockchain. Because of the more complex design involved in issuing paper-based or even plastic-based notes, we will initially assume a purely virtual banknote that exists only in the computer. With purely card-based payments, we need not only banknotes not to be printed, but the individual payment transactions can also be tracked directly and easily settled down to the smallest fractions of the amount of money borrowed. In the case of purely digital settlements, it is even possible to generate the code for the denomination not before the payment process.

In addition to bank cards, which are used to debit directly from the existing account amount, budget cards can also be introduced, where only a predefined sum, the budget, is available for debiting, comparable to the already existing prepaid credit cards. This could then also be combined with foreign currency cards. It would be even easier to implement the budget card or cash card via the smartphone with the new electronic cash exchanges that are entering the market. The receipts and invoices in the secure currency should be standardized in such a way that a quick check is possible at any time and is easy for the customer to follow. In addition, the statements should be designed in such a way that they can be used in math classes. Sent to a cell phone in the store immediately after shopping, everything could be checked immediately without paper and printed out or saved at home at the end of the shopping day. The handling of countable cash does not therefore have to be lost, can be reproduced even on the computer for didactic reasons, and can even be used in the local market to influence everyday life on site. A cash valid only in a special local market could be even useful, one wants to separate the markets against each other, in order to strengthen so the local aspect. At the same time, working with a money that still involves the full sensory system can also better promote and challenge the citizen in his or her wholeness, both emotionally and in terms of learning. A money that is only valid locally could be exchanged for cash in the market with the cash card via digital book money, and the unused money could be exchanged back again at the end of the market aisle.

State institutions can only access the money of the new currency via taxes, fees and rents, and this only if this money is accepted for the payment of debts to the public sector. In order to increase the general acceptance of the new money, it is not unimportant to take care that the state bodies accept this money. It is important for the state organs to accept labor services as a means of payment with the acceptance of NIM and to deposit it in the vault. Safe money could then be used to finance work services for the general public, the state.

Money, in addition to covering the cost of living, of whatever kind, is also used for major purchases such as cars and major travel, as well as for the purchase of real estate, and for the purchase of securities. In the case of larger financial transactions, the use of money is likewise described as the use of capital, which in many cases must first be saved. If money is available in abundance, however, there is no reason to save it. If, however, saving is recognized as necessary in sustainable economic activity, the procurement of credit without prior saving must be limited. A limiting factor in the classical monetary system is, of course, a high interest rate. Therefore, the elimination of interest rates on safe money could lead to an increase in the demand for credit, unless other limiting measures are in place. One absolute limiting factor is the potential work output available during a lifetime, which decreases with each additional year of life. Also limiting is the actual possibility of split repayment. In addition, the value and possible recapitalization of an acquisition must be included in an algorithm for limiting current credit demands.

Nevertheless, in the long run, capital should also increase within the framework of Safe Money.

Now, one might think that the increase in capital, an increase in the capital stock, should strengthen capitalism. But this could also lead to a weakening or even the end of the capitalist system, because an abundance of capital will at some point no longer be able to increase productivity to a meaningful degree. In any case, money and capital can then at some point also cease to be a limiting factor. In the case of "safe money," however, the intrinsic limitation of this type of money must be considered; "safe money" can only enter circulation in the quantity that is actually available as potential working time.

It may now appear as a contradiction that as in the classical system also in the system of the safe money the market value can deviate strongly from the working time value, importantly, the difference may not be balanced by the central bank, which is also not possible for the free banks in the system of the safe money anyway, otherwise the working time value would be changed afterwards, which may not be. Who pays more for a commodity, than in it as work achievement is contained, must pay this simply also with an increased work expenditure for its part? This should also help to limit borrowing in the NIM currency system.

The limitations on borrowing necessary in any monetary system are becoming weaker and weaker in the current classical state system, and not only because of the lowering of the prime rate to 0%, but also because of the almost limitless granting of credit to municipalities and other legal entities.

Dissolving the limits on the money factor was and is the declared goal of the ECB's current policy, not to tighten the necessary limit for municipal and state bodies. Whether this will encourage investment activity as expected, that may be an option in theory, but in fact the abundance of money cannot always replace other factors that have a limiting effect. A fortiori, it cannot make sense to replace factors that are not currently limiting in any way. Similarly, factors whose effects are already maximized cannot be further increased in effectiveness by money. For example, if there are enough workers, exchanging money for even more workers can have no further effect. If, on the other hand, there is a shortage of labor, for example specialists, money may be able to provide more training places, but it can hardly provide the missing specialists immediately. Thus, in many situations, it also becomes irrelevant how much money is available. If money is available in abundance, then even more money can have no effect. Thus, the factor "money", created by social convention, proves to be quite equivalent to the natural factors, such as labor and energy, because, despite its specificity as a super factor, it can only become effective if the scarcity of the factors to be replaced is not generally structural.

Now growth will not always be proportional to the use of money, there will be here, as with all other factors, a saturation limit adapted to each growth process separately. The saturation with money can lead then in individual cases also to the fact that available money is not needed. But what do you do with money that exists but is not needed? It makes sense to put it aside and not use it for purposes unrelated to the project, just because you don't know what to do with the money. Money that is put aside but not used increases the capital stock, the capital that can be used increases, which means that we are addressing the storage function for money that was already mentioned in the introduction. If we understand money as an intermediary object of exchange, the storage function is to be understood as an exchange within the time dimension, the current exchange here and now in the market as an exchange in the spatial dimensions with only apparent neglect of the time dimension, the measurement of value, on the other hand, as an exchange in the relational dimensions. In this context, money does not have to change hands in order to be used as a yardstick that determines the valuation of the competing product.

    The security of money, it should be explicitly noted, is more important for growth processes than all other properties of a currency to be valued.

The secure handling of money and the secure movement of goods also require enough money on the market. In order to be able to guarantee this, a control authority will be needed in the asset money system; in the safe money system, corresponding statutes and laws should suffice. The classical central banks can also put non-credit-based money into circulation for this purpose, but they must then also ensure that superfluous money is withdrawn from circulation again, in the simplest case via tax money.

Since in many cases products are also valued higher in the market than the labor output should allow, there is indeed more to be put into circulation than the working time accounts would suggest. In the case of credit-based liability money NIM, this should be compensated by an increased need for credit, which does not mean that government control would be completely superfluous in the liability money system. In a passive money system controlled via working time accounts, additional money in the balance sheet can also be settled via the non-salaried portions in the accounts. If we assume in a model calculation that each person has to spend about 75 hours a month on his or her own household, i.e. with 2 persons then 150 hours, an accounting per household would result in about 3,000 euros. This would even allow the basic salary to be settled via the working time accounts. If the state appears as a financier, it can draw the money from the taxes, should generate it in no case over credits. If one wants to keep the state out also here, then the increased need for funds can be created only over lifetime credits. It is important to note the nature of the account in the currency proposed here. Since NIM is a credit-based currency, so too must the credit account be given central importance. Therefore, when opening an account, credit must always be included, even if the primary objective is to store accumulated capital. The credit can be credited to the assigned credit account only after the credit has been credited to the clearing account. Therefore, a credit agreement must be concluded simultaneously with each account opening. In practice, this can then look like this: a credit is applied for which covers at least the expenses to be expected for the first year. In addition, money can then be paid into the foreign currency account that is also to be set up. The money on the foreign currency account can then, as soon as an exchange partner has been found, be exchanged for NIM and parked on the credit account. Only when the credit balance exceeds the amount of credit granted, an overdraft can also be granted.

3. Concretely, the new Safe Currency

The new currency is secured on the one hand by the register to the work performances, on the other hand by the credit contract referred to it.

The creation of money by credit contract can be carried out in any of the already existing currencies and is indeed already practiced, but not as a purely private creation of money by a private banking syndicate, a private financial service provider or a privately organized cooperative with a labor services register.

With the new money, all the necessary safeguards can be built into the contracts from the outset, so that the dependencies in the old currencies are not dragged along in the first place. Therefore, it makes sense to introduce a completely new money system along with a new money. Since the hedge to be addressed here is a hedge via the contractual assurance of work performance, this cannot be compared with the credit contracts that are otherwise customary at present. With these contractual hedges, it is also not possible to support or hedge another bank that does not know any of the new hedges.

Since the new money should not be nationally bound, it must be conceived from the outset as an international money. In this context, we should recall the remarks of F.A. Hayek, who was the first economist to suggest that the state should be deprived of its monopoly on money creation and on the issuance of metallic money. At this point, it is also worth mentioning the discussion about abolishing cash, a discussion in which central bank economists are also involved, including the possibility of reducing the value of cash when it is deposited or exchanged. With a new currency, all these considerations would also be off the table, although it would not be necessary to endow the new currency with cash, which might even be more of a hindrance.

Before the birth of the new money, as is usually the case before every birth, a name must be found, in short, what should the new money be called? Because of the international appearance, it makes sense to find an English-language name, suggestion: New International Money. In the abbreviation, this results in NIM and could then also run in German under the name Neue Internationale Moneten, the institutions that publish NIM as "New International Money Maker", NIMM. If one wants to avoid the language preference, also "Moneta" offers itself as a name. Essential is now the assignment to a fixed work unit. For example, one NIM could be the equivalent of 10 hours of work by an unskilled worker, which then determines the basic labor output. If this work is remunerated in euros at 100 euros, it should be possible to exchange one NIM for 100 euros, although this rate could also settle somewhat above or below this if it develops freely on the market. This would also mean that a work remunerated with 20 Euro per hour would be remunerated in NIM with 0.2 NIM, and every hour in Euro remunerated with 40 Euro in NIM with 0.4 NIM. This could therefore also be a first indication of how the quality of work performance should be taken into account in the labor cadastre. Since, in many respects, security is more important to wealthy citizens than possible profit, it can be assumed that, after a start-up phase, a run on the new currency NIM can be expected. By exchanging euros, pounds and dollars for NIM, the NIM-producing institution, declared here as a "free bank," receives foreign exchange, which is useful for offering members other currencies, since not everyone will accept the new currency in trade so quickly. Because of the possible problems in the EU area, one can also establish the actual central bank or mother bank in Switzerland or Liechtenstein and from there feed the assigned national e-money institutions with this money by transfer. It could then possibly look like this, that the customer opens an account at the parent bank and at the same time an e-money account at his place of residence. In this way, money can be transferred from the parent bank to the local e-money account and used directly at the place of residence in a previously advised currency. It makes sense to run the e-money accounts in at least two currencies from the beginning, one in NIM and the other optionally in euros, dollars, pounds, Swedish kronor or Swiss francs. The parent bank can be designed as a central bank, but also as a commercial bank, which will keep all credit contracts both in paper form and electronically and, in association with other Free Banks acting as parent banks for their area, ensure payment transactions in this new currency, IT-based, if desired, for example, also with blockchain technology. However, if deposits are to be credited to an account as NIMs after euros, other customers must be willing to offer their NIM balances for exchange into euros.

A company that wants to pay out its employees in NIM initially has a problem, because how do you get this money? Since this money is created through private credit agreements, the question is more concrete, in as much as private individuals are to be found who provide the company with NIM as a loan or also acquire shares in the company in NIM. If business is subsequently conducted in NIM, it may work to accumulate enough NIM in the cash register to pay employees with it. If it is not enough, foreign currency can be exchanged and money can be used that employees exchange back into euros, for example.

A fundamental problem, especially at the beginning, is the supply of companies and businesses with credit money, since loans in Safe Money can only be granted to natural persons. Hardly any problem would arise if all employees also became co-owners, since then everyone would only have to borrow a partial amount so that the required capital could be raised in total. In the long term, this will also mean that a different business model will be preferred than has been the case to date. The most suitable model is that of a cooperative, as found in the various cooperative banks, the Volksbank, and also the agriculturally oriented Raiffeisen cooperatives.

Since every banknote in the new currency NIM is, strictly speaking, a promissory bill, the registrations of the notes must also be provided accordingly with a registration code that is identical to the registration number on the credit agreement. If each credit agreement is first given a code for the credit-issuing institute, this could look like this: for all loans of the Free note bank in Cologne, the registration code starts with BuD-Koel for "Bundesrepublik Deutschland Koeln". The country code should always have three digits, while the city or area code should have 4 digits. This can be followed by the year, the month and the consecutive contract number in that month, starting with the first and ending with the last contract in that month, perhaps 22 or even 3,560. If a loan of 100,000 NIM is now paid out, attention must still be paid to the denomination; after all, one does not go grocery shopping with 100,000, whether in NIM or euros. For purchases in the local retail trade, the new currency is to be divided not only into multiplicatives of the unit 1 NIM, but also into partial units of a 1 NIM. If the thousandth part of a NIM becomes the smallest denominated credit amount, then the division can be made into 1 NIM x 10 to the power of 3 to 1 x 10 to the power of 4. Thus, we need at least 8 digits to represent this code. A code with about 20 digits should be sufficient to generate the necessary uniqueness here. It is not important whether corresponding notes are printed, or only fictitious notes are exchanged in the digital network. What is important is the exchange at the end of the term. This should be carried out with the bank that issued the loan. Until all the money has been collected to pay off the loan that is due, the process can be recorded in a blockchain or even a comparable procedure so that the exchange process can be handled smoothly afterwards; after all, the repayment is made with banknotes that are currently available and not necessarily with the exact bills that entered circulation when the loan was granted and paid out. To ensure that this repayment is secured in any case, the labor that is used as the first collateral must still be covered by a second collateral a kind of reinsurance, if the borrower through illness and death can no longer fully contribute the deposited labor hours to the still due repayment.

In order to be able to finance residential property also there, where nowadays the social housing construction occupies the field, the appropriate building credits with safe money with the "socially weak ones" should be put on the one hand on hereditary building properties and on the other hand with credits put on on a long-term basis between 30 and 50 years, then the monthly rates could underrun the present rent even.

When opening an account in the Safe Money System, it is also important to have deposits as business deposits, which not only document co-ownership of the bank, but are also intended to provide a safety cushion and, in retirement, residual security for retirement income in the event of health problems in old age. Therefore, the deposit can also be repaid at the earliest when the account is closed for retirement. After death, the remainder of the deposit should be collected after deducting payments to survivors to handle all expenses associated with the funeral and any debt repayment, a surplus as a solidarity contribution, so that in emergencies members can also offer assistance that would otherwise not be possible.

The new money NIM can be used naturally in principle also over credit cards and bank cards digitally, likewise over payment systems by cell phone.

4. Savings agreement (Ansparkreditvertrag) and overdraft more exactly regarded!

As we have seen, any normal credit agreement can serve to create money. In a credit business dominated by normal banks, however, this type of private money creation should generally become the sole type of money creation untouched by government interference, as provided for in the free banking system. Now, this does not mean that credit can only be granted in this way. In addition, lending coupled with savings contracts, as already mentioned, should be seen as an independent way of granting loans and as already shown, of encouraging savings behaviour at the same time.

If, for example, savings are being made for a car, a contract can be made so created that a loan is granted only if half of the required money has been saved. If the desired car costs 20,000 euros, 10,000 euros must be saved, and only when this saved money has been received in the credit account the loan can be paid out in the amount of the saved money. This means that 10,000 credit debts have then been created, which in this case are not secured by a working time account, but rather by the acquired material asset. Thus, then no new money is created, permits however a credit granting also if no other collateral is present, except that from the object which can be acquired.

The Ansparkreditvertrag corresponds thus rather to the old building savings contract, should however in a more general form also enable the acquisition of small objects. If a student is saving for a new cell phone, a bicycle or a car, for example, the savings credit is better than the life-time credit contract, which is used too early and is in principle only a possibility for citizens in employment to obtain money.

Also, the overdraft credit granted with almost every account can be managed as Ansparkredit, if one goes and grants and grants in each case exactly so much at overdraft credit, as before was saved, by leading the account altogether in the plus (1 month with 100 euro in the plus entitles 1 month with the account 100 euro in the minus to remain). Therefore, each account with the new Safe Money must also be linked to a matching overdraft facility agreement, which in terms of the basic principle is the same as a savings credit agreement. In principle, only the credit or clearing account should be able to slip into the negative range, credit account and euro account should only be kept in the positive range.

Such arrangements can always be made, i.e. even with different interest rate models, but are absolutely necessary if you want to work with interest-free accounts.

It should also be emphasized that the waiver of interest makes the bank's services more transparent, since the various services no longer disappear in an interest rate, which makes non-services appear hidden as services, and thus the whole thing becomes intransparent. The aim should be to view money as a kind of pledge on callable working time and to value it accordingly. In the case of mutual services, however, this also means that the service provided can demand a subsequent service in advance. This can also be used to counteract tendencies that no longer reward saving and gradually take control of the citizen's money completely out of his hands. The associated interest-free credit also simplifies the handling of money, since interest and compound interest calculations are no longer required, which can in principle also be implemented in other currencies but is best realized with the new currency NIM.

5. Credit as the basis and promise

The new currency must be able to rely on and build on credit as the basis for the new monetary system. The basic idea is that before any money can be saved at all, there must be money to save, and if not provided by the sovereign, then through mutual credit contracts. So, if one does not want to work with a credit of the national central bank, the citizen must first create the new money over a credit contract, in order to be able to bring it then into the circulation. By signing the contract, the account holder promises to repay the borrowed amount of money with his labor. The basic loan, like all lifetime loans, refers to the work still to be done until the end of life. Even if the expected performance potential is calculable in total until the end of life, this does not mean that this performance is also to be borrowed in total, or even lendable. Here, too, the term can be negotiated individually, although longer terms than for conventional loans can be assumed. Insurance should be mandatory to guarantee repayment even in the event of illness or premature death. Safe money thus also offers better planning in all respects, both for the creditor and the debtor.

In coordination with the requirements of the tax authorities for an annual financial statement, the clearing accounts of NIM accounts could be worked off via an annual credit to be settled annually. The negative items could then be cleared in the coming year with a new credit. This would then also enable account management via a blockchain that terminates after every 12 months. A related decentralized management of the account within a year could also be seen as advantageous in many respects. The bank would then possibly only have to make the annual transfers from a loan to be closed at the end of the year to a new loan to be opened at the beginning of the new year.

VIII. Currency and Financial Capital

Money can be saved in the new currency as well as in other currencies, as shown with linked credit savings contracts (Ansparkredit). In this process, no new money is created, but existing money is accumulated, saved up, so to speak. Saving can be useful when major purchases are not immediately affordable but can also be used to build capital.

Capital can develop likewise from credits with money creation, should be formed however up to the double majority primarily over savings contracts, thus by the accumulation of saved amounts of money, which is unfortunately in the meantime no longer the rule!

Indifferently, how capital originated, it will be able to promote as money factor growth in certain situations and economic constellations. If capital is missing, this can limit the growth even with sufficient presence of the other factors, if for example not enough buffer capacity is available. The conditions under which growth can fail completely due to a lack of capital will be left out here for the time being, since this is to be derived from certain constellations of misguided social arrangements, which may require more space to discuss than is available here, but which can certainly be clarified in subsequent volumes. First, the special nature of capital must be brought to mind. Indeed, with financial capital, other factorial limitations can sometimes be partially or even completely removed. On the other hand, there may well be growth without financial capital if this growth is not deficient in the remaining conditions and factors. In particular, human capital can substitute for financial capital in special cases, since projects can also be advanced with unpaid human labor.

A sufficient endowment of financial capital, on the other hand, can finance a lack of energy as well as the purchase of resources and of labor. This may be the reason why the view has become common that with sufficient capital, nothing else can actually be lacking.

It is true that patents and ideas can also be purchased, but the necessary provision of information is sometimes effective as a limiting factor even when enough capital is available and remains effective. Conversely, energy and human labor, as well as resources, can also be converted into financial capital. More precisely, however, one should assume different forms of capital that can be converted into each other. According to this, financial capital can be transformed into physical capital as well as into human capital or even into educational capital or regulatory capital. A fundamental problem arises precisely with the age of "Industry Four", if the profit margins are not distributed accordingly fair, because then it is to be feared that one day the production capacities are no longer called because the citizens have no money to buy and pay for the products. A positive development could result from the increasing tendency not to buy the products from indifferent corporations, but from cooperative communities, commons and production-customer cooperations, with differently marketed products. In solidary cooperations, production "on demand" could be secured by memberships covering the fixed costs and the zero marginal costs subsequently benefiting only the members of the solidary community, so that the vision of almost zero production costs also finds its beneficiaries on a broad basis and in this way, moreover, production does not come to a standstill.

In addition, in traditional finance, high outflows of capital into grey channels are still to be expected, especially at larger production facilities. If Safe Money is available, it cannot be ruled out that Safe Money may also play a role. An expected return on capital can now be used, no matter in which currency, also for old-age security, which is by no means to be rejected.

Since the capital and the income earned from it can be very different, both in terms of origin and in terms of use, so there should also be no separate taxation. Capital income should be treated in the same way as income from an entrepreneurial activity or an activity in a dependent employment relationship. It makes no sense for the state to tax capital income less, but neither does it make sense for other income to be taxed less. As with other income, in the case of capital income it should be possible to deduct general living expenses and likewise the cost of work-related expenses from profits, so that only the remainder is taxed as profit. Before calculating the profits, the income, regardless of its origin, must be added together. Income as an employee from an employment relationship or from the use of capital is to be treated equally at all levels. Because of the unequal treatment into the 21st century, inequalities arise that would not otherwise arise. Already at the level of company accounts, these inequalities become effective when financial capital receives a higher payout from earnings than human capital. If the capital costs of machinery and buildings used are deducted from revenues as average costs, as are the wage and salary expenses incurred, including all special expenses and nonpecuniary benefits, the resulting profit should also be divided equally between financial capital and human capital. For employees, this could mean an annual payout as profit sharing. It would also make sense to include a 20% reserve before calculating the profit shares. The equal treatment of human capital and financial capital will put pressure on the profitability of the use of machines and robots. If the consequence of this is a reduction in the pace at which the Internet of Things is realized, this is certainly not a negative consequence, but rather a desirable development, since a successful adaptation of people to a robotized world takes time.

1. Capital and assets

In modern economies, we can justifiably assume that without money, capital is not formed, and without capital, the formation of wealth to the extent we know is hardly conceivable.

Over time, wealth and capital solidify through the large inheritances in certain families that dominate the capital market and thus direct economic activity, just as princes once did through their estates within the economy in historical agrarian societies. In this respect, today's economy can also be understood as a capital aristocracy in the wake of the replaced aristocratic land aristocracy. Therefore, it becomes understandable when proposals are thrown into the discussion here to dismantle the aristocratic structures in the economy through the highest possible inheritance taxes want to enforce. But because the inheritance tax, as it is currently handled, is a substantial taxation, this way seems to me to be the wrong way, although at first glance justice is served, but only at first glance. It will serve the good of all and the good of the national economy less. If one wants to reduce the excessive differences in the starting conditions for the next generation, there are certainly alternatives. One alternative could be to encourage the heirs of large fortunes, spread over several decades, to use their wealth to bring the unsolved social problems closer to a solution. If a middle-class person bequeaths a company worth millions to his or her children, they could take on a social task, for example providing housing for impoverished pensioners or free computers for local educational institutions. In addition to donations in kind, money can of course also get socially necessary projects off the ground that were previously not possible, and all of this from the profits generated, expenses that even reduce tax…

We use money as a medium of exchange, but also as promissory bills for easements and contributions in kind, which we keep in order to be able to satisfy future needs, not least also to satisfy power needs. Whoever accepts an inheritance that enables him to shape his future life without having to work, is thus indebted to the society in which he lives, in which this fortune was earned, and is obliged to give back something of what he has received, throughout his life. The debt to society resulting from a large fortune is not settled with a one-time tax payment and is also not tied to the current place of residence.

Existing capital can also be used to expand or rebuild assets. As the name suggests, these are tangible assets and cash reserves that stimulate activity and thus growth; in other words, they can promote growth. One could draw a comparison here with hormones in the plant and animal kingdoms. Capital can promote growth in general, sometimes indicating the direction. But for this we also need the other factors and the exact knowledge of how capital should be used or is used. It certainly makes a difference whether capital is used in the area of logistics, production or order placement and order processing up to and including invoice processing. It is also legitimate to ask in which sub-sector of the economy capital is primarily used, in agriculture, industrial production, health care or leisure. Financial capital can flow everywhere very quickly, it can promote new life, degradation processes and growth and is thus comparable to water in untouched nature.

Many money flows, which are hidden from the ordinary citizen and also hardly comprehensible, run in areas that do not serve the welfare of the population, such as the money that flows into the drug market and thus destroys the health of many people and ruins the labor of many people dependent on it.

If a profit is generated by the use of capital, this often promotes the formation of wealth, if only because the main share of the profits from capital flows to such owners of capital who do not finance their livelihood with it but look for financial investments that are to increase the money and thus use it to increase wealth. This should not lead to the conclusion that the resulting inequality in the distribution of wealth should be compensated for with a separate tax. Only an equal taxation of capital income and income from dependent employment will be able to bring about an evolutionary change in the long run, which follows the natural development trends and does not pave the way for unrest and revolutions.

2. Capital and Money

If a currency is stable and inflation is within a manageable range, capital will accumulate in any currency area. If, on the other hand, inflation is high, capital is likely to flee to other currencies, regardless of where it originated. Since security is an important aspect, so it will be the most important thing to go to the safe place, even if interest rate premiums are supposed to tempt people to put safety on the back burner. Since in the system of safe money NIM cannot be worked with interest surcharges, security alone counts here in the end. Short-term gains through interest effects can increase assets, but they are not suitable to preserve assets in the long term and to promote saving. Those for whom interest gains on money are too uncertain will switch to tangible assets in our classical monetary system, be it gold, art or real estate. In the case of real capital, it should be noted here, not everything is risk-free, the owner must expect wear and tear and poorer valuations over the years.

Nevertheless, only active capital, capital that works, can grow, the multiplication of funds by interest is not growth, but a simple multiplication, to the detriment of stability, because here money is only shifted, but not newly created. Because the shifting usually takes place at the expense of the poor and not of the rich, one can also speak pointedly of a machinery for the enrichment of the already rich. This should perhaps lead to storms of protest and not fuel academic discourse. Money should not be destroyed in value either by interest or by inflation, and yet there is open discussion about how to do this so cleverly that the citizens do not notice it. This discussion will lead us no further if we do not look the facts in the eye, in order to promote afterwards the right use of money, in order to build up fortunes again primarily by work performance or to make also investments, which make this possible. Assets not created by labor belong to the community, therefore to all, and cannot receive a real market price. These values, classified in the tax law as non-exploitable values, should not be privately owned, they should only be usable by the citizen through lease or rent, as far as free use has not been established for all citizens.

3. Capital and investment

Capital is often used to purchase machines that take over the work of people in production, in recent times increasingly not only in production, but also in the office and in logistics. Machine work, made possible using capital, is replacing human labor more and more every year. One could also express it in such a way that the use of financial capital is increasingly replacing the use of human capital. This creates an imbalance that increasingly wrests the tool from the worker or employee, or collaborator, and transfers it into the possession of the capitalist. Marx drew the conclusion from this early on that the means of labor, the machines and the agricultural land, in his opinion all means of production, should be socialized. This approach is correct in some respects, but wrong in many, though understandable in its time because of the historical background of information. First, what nature offers us, that is, provides, is not a means of production, but the raw material that we can work and process. The natural raw materials and the land, the soil, they are given to all of us for responsible use, as well as water and air. Therefore, all citizens should also be taken into the responsibility and the benefit as far as the use and the profit derived from it are concerned. It is different with the machines, which developed over the capital employment from previous work achievement. If saved up work performance is used, then this should be taken also accordingly possession-referred in the profit. It makes no sense to socialize the saved labour, it is like the labor itself always private property. If people work together and conclude contracts for the purpose of manufacturing products for sale, the state must ensure that the contracts satisfy the general sense of justice and do not harm the community of citizens. Those who provide saved labor in the form of capital should not be disadvantaged, but neither should they be favoured. Therefore, the profits from production are not to be distributed unilaterally in favour of the holders of means of production to the owners of capital, but equally to the pecuniary capital and likewise the human capital, i.e. in equal shares. Especially if we imagine that one day robots will manage production almost alone without human labor, it can only be fair and reasonable to distribute the profit between pecuniary capital (monetary means) and human to be divided equally. In any case, this is likely to be more sensible than introducing subordinate redistribution via a wealth tax. This could sometimes reduce the use of robots within a certain period, as it could reduce the prospects for maximum returns on the capital employed if the use of machines is pushed forward at what is now a slower pace. Overall, it is also important to ensure that every citizen is ascribed a minimum working time per week as an entitlement. It is not the minimum wage that is decisive and irrelevant in the case of basic salary and profit sharing, but the entitlement to a minimum working time, because this is important for humanitarian reasons. It should be noted in this context that the use of machines and people should in principle be valued in the same way. This can also be used to address another problem, namely the fact that the products manufactured in abundance in the age of the Internet of Things must also find buyers, otherwise no profits can be generated. Cooperatives that establish cooperation between buyer and producer could communitize profits and thus generate a culture of the commons that is promising for the future. On the commons, I would point here to Jeremy Rifkin's ideas on the subject.

The Internet may be able to help us quickly find like-minded people with whom to set up production on a limited scale along the lines of Industry Four.0, transporting production to customers but not products across the globe. Production belongs where the products are needed. That's where the profits come from, and that's where they should be taxed.

Under no circumstances should the "money experiments of yesterday" simply be repeated, especially if they have not been successful in the long term. The repeated attempts to provide governments and the economy with cheap credit may boost investment in the short term, but in the long term they will generate profits for the banks but will only promote growth to a limited extent in the long term. Fittingly, in his Easter article in the FAZ, Mayer writes a column on the conduct of the financial juggler Law, drawing on the critical remarks of Law's former employee, banker Richard Cantillon, on the new paper money, "He distrusted the new monetary system. In his view, it would work only if people used the paper money to purchase assets. As soon as they wanted to use it to buy goods, services, and precious metals, they would realize its worthlessness. In the spring of 1720, sentiment tilted and with-it Law's company's stock price…There was a currency reform in which Law's paper money was debased and replaced with metal-backed money." This did not abolish paper money in principle, but it did abolish the pegged back to metal money. Important investments are not prevented by currency reforms, but they are disrupted. Whether acquired with metal money or with paper money or in kind, the participation in a company still represents the most important share in the multiple investment transactions. Financial capital is needed not only to build up a company, but also to expand and establish new production facilities or new distribution channels. Of course, bets are also made, on rising and falling prices with barriers up and down. Derivatives, bonds and debentures, which are developing and spreading in this field, should not be a subject here, nor should the various private and state lotteries. No matter what bets are made, however, the winnings, like all winnings, should be subject to a profit tax, contrary to current practice in Germany. In return, all investment activities and, in principle, work itself should not be taxed. It is to be expected that then also more money from saved capital will be available and loans for legal entities such as companies and municipalities will no longer be necessary. If the liability risks are also no longer limited but distributed fairly, then there can be greater security with the loans that are still necessary simply because of the broader distribution, and bad loans will only become a rarity.

B. MANAGEMENT AND CONTROL OF MARKETS

IX. The Control of Markets and Finance

"The value of paper money can obviously be regulated on the basis of various considerations ... though it is more than doubtful whether any democratic government endowed with unlimited power can ever accomplish this satisfactorily."
(Hayek 2011, p.149)

Steering and regulation require a determination of goals in advance; after all, the captain who steers a ship has a destination in mind that he is heading for. Therefore, a short note on which goals are to be aimed at within the markets. If the GDP is to be increased and therefore more and more growth is to be steered for, then the proceeds to be maximized are addressed with it, proceeds or profit maximization as a goal, finally the employment, the costs, is to be profitable. In addition, the degrees of freedom of the acting citizens are to be maximized, among other things with the reasoning that this will have a positive effect on the general profit maximization. A third objective is the secure environment. Security, which permits long-term planning, freedom, which allows a high degree of flexibility in action, and revenues, which can be achieved at low cost, i.e. profitability, these are the goals of any management in the markets. Money is the mediator that is used to achieve the desired goal. The control of money flows must be thought of as highly complex. No matter what money is used in the domestic market, there must be rules and laws regulating the financial sector. Citizens must be able to plan for the long term and be protected from financial sharks and dishonest dealings with money. Only in this way can money promote growth and increase productivity in the desired sustainable way.

If financial capital is capable of boosting productivity, then control over the use of money and capital can sometimes be of central importance, and therefore control is not only necessary but even crucial to the success of an economy. Two contrary views have been established on this subject, neither of which Friedmann believes is acceptable. The first is the view that the economy can take care of this on its own, especially if one returns to the gold standard, which is why separate control is not necessary. The second widespread view assumes that only experts could determine the course. These experts could be located at the central bank or in a monetary office with a team of economists as part of a bureaucratic body. The reference by Thomas Mayer in the Sunday newspaper of the Frankfurter of 13.5.2018, which is to be quoted here, is astounding: "Shortly after the bankruptcy of the American bank Lehmann Brothers, the British Queen Elizabeth II asked in November 2008 why none of the economic experts had predicted the financial crisis. To this day, the guild of economists has not managed to give the Queen a conclusive answer." Now, in the aftermath of the Lehman crisis, attempts have been made to take measures to stabilize the banking sector, while leaving crisis management to those who were partly responsible for the crisis. Measures such as Basel-III, possibly Basel-IV, or simply the demand for higher capital ratios, all seem to me like curing the symptoms, while the necessary measures are not even considered in the first place. Banks that do not sufficiently control their activities, employees who speculate with customers' money and are systemically relevant because of their size, such banks should have their licenses withdrawn. In the case of large banks, splitting them up and keeping them in an association could be a solution.

The central bank, in America the Fed, in Europe the ECB, can control the money supply, first of all, by being solely responsible for money creation and prohibiting the commercial banks from doing so; of course, it could also obtain this information through a reporting system. The requirement that the commercial banks, for every loan must deposit a small part of it with the central bank is a kind of reporting system with a security aspect, but this has increasingly faded into the background over time.

It also seems that people do not really think about the statistical relevance and use it accordingly. Indeed, one problem with private money creation at present is insufficient control over the money supply thus created. In the current monetary system of the euro, this is still halfway guaranteed by the fractional reserve system and the link back to the central bank via bank loans, but overall, it seems to be very difficult to obtain precise information on the current money supply in circulation.

This raises the question not only of the money supply in circulation itself, but also of how it is controlled. The central bank can influence the market via the prime rate, i.e. the interest rate at which the central bank lends money to the banks, or by buying securities from the banks in order to bring new money onto the market.

If it is true that the Great Depression of 1933 was essentially caused by a lack of money in circulation, one can rightly take this to be the result of faulty central bank intervention, or even of no intervention at all. Friedman points out that between 1929 and 1933 the money supply in the United States fell by one-third. It is also interesting to note that about two-thirds of this is said to have resulted from Britain's departure from the gold standard, and Friedman's view that such a drastic reduction in the money supply in circulation could have been prevented by the Fed. This calls into question the competence of the group of experts assembled at the Fed, since it obviously can neither control the financial market in the right way nor intervene in a properly steering manner. The governments' attempt to intervene in a controlling manner is also obviously failing. Wouldn't it be better to prevent governments from intervening in a controlling manner? Of course, this also raises the question of whether monetary policy has the power that is so readily attributed to it. If we look at the historical development, we can show with Friedman that the introduction of the Federal Research System in the U.S.A. did not bring the expected stabilization that was hoped for. The panel of experts can make wrong decisions just as easily as the unregulated market. Nevertheless, wrong decisions are more likely to be expected from the unregulated market, and rightly so. Now this does not mean that the expert panel is necessarily needed to obtain an optimally regulated market. Insofar as self-regulating circulatory systems can be identified in the market, they should be given preference if possible. But what could these self-regulators be? Generally speaking, we must look for laws and private regulations that are capable of neither unnecessarily restricting the freedom of citizens nor destroying the stabilizing control loop in the sense of feedback loops. In any case, money creation should develop out of the needs of the citizens and not be left to the decision of a body.

When the ECB buys up large quantities of bonds and other securities on the financial markets and at the banks, it floods new money into the markets, since the money for the purchase of securities does not come from savings contracts but is created specifically for the purchase of these securities. This is done to avoid deflation, even with the explicit goal of 2% inflation. Both the natural inflation and the purchase of securities by the central bank provide in each case already alone for a devaluation of the currency. Actually, the central bank's control should ensure that the currency remains stable in value, i.e. that no devaluation takes place. The main problem here is the mixture of private and state money creation and not the question of whether it is asset money or liability money.

The central bank as a state institution can flood the market with money, as the ECB shows us, but it is questionable whether this will allow the desired control in the long run. On the other hand, with purely private money creation, there can be no central control of the money supply in circulation. However, there is no need for central control either, if in the market every market participant creates exactly the money supply through his credit, he needs. Thus, enough money should come into circulation so that business does not falter, but on the other hand, not too much money either, since it is to be hoped that only a few will make full use of their borrowing possibilities ahead of time. A purely private passive money system, we must realize, lives from borrowing from the outset, which is why it must be assumed that every citizen will take out at least his first citizen's loan. Citizen credit can be said to be the credit necessary to finance one's contribution to the common treasury as a citizen. By the fact that the circulating money supply depends on the number of participating citizens and their activities in the market, the money supply should also automatically increase with a growing population and decrease in the same way with a contraction in population growth. In this way, we achieve self-control that is superior to any panel of experts. As a reminder, the self-control referred to here is not the market left to its own devices, but a control loop secured by laws and contracts and establishing itself in many cases, which promises stability and growth at different points in the overall economic structure of the economy.

In each of the different control loops, which can ensure a regulated money supply, control is governed by different target values on the one hand, and on the other hand by the actual values tapped at a unified controlled system and the target-actual value differences to be derived from them, which lead to changes in control values with which the deviations are minimized. Since everyone tries to minimize the differences optimally, a better control effect should result on the whole average than if this is to be found out in discourse via a commission of experts. In this context, discourse in the immediate environment of borrowing is not only part of transparent information transfer, but its relevance should also neither be underestimated nor prevented.

In this context, the conscious establishment of control loops for self-regulation in the financial and monetary system with the necessary rules should be largely compatible with the principles of ordo liberalism of the Austrian school. If the necessary rules are prescribed by a commission or the central bank, this may work just as well, perhaps even better, under optimal conditions, but the democratic component is then missing. The rules must therefore be drawn up and laid down by the legislature, in Europe by the European Parliament, and confirmed by the national parliaments. It would make sense if the corresponding draft laws were submitted to the national parliaments for revision before they are voted on in Strasbourg. In this way, the missing political-democratic component could be incorporated several times over. To ensure that the rules are both effective and can be adapted, an institution to be set up by the executive branch should be charged not only with monitoring, but also with forwarding any necessary corrections to the legislative branch in the form of bills.

1. Financial control over the means of production

In general, one will hardly expect any contradiction when it is asserted that the owner of capital in an enterprise, i.e. the owner of the financial means = capital, is also the owner of the means of production. As a capitalist, the owner of capital becomes the master of the means of production and thus vulnerable to attack. After all, the means of production should belong in the hands of those who also drive production with their labor, since no production can take place without labor, no matter how many means of production are available. The socialization of the means of production, a tried-and-true reaction since the Communist Manifesto, unfortunately does not lead to control over the means of production by the workers, as conveyed by Marx and the authors inspired by him. What is correct is only that the means of production belong in the hands of those who work with them, in the correct conclusion in the private hands of those who are involved in the production and marketing of a product. Involved, however, are not only those who work on the municipality should never act as a financier, because then it cannot take over any external control without having to control itself at some point, which is clearly a dilemma. It should be pointed out once again that the municipality should not act as a financier under any circumstances, as it cannot then take on any external control without getting into the quandary of having to control itself at some point, which clearly contradicts the principle of the separation of powers in democracy. The public sector can levy taxes on the profit but must not be directly involved in the generation of the profit. In this respect, the privatisations that have already been carried out and the privatisations of public sector holdings in business enterprises that are still being demanded can only be seen as positive. However, it is usually forgotten that the land on which the business buildings are located should not be part of private property. The participation of the state of Lower Saxony, for example, should be handed over to the VW Group in an exchange for the land owned by the company, i.e. participation for land. A lease could then be agreed for the land used, which could at least partially compensate for the loss of dividend income. This would immediately exclude all entanglements of politics and private business without having to fundamentally forego a share in the revenues.

In the case of newly founded companies and smaller enterprises, as well as trading businesses, the necessary land should be made available by the municipality as leased land and the enterprise should also preferably be founded as a cooperative. Only the cooperative or cooperatively structured commons can ensure from the outset that every employee, every worker and everyone who contributes capital is both actively involved in the business and is guaranteed a share of the capital stock and thus also a right to say. The municipality, it should be explicitly stated once again, should not be granted any influence on the management, and control should only be permissible to the extent that it is fixed in the public interest as a necessary external control. External control also includes ensuring that financial capital and human capital have an equal share in profits. It is in the interest of the state organs that productivity per capita and income per capita be kept in a state of equilibrium; after all, buyers must also be found to ensure a continuous decrease in the stock of goods through purchasing.

2. The tool in the hands of the workers

In the modern production enterprise, machines are indispensable, and without capital they cannot be acquired. Therefore, new companies can hardly be founded without the use of capital. Another trend, however, is that smaller and fewer machines are being used, while new ideas tie up capital. New ideas and innovations need capital and have always needed capital to become a viable business, but now seem to be increasingly more important than financial capital. With debt capital, one usually brings the investor on board as well as the necessary money. The investor is primarily interested in increasing the return on investment, which is why he financed the machines, the tools, the development of patents. However, the profit from the sale of the produced goods can only come about if machines and people work together, which is why it should be a matter of course to share the profit between capital owners and employees. The employee, the worker, whether manager or just a controller at the machine, they are essentially involved in the success and not just a cost factor in the balance sheet. If it is the explicit will of politics to give the employee his means of production, this can be done by promoting employee share ownership. The expropriation of investors would perhaps satisfy the sense of justice of many fellow citizens but would drag the economy down in the process. Only cooperation between capital and labour on an equal footing will achieve the necessary bring evolutionary progress. In this context, it could also be helpful if, as a matter of principle, legal persons are not allowed to take out loans, sofar no capital can be created by legal persons through borrow. Instead, the use of employee capital should be promoted, which is also necessary if the capital of legal persons is eliminated. Due to the elimination of capital from institutions in which it is held through legal persons, this can only be replaced by capital from natural persons, whereby many small contributions are initially more difficult to collect, a distribution among all company employees could be a solution here!!

3. Are payments processed efficiently and in a controlled manner?

To ensure that everyone is properly remunerated for their services, it is necessary that they are remunerated with an appropriate amount. Not only the payment of money by the farms, but also the quick transfer of instructed money is important for an efficient circular economy. Control should primarily be the task of the tax offices! Measures such as the minimum wage and direct capital controls are necessary to prevent the labour market from getting out of control. It is enough if vacancies are also consistently reported to the labour offices! New payment services and cryptocurrencies shine above all through faster processing, especially in international transfers; banks are sometimes still too much stuck in the old national structures.

4. Interest rates, price formation and the labour market

In principle, it can also be assumed for the level of wages and salaries that the price on the market is formed by demand and supply, as is the case with goods. It must be considered that services and goods that cannot be increased cannot be traded on the market. Likewise, goods and services that are permanently available in abundance cannot be traded on the market. It is often forgotten that the permanent scarcity, which cannot be eliminated through the purchase price, also prevents the formation of a fair real market price. The resulting unreal market price in no case even comes close to a work performance and thus to the necessary secondary conditions for the emergence of fair market prices. The market price should evolve between scarcity and abundance along justifiable labour inputs and value estimates. The relationship between scarcity and abundance should therefore not be discussed without reference to labour performance. It was only the division of labour that led to the fact that products that citizens could no longer produce themselves also became scarce, for example because there was a lack of specialists who could produce these goods. This addresses the labour market, since there is obviously a need for these specialists. On the other hand, if these specialists are no longer needed, they become unemployed with the resulting social problems. The pendulum between scarcity and abundance of goods determines, on average, the balance between demand and supply on the market, which has to be adjusted again and again, but also depending on the labour market and the capital market. One could now construct and analyse the labour market in a model in the same way as the commodity market. However, this transfer to the labour market does not seem permissible to me for several reasons. An economic devaluation of humane work performance must not be permissible for ethical reasons alone, even if so, many superfluous work performances can be tapped. The market must be oriented in such a way that it first considers the basic human needs for satisfying work. However, the labour market as organised today cannot function according to the principle of supply and demand like the commodity market, since the dependencies on long periods of education and state educational institutions only permit equilibrium situations to settle in the long term, which can then only follow current market events with a time lag.

With the diversification of human labour, i.e. the division of labour into ever more specialised areas that require ever more detailed knowledge, scarcity is in principle determined by the amount of labour available. With the transfer of labour to machines, however, the scarcity of labour is eliminated and thus ad hoc the labour itself is devalued. This follows the same principle according to which the real value of money loses value with the quantity of money. This is immediately understandable in a short-circuit of thought, since labour performance expressed in money is also tradable and usable like money. Nevertheless, it is dangerous to lump the labour market together with the financial market and the commodity market. For the entrepreneur, the labour saved is a saving of money and means lower costs. However, the employee who is made redundant and can no longer find another job must then be financed at the expense of society. An economy must therefore ensure, not only for ethical reasons, that as many citizens as possible are in work, i.e. that they have a job that is subject to social insurance contributions. If workers are made redundant in the manufacturing sector, in the future probably increasingly by robots, society must find a way to compensate, for example by financing jobs through the profits of the companies that make workers redundant. A society that replaces all jobs with robots without creating new jobs could eventually suffocate from technical waste, from a modern antiquarian bookshop that no one wants any more because no one can pay for it, even if the market price falls below the fixed costs or the marginal costs tend towards zero. It is precisely the fixed costs that always must be taken into account that show us that the market cannot be kept stable solely in the equilibrium between supply and demand, but that the question of investments also has to be taken into account. If investments are co-conditioned by interest rates, low interest rates can tempt people to invest even when demand is low. Wrong investments and thus also wrong investment impulses can lead to high losses up to insolvency, and in general to a recession. More helpful than cheap money could be public sector contracts, which keep citizens in work or even bring them into work. The labour output of citizens can ensure sustainable growth, but it must also be financed. Since work performance is the cornerstone of general prosperity, there can be no truly unconditional basic income, at least not without considering working life.

5. Making a welfare society with the consciousness to respect human right-

The basic income as largely unconditional, a basic income based on solidarity, is one of the best approaches to making a welfare society stable and worth living in for the future. The willingness of the recipient to give something back to society in return for an otherwise unconditional basic income should be the basic condition for enjoying a basic income. This basic prerequisite is not an if-then demand, since it already results from the requirement in the Basic Law to respect human rights, because work for the Community should be part of the work to which everyone is entitled in order to be able to live in dignity and participate in community life.

In the real economy, the satisfaction of these demands can only be realised if there is a general awareness of necessary interdependencies. A consciousness must be created that makes life in ever more condensed environments still appear bearable and responsible. This awareness can be promoted by a money economy based on credit, which does not only have enrichment in mind and does not satisfy the greed of individual citizens, but rather secures basic needs, as in the case of the Safe Money favoured here and work in cooperatively organised fields of work.

The increase in productivity is now often paid for with a devaluation of human labour power, which can also lead to the mass unemployment that can be observed. This does not have to be the case, otherwise we would have to go back to the Stone Age to become happy people. No, however, we must adapt the valuation of human labour to the new conditions, and we must do so again and again. The rampant disregard for intellectual capital is a problem here. Intellectual products, once created with a lot of work, can then be copied at the click of a mouse and disseminated at will. It is not for nothing that the old family recipes of a baker were subject to strict secrecy, since they were the true capital of this family, the intellectual capital, addressed here in the book and especially in the subsequent volume with the educational capital.

Today, all this is offered for free on the internet or simply stolen through targeted industrial espionage and, in the best case, acquired by buying the company. This may then be ticked off as the interest on the knowledge horizon. As a rule, however, it is not so much the originators who gain from the new achievements, but rather the managers in the sales organisation. If large corporations now buy the specialised knowledge that has emerged in the division of labour, the knowledge is retained, but a niche, an important market participant, disappears. Oligopolisation with subsequent monopolisation then leads to impoverishment in the relational space. Only the diversity of niches guarantees the stability and robustness of an economic system. Therefore, one of the most important tasks of the state is to ensure that oligopolies and monopolies cannot arise in the market. Nevertheless, size can also be advantageous, especially when the associated rationalisation gains are considered. If two firms that operate in the same niche merge, this is beneficial, both for the firm and for the associated economy. If, on the other hand, firms that serve different market segments, i.e. operate in different niches, merge, the diversity of niches is reduced, which can have a negative impact on the stability of an economy.

The market, which can only form fair prices between scarcity and abundance, must be able to draw on the diversity of suppliers. In the case of unfair prices, this leads to insolvency or, in the case of misguided expectations, often to overproduction and the wasteful use of scarce resources.

If only what finds a buyer is produced, since production is only on demand, the price can settle far below today's usual prices without reducing profits. If, in addition, there are joint structures between production and consumption that guarantee the producer permanent sales and the consumer the best quality of goods, a price can be formed on a reciprocal basis. The use of common means of production can be compensated with a fee for the individual user. Offsetting wear and tear with interest is only acceptable if the provision of financial resources is not additionally included in an interest rate. The interest rate, which includes different calculations, unfortunately usually leads to a lack of transparency in the cost estimates and can only be just right for those who want to conceal the true costs in order to make higher profits. In any case, investments are also easier to calculate if no interest payments must be made for the required capital. This is possible with "safe money", but it requires different regulations from those currently in use, which are sufficiently described in principle here in the book.

At present, the central banks try to change the general interest rate by raising or lowering the key interest rate and thus exert an influence on investment activity. Since with Safe Money the accounts are kept interest-free, this makes the discussion about the influence of interest rates on price formation and unemployment, a structural variable that is quite important in classical economics, superfluous. It should be noted that secure money and secured capital can also be used to finance job creation programmes, as has been done so far. This way of trying to eliminate unemployment has been used again and again in recent decades, but it has also regularly increased the debt ratio of the public sector, because there are currently no really helpful prohibitions on the public sector borrowing money. Another way in the current monetary system is to lower the key interest rate and increase the money supply. In the short term, small successes are always possible in this way, but a breakthrough has not yet been achieved. The idea of increasing government spending in times of high unemployment in order to create new jobs and paying off debts in times of full employment almost doesn't work at all, perhaps because it is simply too easy for politicians to keep creating new debts and to wait to pay off debts after the fact, since no election promises can be realised in this way!

In the safe money system, this debt trap does not exist for the public sector; on the other hand, many possibilities of financing, as mentioned above, are eliminated because the public sector cannot take out loans in this currency. One may regret this, but there are also good reasons to note this with a certain amount of joy, since the measures mentioned are ultimately ineffective in the conventional monetary system if the debts of the municipalities continue to rise and rise. If, on the other hand, it is possible to create jobs without getting into debt, this should be conducive to the desired growth, and conducive in the long term. On the other hand, if there is too little money in circulation, this can have a negative effect on growth processes, can even stop them, money becomes a limiting factor. Money can nevertheless not cause more growth than the other factors allow. In the safe money system, the money supply is controlled by the citizen as a customer, it is produced according to demand, therefore safe money should always be available in sufficient quantities in the corresponding money system, so that this cannot inhibit growth in this respect. The decisive factor in the Safe Money system is the target with which new project ideas for building new structures are launched, and not the money, as this only comes into play as a secondary factor. Should liquidity problems nevertheless arise, the national central bank can selectively channel money into the market by pumping a certain amount of money into the market without a loan agreement, quasi like a gift, and this sensibly with a limited validity. If there is no interest on borrowed money, there can be no inhibition of growth by the interest rate, the only thing that is important is the correlation between money and labour output. If, for example, a property is bought that corresponds to the security through work performance for the money received, it is only necessary to ensure that the monthly repayment instalments can in all likelihood also be raised by the customers, and in an appropriate amount to the expected loss in value of the property.

Generally, in the Safe Money system, unemployment would not be eliminated with public money, but with projects in which the municipality can participate with ideas, free licence agreements and temporarily free leasehold land, and otherwise raise the necessary funds privately.

The ideal state in the Safe Monetary Area would be when there is no inflation and employment remains borderline to full employment, so there are also no price bubbles or mass unemployment. If price formation is oriented towards labour output, one could assume that there is also no inflation and insofar the Safe Currency even promises full employment with stable money of value in the ideal case. Since inflation primarily reflects the loss of value of a currency, a safe currency without loss of value should also know no inflation. The reality could be very close to this if binding working hours with the right to a minimum working time are fixed. In this way, the basic salary can also be securely financed for everyone. Working hours, wage development and profits must not be decoupled. By decree and law, for example, on-site customer service in the local market must be made compulsory even for large corporations. It is time to think more about the jobs of the future and not to assume that the market itself can regulate this. Regulatory laws must be passed that can regulate employment in such a way that every citizen can find a job without the need for state administration of unemployment. Above all, we should not underestimate the innovative power of competing companies under pressure to come to the market with innovations in order to conquer a niche for themselves as the sole representative of this niche. Misunderstood competition, on the other hand, leads to precarious working conditions and the administration of the superfluous unemployment that thus also arises, which is certainly not conducive to lasting and sustainable humane economic growth! The necessary regulations, the counteracting regulatory laws, also include those that efficiently maintain and expand diversity in our markets. Self-regulated democratic local markets and local production cooperatives are important here, as well as family businesses that are to be stabilised in such a way that they can take on the large corporations. If necessary, it will also be necessary to break up oligopolists in the market in order to maintain viable smaller units in the market and even create new ones if necessary. At some point, it will be necessary to agree to distribute and thus limit power in the market, just as power in political systems, according to objective considerations. Neither money nor voting majorities in democracy are suitable for maintaining and even expanding the democratic-republican achievements of power-sharing. This requires a strongly anchored awareness of the corresponding democratic values in the minds of the citizens. This can be achieved solely through education, equal educational opportunities and performance-based remuneration.

6. How are services to society rightfully remunerated?

Many activities that are harmful to society are financed with money that comes not only from private funds but also from public budgets. In many positive activities, on the other hand, funds sometimes flow only sparingly. Payments made for purely power-political reasons are also harmful. The farmer, as an environmentalist and helper in the goal of achieving climate neutrality, should be supported more strongly, as should the citizen who is willing to forego his own comforts for the sake of a positive climate policy. Likewise, more money should flow into supporting voluntary and honorary services.

If a basic salary is also paid in retirement, this should be increased appropriately for voluntary workers. Voluntary work should not go unnoticed, nor should commitment to family, children and the elderly, especially in the private care sector. An increase in the basic salary or consideration in the calculation of the pension should be a matter of course. Here, the emotional lines should consciously lead to a strengthening of the community on the rational level as well. Rational strategies need emotional support for their success balance. This applies not only to the individual citizen, but also at the national level for the balance in the international movement of goods and money.

7. Common currency and national currencies

Since the introduction of a common currency in the EU with the aim of introducing the euro as the common currency in all states that belong to the EU, many of the member states are still not part of the monetary union until 2020. In addition, there is a great disparity in economic strength between the states that belong to the monetary union. This makes financial control more difficult, although the control possibilities are comparable to those of a national central bank. The national central bank can take appropriate measures for the respective economy relatively quickly in accordance with the economic development. The ECB does not have such an easy task, as it must take into account the development in all member states, especially those within the monetary union, which unfortunately are not uniform. The central bank of a common currency always runs the risk of not keeping the currency in the right balance for all member states, of accepting an exchange rate that is too high or too low. Because of the lack of possibilities to precisely adjust the currency for the individual member states, government securities should not be permitted in this common currency, the existing securities denominated in euros, for example, should be allowed to expire and further issues stopped, sometimes hardly feasible, a dilemma. A way out of this dilemma could be the introduction of parallel currencies. To do this, only the old currencies would have to be re-admitted as second currencies, and EU states without the euro could introduce the euro as a second currency and let their own currency continue to run as the main currency. Once people have become accustomed to two parallel currencies, it could also be easier to accept a third currency in circulation.

Payments for work done and for the purchase of services and assets can be made more quickly today than was the case 50 years ago, and cross-border payments in the euro area in particular are easier and more efficient to process. Nevertheless, several steps and sometimes several banks are still required to get the money from A to B. The digitalisation of the processes promises faster processing as far as only the forwarding is concerned, but the necessary control is still time-consuming. Only direct processing from account to account could fundamentally change this. Sometimes it can be quite important that the processing of a financial transaction takes only fractions of a second. That is why international transactions are usually conducted in one of the reserve currencies, most of them in US dollars. In the same way, the transfer between two Free Banks in the NIM currency could be straightforward and direct if the partners have an account at a Free Bank. But the future may also present us with another reserve currency, sometimes the Chinese renminbi, or perhaps more cryptocurrencies will be used.

Even if payments are made in the same currency, this does not automatically mean that everything is done at the speed of a phone call. If one analyses the current processes closely, it is noticeable that secure transfers are controlled via transfer systems, such as the Target2 system, where detours and multi-step processes not only consume time, but also bring to light imbalances that are easily misunderstood. Higher balances in favour of the northern regions in the EU and the corresponding debts for the southern regions point to an imbalance, but not to legally enforceable debts. Kranen shows very clearly in his essay "On Bogus Giants" that the unbalanced Target balances can be offset by annual transfers to an account at the ECB. Admittedly, this does not solve the problems that such an imbalance indicates. Since money can also bypass the banks in the case of direct purchases, even in cross-border transactions, if these are paid for with the banks' own currency reserves, the Target balances also do not provide all-embracing information on monetary transactions. Direct transfers between two free banks should not affect the Target2 balances either. Whether direct settlement or transfer via special transfer systems, it is important to have rules and laws that guarantee secure payment transactions. A distinction must be made between international payment transactions and local payment processes. Even if globally digital processing promises security with high speed, in the local area cash or a corresponding substitute could be more efficient and secure. A partial shielding of the local market would be desirable and would also give the citizen in the market of his trust more of a feeling of security than can ever be possible with international safeguards. If one were to work with local cash in the local markets, it would be possible to keep a better eye on one's own finances, better in one's private purse, despite the digitalisation in the financial system, and to continue to be able to teach young people the right way to handle money in a form that includes all forms of sensor technology. If the cash is initially exchanged with the card at the locally valid exchange rate, it can be exchanged back accordingly after the purchase. The exchange fees can be charged directly or can also be settled via the general market fees. In the local market, however, only cash cards and local cash should be accepted.

8. Is performance-related pay being paid?

In an article in the Frankfurter Allgemeine with the headline "How performance is punished" one gets a partial answer for the low-wage sector with a look at a hardly noticed phenomenon, the "social saw blade". Between 15000 and 40000 Euro annual income there are several jump points, which means that there an increased gross salary leads to a minus in the net. This rightly raises the question for those affected whether it is still worthwhile to work harder. Further examples can be given with the help of tax progression. In all these cases, money does not promote growth, as would normally be expected, but blocks it. Such effects can arise when parallel developments are not sufficiently coordinated and the administrators, and even more so the legislators, do not have the necessary overview and insights.

If everyone receives a basic income with which the basic needs can be satisfied, and in the best case they do not have to pay income tax up to twice the basic income, then such effects can basically no longer occur. On the other hand, if such a basic income is introduced, social benefits such as Hartz IV can be abolished, as well as housing benefit or education allowances. If then only that which exceeds twice the basic income is taken into account for tax purposes, the jumps like the "social saw blade" are probably no longer conceivable. In general, one should consider that remuneration that is not performance-related will lead to disruptions in the growth process. On the other hand, bonuses that are not performance-related can also have a growth-inhibiting effect. The ownership of the means of production alone is not to be regarded as a service to be remunerated, but the labour services saved with it and their management are.

Money can be used as remuneration for any kind of work performance, to finance wars, to pay for criminal acts, generally to intervene in the development and processes of a country. society, both positively and negatively. Both construction and deconstruction are controlled with money. Money is neither good nor evil, but it is also not rationally bound. In the market, the flow of money will also follow emotional lines more often than assumed. The relational patterns tend to obey the rational lines, the psychological patterns tend to obey the emotional lines. Reward often follows both rational and emotional patterns. To the problem of performance-related pay, there is sometimes a lack of clear rational comparative analyses that promote fair pay. Of course, people are also not paid according to their performance if they take advantage of people's hardship, are hired and paid according to gender or the vitamin B principle in order to maximise their own profit and that of their family and friends with below-average pay. Especially in many developing countries, but also in various sectors of highly developed countries, the performance rendered is not always adequately rewarded. It will also not always be possible to exclude the possibility that work that is currently not in such high demand is temporarily not remunerated and paid according to performance. This can be tolerated in the short term but must not lead to the creation of customary rights in the longer term and thus to a widening of the gap between rich and poor.

9. Can the financial market be controlled at all?

If only local money is used for payment in the local market, this is relatively easy to control. It is only with the global transfer of money that control becomes extremely difficult or even impossible. The control of suppliers to the local market should still be sufficiently successful. The control of stock markets as well as bond markets and securities not traded on the stock exchange should be more difficult, especially if there is no legal means to control financial jugglers outside the regulated markets. Without the obligation to register every financial instrument that is traded with the financial supervisory authority and to regularly provide data for a controlling analysis of business practices, the capital market will never be brought under control. It is still too easy for financial sharks and small-time crooks to use all kinds of tricks to pretend that they have the necessary business capital and to transfer the money they have collected to a tax haven and then apply for insolvency. It is to be assumed that 50 to 60% of insolvencies are arranged with sufficient criminal energy and that the insolvency could have been avoided by the honourable businessman. The question is somewhat different if we change the perspective and do not look at the control of the individual, more or less defenceless citizen, but scrutinise the control from the point of view of the global corporations, where in any case only the weal and woe of the corporation counts! When it is no longer the bank that controls the transactions of the money but the payment service of the corporation, then the question arises whether and when the state and its central bank have finally lost their influence on the money markets. One could point out this state of affairs as the state with the desirable private control, unfortunately the control of the oligopolists runs over the heads of the citizens without establishing a democratic reference. The acquisition of information by the corporations generally does not serve democratic transparency, but rather their own manipulative objectives.

 The question is somewhat different if we change the perspective and look not so much at the control for the benefit of the individual citizen, but for the benefit of the corporation. If, on top of that, financial transactions are no longer processed via the bank but via the corporation's own payment service, then at some point in the future it will hardly be possible to control these corporations. Multinational corporations will do everything in their power to the aim is to elicit all conceivable information from the market in order to better manipulate the transparent citizen. Those who know exactly the buying behaviour of customers and their financial situation can influence the market in a targeted manner and thus occupy positions of power, and this worldwide. Therefore, in a democratic state, the citizen must also be protected from the free appropriation of information by commercial institutions and organisations; the passing on of personal information by public authorities should be prohibited by law. Non-democratic control over the market in its full complexity should also be prohibited for all institutions that are not democratically legitimised to do so. If the information about customers stored and managed by the banks is protected in such a secure way as can be expected from free banks in the Safe Money System, a floodgate should already be closed through which information can get into foreign hands without the explicit wish of the citizens. Therefore, direct control of account holders within the banking system is also important, perhaps best done by a bank owned by its customers. Without a clear position on this by society and its institutions, individual citizens will find it very difficult to assert themselves against the global corporations. The nation state or a superior power structure legitimised by the citizen must hold the social control and carry it out against everyone without exception.

This does not mean that the state should always and everywhere interfere; on the contrary, it should neither seek stakes in companies nor carry out financial transactions on its own, not even through the central bank as a state organ. Central banks should exercise control together with the financial supervisory authority, but not intervene in transactions themselves.

Those acting in the market need higher-level control but can only control themselves in democratic bodies and institutions on the basis of clear regulations, which is why clear laws are necessary here, with which a controllable coexistence within self-determined limits becomes possible. Central banks, which are entrusted with the state task of being the only institution in the state to create national money, can certainly also control the commercial banks to which they hand over the money, but they can then no longer control the creation of money themselves; this would have to be done by an institution independent of the central bank.

Since the financial market in particular crosses national borders very easily and quickly, it applies to national and local markets that legal transactions in the market must be brought down to the local institutions. We must distinguish between social control, community control and private control, which must be clearly separated in legal terms.

X. Social control

"The essential condition of the monetary order currently in force is the monopolistic position of central banks, since private money production through book money is also subject to their supervision and quoted in the state currency unit."

(Kowalski, 2018)

The still existing control of money creation by the central bank cannot be equated with efficient control in the EU, for example. One problem here is the shared control, namely by central banks and commercial banks! What is missing is democratic control, democratically legitimised control, which is to be brought in either through an institution established and controlled by parliament or through legally regulated processes of a self-regulating credit system. One could also say that capitalism must be brought into democratically controlled channels. Whether we strive for a free liberal order or a more centrally directed economic order, in either case there is a need for good laws that make trade possible in peace and without lasting disputes.

Even if the controversy between capitalism and socialism as in the times of the "Cold War" no longer exists, the ideological disputes have not completely disappeared. Apparently, since the end of the 20th century, new religiously based disputes from the Islamic region have joined them, sometimes even more aggressively than is known from the previous religious wars and the disputes in the secular sphere. In addition to the demand for the practice of religion in a humane manner, which has made its peace with the political system and is accordingly allowed to claim its religious freedom, an open political discourse should bring the religious ideological dispute down to a factual level. In an effort to establish factual political control, one can also ask whether there can be a humane capitalism and how capital in a social system could positively and humanely ensure the continuance of the community. And what could be a humane socialism, both integrated into a humane and free democracy?

In any case, control over laws and regulations with levies and taxes is exercised by state institutions, which ensure that regulatory requirements are followed. In addition to laws that control behaviour, laws that regulate ownership are of paramount importance. Which of the goods should be private property, which communal, which social property?

Means of production, be it only the hammer and the folding rule or even a machine, may not be socialised, they clearly belong to private property and can at most be freely communalised on a contractual basis. The socialisation of the means of production does not guarantee better control in the sense of the working people. On the other hand, a community of craftsmen can jointly acquire machines that the individual cannot pay for and declare them as common property. Such communitarisation is to be clearly distinguished from socialisation, and this regardless of how the state is politically organised. Similarly, it cannot be denied that the accumulation of capital in the wrong hands can lead to a private constellation of power in which those who do the work in this society are no longer masters of the means of production with which they create social surplus value. The past decades have shown that the socialisation of the means of production does not provide a remedy here, perhaps rather communitarisation in cooperatives and self-help groups, as well as in communities of solidarity.

From the point of view of control, it is very clear that socialisation largely lacks the control that is given in communitarisation by the control set by the legislator through enforceable legal regulations. The legal regulations are precisely the means by which the state should and must intervene. When, according to a report in the FAZ, the Deutsche Bank calls for a legal framework for green bonds, as this is the only way exponential growth is possible, this is a good example of the state's control function. How the money flows depends not only, but also, on the legal framework, framework conditions. Stock corporation law and the legal framework for limited liability companies have a significant share in the structural conditions for the formation of corporations. If you want to prevent capital owners from pocketing the profits and charging the losses to the customers and the community, you must fundamentally change the legal provisions on liability. Moral appeals and ethics seminars for managers are of little help here. Apart from changes in liability in company law, it must be possible to integrate internationally operating large corporations into local markets for the benefit of every citizen, not only in terms of liability, but also in terms of customer contact and local presence. The local customer must have a say in how the goods sold in the local market are produced and brought in.

It is to be hoped that it will be possible to bring together financial capital and human capital worldwide and to consider them equally in the determination of profits. Instead of creating a capital equalisation via the rich tax that is repeatedly brought into the discussion, it could make more sense to change the distribution of profits at the place of origin of the profit, which would be fairer and, moreover, in any case more cost-effective for the economy. If one wants to tax the labour output of machines in the same way as the labour output of humans, one could divide the pre-tax profit equally between the financial capital and the human capital used, whereby the costs would then also have to be allocated in advance in the same way when calculating the tax. For an exact cost-profit calculation, both the costs of using the machines and the costs of wages and salaries, as well as other expenses for the employees, should first be deducted from the revenues before the pre-tax profits for financial capital and human capital are shown.

If we look at the inequalities in the world, the question immediately arises as to how these come about and where we find the greatest inequalities. Conversely, one can of course also ask where the least inequalities exist. According to Friedman, these are the capitalist systems. If this is true, then the question immediately arises as to how it comes to be the way it is. Capitalism obviously uses the forces inherent in the system that arise from the potential differences between inequalities. In non-capitalist systems, inequalities are either negated or attempts are made to systematically eliminate them, as well as to systematically attribute them to higher powers. In many cases, even the natural tendency to abolish inequality is blocked, or in the active effort to eliminate inequalities, one encounters differences that can no longer be balanced peacefully, and which are heading for system destruction faster than can be grasped. Only the smaller imbalances can always be resolved shortly after they have arisen. Therefore, the primary goal should be to maintain diversity and not to bring the various subsystems and niches all into equilibrium at the same time. The stability of the system, however, cannot therefore be determined from the sum of the system elements concerned; it is always more than the sum of its parts, since the relations between the individual parts and here between the individual niches can only determine and explain the whole.

When we speak of inequality and think of inequality in access to the achievements of the affluent society, we should not just work it up in a blanket way. In addition to inequality in the ownership of assets, inequality in the distribution of income and inequality in talents and starting positions at the beginning of life should be addressed and not forgotten. It is entirely laudable and sensible to want to eradicate unjust inequalities. However, the natural drivers to eliminate and curb inequalities should not be ignored. Under no circumstances should we give in to tendencies that try to eliminate inequality by bureaucratic means, because this disregards the natural forces that can do this better. In the process, useful energies are also dissipated, and the result is Instead, frictional resistances that can erupt at some points and are reflected in revolutions. Capitalism in its diversely fractured form may never make the existing inequalities disappear completely, but it can always bring them back into the central equilibrium of the system, but certainly only insofar as a high diversity of niches keeps open the necessary possibilities for this. As soon as this diversity disappears and only a few monopolies embody the capitalist system, one will have to reckon with more and higher inequalities and imbalances, which at some point will also lead to an undesired outbreak and ultimately to civil war!

1. Inequalities and imbalances!

From the perspective of finance capital, wealth and income are the two central poles of imbalances in the economic process that generate inequality. If Piketty assumes in his book that a comparison over many decades obviously shows that at certain points the gap between rich and poor is continuously widening, although in general the tendency cannot be denied that the poor are also better off in our century than in the centuries before, one can, like Piketty, call for a redistribution through a wealth tax. This is an attempt to minimise the effects of wrong development through rules on redistribution. But, it would be better to remedy current financial problems with a one-off levy, for example, a one-off levy to renovate schools, or to financially support the need for digitalisation in educational institutions. Another way to tackle poverty directly is the idea of a negative tax, as Friedman proposes. Of course, the basic salary derived from the negative tax, for example, in a practical endeavour, must be financed with tax revenues. However, in my opinion, it is not in line with Friedman's ideas to accomplish this with an additional tax. Friedman's concept is rather to finance these expenditures by eliminating benefits in kind from the social budget, because it is better to give the money directly into the hands of the needy and not to favour a control through benefits in kind, so as not to take the responsibility for one's own life out of the hands of the "social welfare recipient". A basic salary is not so much a means of fighting poverty as a means of helping people to help themselves, which is more humane than the oppressive social assistance of the past hundred years. Of course, this approach also requires psychological support, only if necessary, and, if necessary, restrictions if, despite help, the money provided is not used to maintain a dignified life. The point here is that inequalities and imbalances are not reinforced by bureaucratic measures and state intervention.

This does not exclude counselling in state counselling centres; this can even be done better if job placement and the payment and granting of financial aid are not linked to it.

Positive effects from imbalances can only be expected if the resulting differences in potential can freely exchange themselves in a system-theoretical view and, moreover, if the differences are not too strong. Translated into everyday language, space must be left for free activities to fit positively into the social environment and state intervention must only be undertaken when the imbalances reach a level that cannot be tolerated any longer. However, the state should always be in the driver's seat when it comes to control functions, be it to protect the private sphere or to protect economic freedoms of action. Nowadays, a national economy is no longer conceivable without banks and bank-like institutions, which is why the control of these institutions is unavoidable, especially since they are largely systemically relevant. Private banks can now no more be protected from insolvency by state intervention than can transport companies. Providing the infrastructure is the primary task of the public sector, not filling the substantial positions. How this infrastructure is used by private companies should basically be up to the state remain a private matter as long as the public interest is safeguarded, and this can be ensured through controls. Care must be taken to ensure that no institutions and companies can emerge and assert themselves in the financial sector that contradict the rules of good commercial management and give rise to unnatural, non-legitimisable disparities in relative valuations.

Addition to the diversion of funds in the social sector, tax measures are also conceivable. These should not be done simply through more taxes, but through restructuring that also makes loopholes disappear and simplifies the tax system as a whole and makes it more transparent. Transparency should be improved by a profit tax alone, with the elimination of turnover tax and income tax. Moreover, the loopholes will also disappear if profits are consistently taxed only where they arise.

There is no need to worry that this will cause an export-oriented economy, such as Germany's, to lose an excessive amount of tax money, since in the long run high exports also imply high imports, especially if VAT is abolished at the same time.

The accumulation of financial capital is not only problematic because it makes the rich richer and the poor poorer, it can also gradually have a system-destroying effect even without the rising tensions between rich and poor. If the increased use of financial capital and a retreat in human capital creates an imbalance with tendencies in the same direction in the market and in the political centres of power, this can be counteracted if capital is not chased away with a profit tax replacing sales tax and income tax and if inheritance tax and wealth tax are waived, but instead the profits from it are taxed heavily. The equality of citizens before the law should also apply in the market, capital gains should not be taxed less than the profits from hard and tireless work. It might also be fairer not to tax more tangible assets in general, i.e. substantially, but only functionally the profits where they arise. Profits from internet purchases always arise where the user is physically located at the time of logging in, usually the buyer's place of residence.

The pure profit tax could cause problems if everyone reduces their profits to as close to zero as possible by increasing their costs. To do this, however, either the investments must be increased or the wages of the employees have to be raised. If investments in machinery, for example, do not promise a higher return and no increase in the value of the company, then the only way is probably through better remuneration, which may well be desirable. Costs that do not serve the goal of making a profit can of course also be disregarded; this option also remains open to the tax office in the case of a changeover to profit tax. However, efficient social control is only possible if all profits are taxed equally and, moreover, if they are taxed in the first place.

It is not only the large corporations that prefer to pay no tax. Legally, according to current law, every citizen can avoid paying taxes if he first lives in the property, he wants to sell himself. This cannot be maintained in a pure profit tax system, nor should it burden the ordinary citizen more than it does now. If, when selling the owner-occupied property, the profit is taxable, this will increase the sales price, which does not automatically lead to higher costs for the buyer, since at the same time the substantial land transfer tax for the buyer is omitted. The profit of the owner-occupied house as in the case of the rented house is taxed, but costs for refurbishment and renovation of a property could significantly reduce a profit tax when selling, so that this change does not usually lead to increased tax expenses.

Business tax is also fatal if it causes the entrepreneur to register his business in a tax haven. It is precisely large companies that like to choose this route and thus generate wealth that is by no means the result of the owner's tireless work. Likewise, interest on money lent out can generate wealth that is not performance-related, but simply due to the better algorithm. The abolition of the trade tax and the increase of the capital tax could be demanded from this with full justification, especially since in further consequence a fusion of trade tax and capital tax would correspond to a fairer tax.

The proposal of a global capital tax could possibly promise a faster equalisation of the diverging ownership structures. However, the global capital tax could only keep this promise if it does not undermine the profit tax and does not allow any loopholes due to international agreements. It then remains to be clarified where the capital tax is to be paid and how an associated reduction in global capital is to be classified. If one assumes that the tax is always to be paid where the profits arise, then this is quite unproblematic in the case of food purchases, but not in the case of capital gains. Strictly speaking, the capital gain from shares naturally arises at the company headquarters, just as the gain from wages and salaries also arises there, at the workplace. Because of the splitting of a shareholding into many different shares with different company headquarters, this can cause problems; it should therefore also be possible, in the case of capital ownership, to consider the residence of the holder of a security as the place where a profit arises upon application. However, only the place of permanent residence where other proceeds and income have been registered can be considered the place of residence.

However, profits can also arise when money of one currency is exchanged for another currency, whether in an exchange office or also in the bank. In principle, the profit on currency exchange should be calculated based on the difference between the baskets of goods involved.

Whether it is fiscal sovereignty or legislative sovereignty, the state and its organs are always called upon, also and especially when it comes to maintaining and expanding civil liberties. Therefore, for the sake of preserving freedom, state intervention and control systems should not be rejected in principle. The market can only function and be self-regulating if the necessary laws and control systems work, control systems that guarantee fair competition. Leaving the market to its own devices in a laissez-faire style without setting the necessary limits with a generally accepted regulation is quite simply naïve and has nothing to do with liberality, but rather with irresponsible laissez-faire behaviour that promotes the power of the strongest and thus restricts the freedom of the individual citizen. If no action is taken in time, the argument will soon be put forward that the company, the bank, is too big, even systemically important, to be wound up through insolvency. As with other companies, the size and interconnectedness of large corporations and systemically important banks must, without exception, be kept under control even before an impending insolvency. What form this control must take depends not least on the monetary system in which we find ourselves. Financial transactions should be controlled and registered even if they are not carried out through the banking system.

2. Monetary policy, control or enrichment?

"Above all, we must not want to achieve a sham success by entering into a new inflationary development through a progressive dilution of our money, which has become stable again in the meantime, and thus once again invisibly taking the honestly earned money out of savers' pockets. This would truly be the most curse-worthy method we can think of."

(L. Erhard 1957)

Monetary policy can have an impact on society through the central bank, through the spending policy of the public sector and through tax legislation, but also through the creation of money itself. Since time immemorial, and even more so since the link to precious metals was removed, it has been customary when creating money, which is still a shelf of the rulers, to retain part of the virtual value created with it, seigniorage, money that is taken away from the citizen without being asked. Instead of printing, creating money, the state should, by means of the executive organs, supervise and control the laws of money creation in their law-abiding execution. In the active money system, the main control can be exercised directly over the state-ordered creation of money; in the passive system, on the other hand, this process can already be controlled only indirectly through laws. In both systems, the guidelines should be determined by parliament, in its task of initiating the necessary laws. If the introduction of full money completely abolishes the creation of money through credit, the state with its central bank can control and steer the money supply and circulation relatively well, which, however, is more in line with a planned economy and favours the wise ruler. Democratic control is more complex in any case, can be realised in the active money order with an elected council of experts, in the passive money order with institutions which, like the free banks, keep a register of the potential labour of their customers. However, as with other initiatives in democracy, the control here should also come from the legislature, since it can set the rules for this in laws, which should then be given the necessary local control in a financial executive. Whether this is assigned to the tax offices or rather to the Bafin, it is important that it is independent of the political power centre so that the state cannot reach into the money pots without hesitation. Without special democratic legitimacy, no one should be able to determine the money market. Even if one votes for full money, as Thomas Mayer did in connection with the discussions on the Swiss vote on full money, one must think about better corresponding regulations and possibilities of control by the citizens. Such regulations are becoming even more important because the large international corporations are setting up their own payment systems and will probably also take over the creation of money in the future, in any case take control of the monetary system in their area. Digitisation accelerates such processes and leads to global intra-corporate money circuits, which could help this corporate currency to emerge from the corner of cryptocurrencies. With sufficient currency reserves, employees could be paid in the group currency and thus create an independent international currency! As long as the state does not allow its citizens to use it to pay their tax debts, it is not yet a state-accepted currency, but the road is sometimes not far away. Even if this is made palatable to the customer with many conveniences, the internal control and steering sovereignty thus achieved deprives the citizen even more of the much-needed individual control than the banks already do today. Regardless of how money is created and who controls it, the state must take money into its hands in order to be able to fulfil all the tasks that are expected of it. Therefore, it is important to generate sufficient revenue for the state, but not through the money creation process. Revenues for the public sector should flow through taxes, fees and rents, as well as licence fees, i.e. they should be part of fiscal policy, not part of monetary policy. Money should remain stable and not be devalued by the enrichment of those who manage it and the creation process itself. The money to pay the army of people who work for the state, it seems obvious to me, is to be generated through taxes. Investments in road networks, communication networks and the education system, on the other hand, can also be financed by the participating users, so that costs in these areas do not have to be too high. However, since a good education system is essential for survival, the basic needs of a general education will also be financed through taxes. Because of the great economic importance, investments in education and infrastructure in particular will be made in interest-based monetary systems via credit financing. It is then considered reasonable to stimulate the economy with credit money in times of cheap credit in order to pay it back in times of expensive credit. To neglect important investments, even if the money is available at negative interest rates, is unreasonable. It must not be the case that vital investments fall victim to a debt brake when the interest rate falls below zero. In an interest-free system, however, different standards will have to be applied than are currently the norm.

In principle, however, it seems better to me if the money supply and the value of money develop out of the activity of citizens, as is to be expected in a monetary system based on personal credit. Regardless of how money is created, and to a certain extent independent of it, the state must take money into its hands to finance its civil servants and employees, to further expand the transport routes, and to finance the education system, to mention only the main tasks. Investments in road networks, communication networks and education systems are vital and can control and boost economic activity more than all the money in the world can. Of course, investment is not free, and yet such investment must not be allowed to fall victim to a debt brake. In an interest-based monetary system, it should be reasonable to borrow in times of cheap credit and deleverage in times of expensive credit. To neglect important investments when the money itself is available at negative interest rates is unreasonable. In an interest-free system, however, different standards will have to be applied, but even in such a system one will not want to postpone necessary investments unnecessarily. If we therefore want a debt-free state, we will have to find other ways to finance the necessary investments. One possibility would be to allocate the costs to the beneficiaries of the state investments, for example through fees and user charges. Another possibility would be to adjust or increase taxes. In most countries, taxes have almost always been used to finance government expenditure. However, many taxes were justified at the time of their introduction as having a controlling function, which is then very soon forgotten. Taxes on alcoholic beverages, coffee and sugar were and still are introduced, among other things, to deliberately make the corresponding goods more expensive and thus curb consumption in these areas.

Recently, the sugar tax has been discussed and already introduced in several states in order to curb unhealthy sugar consumption. In a country with customs borders, this may have the desired effects, but in a customs union, different taxes in this regard should be undesirable; one would have to agree on uniform tax legislation. The reintroduction of a unified profit tax with the simultaneous abolition of the many substantial taxes may also initially meet with rejection out of fear of giving up control functions, since one can apparently no longer intervene in economic activity with the profit tax. In fact, a rethink is necessary, but with a small auxiliary strategy it should be easier than initially assumed. Let us go through the current taxes and ask ourselves why they were introduced and how they appear in cost terms as taxable expenditure or even pre-tax revenue. Let's take the coffee tax, which makes little sense even from the point of view of health care and is therefore best simply abolished. If one nevertheless wants to continue to tax excessive coffee consumption, this can be achieved by making coffee ineligible in the individual offsetting of deductible costs. All luxury goods can be excluded, as well as substances that are hazardous to health, when the deductible goods are listed, to the Reminder, it is a matter of deducting the cost of living from income when calculating profit. In the case of products whose costs are not to be deducted from income, this increases the price of the product after taxes, which is more or less equivalent to a separate tax.

Another question is whether tax giveaways, as often promised in election campaigns, can be part of positive governance or rather serve to enrich a specific clientele. If the aim is to improve the tax situation of car drivers by lowering petrol tax or even vehicle tax, the focus is certainly on favouring a specific clientele, but in certain economic situations it can also be sold as a successful monetary policy measure. In the long run, a short-term positive effect can turn into a negative one, which is of no great concern to the politician who is then no longer in office.

Before we discuss further the steering effect of tax legislation in the context of monetary policy, we should first clarify who would directly benefit from the abolition of a certain tax. It is the trader who will benefit first from the abolition of trade tax and not the buyer. If the buyer is to be relieved in the market, one will probably rather have the turnover tax in one's sights. If the employee is to be relieved, the wage tax should be reduced. As a rule, such selective relief is quickly withdrawn again when the original promises are no longer so acute in the mind. It would therefore be better to make structural changes that do not directly favour certain client groups and in the short term sometimes even bring tax relief for none, but in the long-term promise simplification and transparency for all, so that in the end financial relief will also result.

Let us return to the creation of money and look at the state's direct possibilities to intervene in this area. In the case of credit-based money of the citizens, direct steering intervention sometimes becomes almost impossible, but is not necessary if the money market is self-regulating. For self-regulation to work, however, complete control and the necessary legal framework are indispensable prerequisites. Private money creation within a clear legal framework would also wipe away the problems of Target 2 balances, as Sinn describes them. This can be read in the essay: "Fast 1000-Million Target – Forderungen der Bundesbank: Was steckt dahinter?" (H.W. Sinn, 2018)

If the state and the banks are also no longer allowed to take out loans, the risk for the taxpayer of having to pay for their interest and repayment is also reduced to zero. The almost free public debt in the euro countries will impose more and more financial burdens on our grandchildren. Without a debt cut, we will end up in a dead end here, the desired controls will become impossible at some point, or will be carried out independently of political influence by the corporate administrations! This also raises the question of whether and when, if at all, a currency can still be saved, even with high national debt. For the euro, Stiglitz proposes granting the individual states in the euro area more competence from Brussels, so that Italy, for example, could solve its problems with a parallel currency to the euro. Since this is not fully compatible with EU directives, Enrico Grazzini proposes the TDB (TaxDiscountBond), which does not directly burden the state balance sheets but, like all bonds, has to be repaid, albeit not in money but in forgiven tax debts. It seems to me that it would be better to convert the debt directly into another currency. in order to obtain a debt-free euro. With parallel currencies for all EU countries, one could also immediately create the desired single currency area, which does not yet exist.

If the euro were to become the official currency in all EU countries at a stroke and at the same time the old national currency were to be accepted alongside it, Sweden could also introduce the euro and create the digital Swedish krona alongside it as the new central bank money.

As long as the state maintains its sovereign monopoly of power in the monetary sector, it can determine the money supply and only permit foreign currencies in external transactions. In addition, there are the taxes with which the state can exert an influence on the economy. One can reject the influence of monetary policy on the economy, but then one must create the regulatory conditions for money to accompany and stabilise economic cycles in a positive way and no longer play a dubious role in political intrigues. Tax legislation that indiscriminately launches new taxes here and there without keeping an eye on the overall context certainly cannot achieve this. The tax laws must form a canon that makes a self-regulating national economy possible. But what could such a canon look like in its basic structure? It would make sense to reflect on some axioms of tax legislation that should be considered irrefutable in a democracy like the Federal Republic of Germany!

1. taxes should be able to generate sufficient financial resources, flanking the revenues from fees, charges and rents, to enable the state to meet its obligations.
2. taxes should not slow down economic activity!
3. substantial taxes should only be allowed in extreme special cases and then only for a limited period.
4. taxes on the means necessary to maintain basic necessities of life should not be allowed under any circumstances.
5. the total burden of taxes should be higher than 60% of income only in exceptional cases that can be well justified.
6. taxes should not be a substitute for rents, leases and fees, including, for example, royalties.
7. tax legislation should be so insightful and transparent that every citizen understands it immediately!

A profit tax that grants everyone the right to deduct from their income the vital expenses to determine profit already fulfils in its basic structure the axioms of a fair tax legislation listed above! If it is now still the goal of the state to help the citizen to achieve the highest possible profits without getting into debt itself, then the basis could be created for a truly just and sustainably efficient tax legislation. The attempt to gradually move in the direction outlined here could begin by combining turnover tax and income tax into a uniform profit tax. If, in doing so, a uniform calculation of profits is prescribed that allows each citizen twice the means necessary to satisfy existential needs, this would be a good basis. In order not to unnecessarily truncate the also money-based driving force for services in the work enterprise, the tax burden should not exceed 60% of the annual income. For the sake of transparency, it makes sense to tax profits at a uniform rate of 50% or even 60% rather than on a percentage basis. The uniform tax rate not only creates transparency, but also better predictability with the effects of less bureaucratic effort and greater planning security, which is not insignificant for sustainable growth. Those who are afraid that important control functions of the tax will be lost, as for example with the tobacco tax, should think about alternatives to the profit calculation, such as with the abolition of the deductibility of previously deductible costs. It is true that with the increased tax on tobacco, consumption is declining. However, if one takes a closer look at the interrelationships, one will quickly come across possibilities to achieve this by other means as well. Control effects can be achieved in the same way if the costs for all stimulants that lead to a strong addiction cannot be deducted as costs of living and in addition may only be dispensed on a personalised limited basis per capita. In the case of unruly use of drugs and substances harmful to health, a restriction could generally be imposed on the receipt of social benefits, even though I do not consider this to be the best solution. If certain special taxes are nevertheless deemed necessary, they should only be introduced with limited validity. It is also important to examine the tax laws to see whether certain principles are observed. Labour and property should not be taxed as a matter of principle, since they are the sources of all profit-making, without which there can be no profits. If the normal profit tax rate is 50%, a profit tax rate on drugs could justifiably be set at 90%, without removing any illegality that may exist. If any possession is not taxed because of fundamental considerations, drugs as a commodity will not be taxed either, but illegally acquired drugs will be confiscated and any trade will be taxed heavily. Of course, the possession of land is then not to be taxed either, as far as private ownership of it is allowed. It is unacceptable that citizens who are heavily in debt have their debts further increased by taxes on their property, while others reap high profits tax-free and, if possible, still use the common goods free of charge. User charges on the use of common goods could not only generate revenue but also perform important controlling functions, not least to protect our climate and the immediate environment, which could otherwise be exposed to irreparable destruction. Those who share responsibility for climate change and generally for the pollution of air, water and soil should also bear the actual or even fictitious costs of repairing the damage. Unfortunately, this has been inadequately implemented so far. Plant closures instead of offsetting costs promise short-term success, which makes their popularity with politicians and activists understandable, but will only marginally curb climate change. In the long term, only cost accounting will produce the desired effect. Only when the polluter must bear the costs, only then will there be direct pressure to minimise this pollution of the environment, not only by finding alternatives, but also by using, for example, effective filters to keep the air and water clean.

Perhaps the financial crises that have occurred again and again in recent decades and centuries will also occur less frequently if more reliance is placed on self-regulating cycles instead of intervening directly in the economic cycles, be it with bans or also with company closures.

Moreover, tax legislation should never be used to conceal the consequences of missing and faulty structural changes with new tax laws. What has long been true for individual citizens also applies to the state: if you have put money aside in good times, you can fall back on it in bad times without having to incur debts. The state must take precautions both for bad times in its own country and in general so that no overexploitation of the environment destroys vital resources. Climate protection measures also require international treaties so that the measures adopted have the necessary global impact. In the case of goods that belong to everyone in the state, the community of states, control begins with the appropriate formulation of use and licensing agreements. Private property, on the other hand, is subject to the legal regulations laid down in the Civil Code and the Criminal Code. Here, direct control is exercised by the judicial apparatus, not without the direct participation of citizens. In this respect, the control function of the laws is an indirect one, with parliaments setting the guideline. Law and justice are also intended to guarantee cohesion in society by resolving disputes before the courts as fairly as possible. The law should also enforce respect for human dignity and ensure a livelihood in old age.

3. Welfare state and basic income

Not only, but in its special commitment to solidarity in the system of the social market economy, the Federal Republic of Germany is a model example as a welfare state with far-reaching social safeguards provided by the state. The ever new laws in the social sector are supposed to bring about more justice, but above all they lead to a complexity and intransparency that is no longer transparent, to complicated regulations that are not always coordinated. For example, in the sense of a "wage gap", it must not be the case that the social welfare recipient (Hartz IV recipient) is better off in a comparable situation than the hard-working citizen. Every hour that a citizen in need of help works and thus responsibly generates money through his or her own work must be tax-free up to a social break point. The cost of living of a worker can be used as the basis for a calculation, which, simplified, can be assumed to be twice the subsistence minimum. For those who want a simplification, the idea of a basic income can create a new transparency without excluding the idea of justice. In addition, the responsibility of all citizens for their state is strengthened if the citizen does not have to act as a supplicant but uses the basic income to cover the necessary costs of his or her own life on his or her own responsibility.

The consideration of social concerns in Ludwig Erhard's idea of a social market economy does not go as far as that of the unconditional basic income, but it comes close to it in many respects and has not least contributed to the upswing in the Federal Republic of Germany, in any case it has had a positive influence. Unfortunately, in the course of time, a great many laws and regulations have come into being that are supposed to strengthen the social market economy, but which are only poorly coordinated with each other, so that even the case workers involved in the process have problems seeing through this maze of laws in order to be able to help their clients adequately. A basic income based on solidarity as a replacement for the various regulations currently in force in social law could put an end to the confusion and, on the one hand, take those affected out of the role of supplicants and, on the other hand, give them more responsibility of their own and trust them to do so. Because more citizens would then feel responsible for their own concerns, we would gain more democracy and greater stability in the entire economic system. Simply by giving individuals more money to manage and control their daily needs on their own responsibility, we can expect better control of the demand for food and clothing in the market, which will also make it easier to keep the market in a stable situation. This is precisely what should be of interest to the millionaire, the billionaire, since no one can be interested in the market being destabilised. Unstable markets, as they arise from excessively large differences in income, must eventually lead to revolutionary eruptive changes, which are usually accompanied by major losses for all. A prerequisite for stabilised economic markets is the protection of citizens from the possible fall into areas below the subsistence level, which is why protection in this sense is not only socially appropriate, but also important for sustainable growth in the market! In this sense, there is much to be gained from Müller's proposal in Berlin, with the solidary basic salary, even if on closer examination a sour feeling in the stomach cannot be denied.

One problem that is inherent in the social system, not only in Germany, is the fact that there is indeed a security system, but it functions in such a way that in the low-wage sector the hard-working citizen sometimes has less to live on than the citizen who takes advantage of all the blessings of the welfare state without contributing in return. In combination with a profit tax system, a basic salary to which everyone is entitled can also prevent these strange blossoms of a welfare state. However, without a fundamental restructuring of the markets, of the national economy, in several successive steps, it will not be possible to achieve this. If the taxable profit is calculated in such a way that all costs of living, including the costs additionally incurred by taking up a job, are deducted from the income, then taking up a job is worthwhile in any case. The lump sum can be set at 750 euros, as can the basic salary, which makes perfect pragmatic sense in the first step. Only by approaching the problems step by step will it be possible to change the system, and 500 euros may be enough in the first step, so that the state coffers are not burdened more than before. For the calculation in the case study, however, it makes sense to assume 1000 euros each, which should not even exceed the current costs in the social system. If we assume 1000 euros as the basic salary in purely mathematical terms, then a person earning 1200 euros, for example, can have the basic salary set as a flat rate of 1000 euros as a cost rate, and thus only must declare 200 euros as profit. If he additionally needs a car to get to the place of work, the 600 euros to be spent on it should also be counted as costs. This employee can thus have costs in the amount of 1800 euros imputed. Since he has to reckon with a loss of 600 euros on income of 1200 euros, this does not result in a tax liability but in a tax credit. One could now decide to pay out such tax credits, either generally or only to the extent that they do not exceed the basic salary to which all are entitled. If only a maximum of the additional loss of 1000 Euros is compensated, this would mean for the present case that the higher expenses are fully compensated by a payment of 800 Euros. This makes it quite interesting for the employee to take up a job that would not be feasible without a car. If taking up a job in this case does not bring in more than the additional possession of a car, it is nevertheless a general increase in the quality of life for which it is worth working. The welfare state must not encourage its citizens not to work! Work must be worthwhile, whatever the wage is now and tomorrow.

Basic income and profit tax must be coordinated in such a way that the self-responsibility of citizens is strengthened, and the self-service mentality prevented, then the introduction of a basic income, ideally as a citizen's income, could be a big step towards more freedom for citizens and a gain for liberal democracy. Everyone who receives a basic income should be able to earn up to a reasonable amount above this without having to pay tax on it. In the case of a profit tax, the simplest way is to adjust the cost allowances accordingly. In the context of cost accounting, greater fairness is also gained by the fact that higher rents in urban centres minimise profits in the same way as cars, motorbikes or bicycles do. To finance a basic solidarity wage, in addition to taxes and fees, citizens can be required to work for the community within the limits of their personal possibilities, which can also be converted into cash benefits upon application.

With good social legislation, the free welfare state can also direct capital flows and thus ensure that there a good balance succeeds or is strived for after all. If we succeed in involving at least 90% of the citizens in the process of further democratisation, our children and grandchildren will still be relatively well off. However, we must never forget that neither money nor majority rule is a guarantee for the prosperity of all citizens.

One question, however, absolutely must be clarified: Can a welfare state also open its welfare system unconditionally to all guest workers, or should there be different ways of accessing national welfare systems? With all love of justice, a basic salary can only be granted to one's own citizens, but it can be made easier for all citizens with foreign passports who have already lived and worked in the country for several years to become naturalised citizens. If one wanted to offer all people living in Germany, whether as Germans or as guests, an unconditional basic salary, this can only be understood as an invitation to all people of this world to make their way as quickly as possible to the land of milk and honey, Germany. Nobody can really want that, because it can only end in chaos!

4. Prosperity in old age for all citizens

In a society in which the working population can no longer finance the well-earned pensions of the retired, there can be something wrong with the distribution of the profits from productive revenues. Low birth rates cannot be used as a reason for the lack of financial resources; rather, the question is whether financing the pension from the income of those liable to pay pension insurance is not perhaps the wrong way to go. Of course, in purely mathematical terms, it is possible to secure the pension by postponing retirement. In doing so, one can postpone the start of the pension until the balance is balanced. If everyone works until the age of 70 instead of retiring at 65, then 5 more years of contributions are generated and 5 years of pension payments are saved. Whether citizens want this and can afford it is not asked, just as little as whether the labour market really needs more citizens to work longer in the long run, or whether these jobs are not taken away from the next generation of citizens. In the future, we must reckon with the fact that less work can be provided for citizens, and this also if we take into account that new jobs will be created for those that are lost. It is not a question of too little working life, but of the fair distribution of productivity gains. One can think of redistribution in order to alleviate hardship, or one can think of a distribution that is beneficial for all at the place of the gains and not downstream. Since redistribution is generally accompanied by social and financial friction, a direct solution is sometimes the better choice. But what might this look like in detail?

If everyone is guaranteed the necessities of life, redistribution can probably be dispensed with in general. But what does that mean? One conceivable solution would be to give everyone the same old-age pension financed by taxation; there would be no need for private provision, unless this is to cover additional needs. It could be simpler to guarantee everyone a basic salary until they die. Pensions paid on top of this could then also be set at a lower level and are thus even more likely to be financed. No matter how the provision for old age is secured, social control that also guarantees basic provision is necessary. Once the basic needs are secured, everyone can take care of shaping their own comfort zone.

5. Socialisation and state planning

Not all socialisation is part of or the beginning of socialist socialisation. The free country, as Gesell conceives it, is rather the commons, to be listed here only as an example of a socialisation that is not rooted in socialist ideology. (Gesell, 2015 [1919]) This is a partial socialisation, not comparable with the socialist socialisations of whole areas of life, such as that of farms or even industrial enterprises, up to and including the socialisation of the private sphere. These socialist socialisations must be distinguished from the socialisations that have a more private character. We must also distinguish between socialisation at the local level and that at the state level. Municipalities and cities in all countries of the western industrialised nations still own land today, with and without real estate, but they are not the sole owners of real estate and land. The overwhelming majority of real estate in the Federal Republic of Germany is still in private hands, which is also true for forests in Germany. Neither in the capitalist states nor in the socialist states have clear criteria ever been developed to distinguish between private property and common property; ownership is always the right of possession recorded in the land registry. Under existing law, ownership rights to land can be acquired by both natural and legal persons, with the municipality, for example, acting as a legal person. In the socialist states it was and is true that the means of production are to be socialised, since the means of production belong in the hands of the 'labourers'. Socialist socialisation, however, completely removes the control of the non-independent citizen over his means of production, because after socialisation they are controlled by a state bureaucracy. Socialist socialisation does not abolish the dependence of wage and salary earners on the owners of the means of production, nor does it abolish the dependence of the economy on money and capital. Every socialist or communist regime has its own currency and capital, not only for the private domestic market but also, for example, for buying goods and shares abroad. With only minor restrictions, the stock exchanges in socialist countries also function according to the principles of stock exchange trading under capitalism. Socialisation was and is not carried out, also in terms of legitimacy, in order to subsequently relieve the citizen of tax burdens, but to build up planned economic structures. Nor does the money economy disappear with all its problems. Even the interest economy has not died out in communist regimes. Here as there, interest-free economic activity takes place only in the private sphere, in the family and as neighbourly help. If, in a land reform, all land in the state sphere, i.e. in the sphere of the state sovereign, were declared the property of the public sector, this would be a socialisation that could strengthen an enlightened capitalism. At the same time, the public sector would have to renounce all ownership of private businesses and corporations. Capital gains should only ever be able to arise privately and should also be distributed privately.

On the other hand, state planning always takes place in capitalist-oriented state structures. In any case, the state must have control over the maintenance of clean air, water and soil, even if private-law uses are permitted which do not always protect the common interest from the outset. The maintenance of clean water, air and soil must be subject to social control. The establishment and control of the framework conditions for local markets is also subject to social control. This also includes tax sovereignty, which in my opinion, however, must be constructed from the bottom up and not the other way round. Even a pure profit tax assumes control functions through the institutions involved, if the institutions concerned conscientiously carry out a control of the costs charged, in order to prevent in this way, the charging of luxury goods as costs of living. The control of the cost structure of a company abroad indirectly even enables the control of the quality of goods up to the place of origin, for example in the case of suspected impurities.

Accordingly, state planning should primarily operate within the framework of state tasks and not attempt to solve problems that can be solved well by private enterprise. The funds necessary to fulfil the state's tasks are to be collected through fees, leases and taxes. Credit and private-sector profit, on the other hand, should be absolutely taboo for any state fundraising. Otherwise, the principle of democratic and republican separation of powers is grossly violated, so that it is not surprising if the state is no longer able to carry out its inherent control functions because of the conflicts of interest that arise. In the long term, non-observance can even lead to fear that democracy is abolishing itself, not through external attacks, but through internal disintegration. Attention must also be paid to the attacks from the economy and in particular the ever-accumulating concentrations of power there. Oversized corporations must be broken up into smaller functional units; a chemical giant that develops and sells chemicals for agriculture and industrial use in addition to medicines should first be broken up into these three subdivisions, then into regionally oriented successor companies. Politics must guarantee, for example, that important medicines are also produced in the local region and not just far away on another continent because production in large quantities is cheaper there. Within the national framework, this can be achieved with laws and, if necessary, also through massive interventions in the management of corporations that have become too powerful.

Another possibility is to impose a profit tax surcharge on the products of companies that have exceeded a maximum accepted size.

Exercising a direct control function via the supervisory board may perhaps be helpful in the case of medium-sized companies, but cannot be a generally preferred goal, if only because this is not feasible in the case of companies abroad anyway.

Under no circumstances should the public sector be involved in commercially operating companies, except in the context of a restructuring for a precisely defined period.

In principle, it will also not be advantageous to entrust non-profit companies with state tasks. For this, the social networks must first provide an infrastructure in which production and trade can develop freely. Networks and infrastructure must be provided and maintained by society; they must remain in the hands of public social institutions. Road construction in a municipality, for example, belongs to the competence of municipal planning, which does not exclude handing over individual contracts to private companies. Maintenance and repairs to be carried out at short notice belong preferably in the hands of a municipal enterprise. In the same way, however, maintenance and expansion of the internet belong in the hands of public planners and companies that do not work for profit, but above all have the common good in mind. There is nothing to be said against charging citizens a user fee afterwards. Secure internet connections should be worth paying the necessary fee for. Public buildings that are not part of a public infrastructure should therefore be privatised. However, the education network also includes school buildings and the buildings of university institutions. The public administration, the judiciary, as well as the police and the armed forces are also part of the state network, but not the banks. The financial network should only consist of the central banks and the financial supervisory authorities as well as the tax offices. The commercial banks should be organised privately, with communities as operators, but not a public sector institution. However, immunising the banks for the next crisis with capital adequacy requirements is not the real solution, but only an interim solution. If, in the next financial crisis, the currency reserves are not sufficient to stop the currency collapse, the capital earmarked for rescue could perhaps be worthless overnight. With Safe Money, as proposed in this book, one can certainly sleep better in such times of crisis than with the euro, the dollar and the like. A financial-economic control network within the framework of legal rules could be of more help in other currencies as well. If a financial structure network is specified within which all financial transactions must take place and, above all, also take place in a secure manner, even banks and bank-like institutions could, if need be, go bankrupt without harming the system.

6. Monetary and sovereign communities

If several states join together to form joint economic zones and currency zones, institutions must also be created to manage and control these joint activities. The structures of the existing nation states can be used as a guide, but new approaches can also be developed. pursue. A novel institution in the EU is the ECB. Although it is modelled on the state central banks, it is a different and thus novel construction, especially since it is supposed to act decidedly independently. It is no longer supposed to finance the nation states, which unfortunately it is trying to do more and more, albeit in a roundabout way. National debts should be transferred to other currencies as soon as possible so that the common currency, as intended, is not burdened with them. If local currencies are allowed alongside the euro, it will also be easier to make the introduction of the euro obligatory for all EU states. A new approach is worth noting here, as Salvini's proposal at least moves the direction of the possible solution in a federal direction, which could offer a solution. Salvini "explained that the high level of private wealth in Italy could help to lower the high-risk premiums.,,,,,,,Italy's public debt is high, but it is matched by a high level of private wealth in Italy". Therefore, solidarity bonds could be issued, which would not transfer Italian government bonds into national solidarity funds via the ECB or European funds, but as a national instrument. As Karsten Wensdorff describes it, the associated new loans to households in Italy "would, on the other hand, be highly diversified and backed by robust collateral". (Wensdorff, 2018) A dual-track monetary system could further support this approach. It would also be important to redefine the position of central banks in general. Central banks can take control of the money market, the financial economy and the banks, if they do so on behalf of parliaments and without involvement in money creation; cooperation between the central bank and Bafin would also be necessary.

7. Global Markets and Regional Interests
(The Globally Acting Corporation)

Global markets can be regulated by international agreements, but they cannot also be tamed in the interests of individual local markets. Here the regional community, if necessary, also a community of states, must intervene and strengthen the local market by law.

The globally active corporation will not serve local interests; for it, only internal profit maximisation is important. But how can we persuade them to take local interests into account? Public institutions can impose conditions, as well as tariffs on undesirable products. It seems to me that it would be better to tax the profits according to regional interests and to look closely at how the deductible costs were incurred. The municipal representative on the supervisory board will not be able to do much about this, especially since he will not sit on the supervisory board of companies based abroad. A local market with local jurisdiction and local tax sovereignty will better meet the needs of local citizens and protect them from the encroachments of multinational corporations. In global competition, national non-profit companies, as Wagenknecht proposes, will not help much either. More important are international agreements, which, however, should not allow legal intervention in favour of the big corporations, but in favour of local citizens. Profit taxation and jurisdiction at the place of purchase, i.e. the place where the profits are made, are also important to give the local buyer in the local market the power that makes him king, the power to sue, which he also has on paper but can usually hardly enforce at the company's headquarters. The local trader, the wholesaler would have to change if the profits were to be paid at different locations, the retailer locations. The wholesaler would probably have to change if the profits are to be paid at different places, the locations of the retailers. The solutions are not so obvious when it comes to free services and goods. It could simply be seen as a cost, but it also means that there is a location where something is sold, even if it is only information that goes over with the free deal. One can book this under advertising costs, although it remains to be clarified how and whether advertising costs are to be deducted as costs from income. Advertising costs and equally free deals should only be charged where income is also generated. If prizes are offered, they are taxable, whether paid out or not; anyone who organises a lottery should also pay tax on winnings. Free offers, like prizes, are in principle to be regarded as profit with the value of the offer, which is not to be taxed by the recipient but by the organiser. In the case of small gifts, the already existing attributions can be maintained and should certainly continue to be possible.

Also justifiable are laws, rules and measures that are intended to prevent known negative changes of global proportions, for example to counteract the worldwide increase in temperature. Neither the CO_2 tax nor a related transfer of money via purchased certificates will bring us any further. What we need above all are intelligent solutions for necessary changes on the ground, in the industrialised countries as well as in the not yet industrialised regions. It is not the transfer of money that will have the desired effect, but rather the accounting of costs that protect our environment and prevent negative impacts on the climate. In any case, not all costs may be classified as tax-reducing.

In the case of internet currencies, which are created with an enormous, hardly justifiable expenditure of energy, it is important not to forget to take a close look at the cost structure. Profits from money creation processes and currency gains are just as taxable as other profits, and here, too, the profit always arises where the beneficiary makes it.

Here, attention must also be paid to the global interconnectedness of the drug markets. Legalising all drugs and regulating them could also bring the money that disappears into dark channels here under the control of society and reintegrate addicts into society sooner and help them come off drugs. The illegal drug market costs the industrialised countries billions and prevents the desired normal development in the poor countries, as agriculture that could feed the people cannot take root there in many cases, as these fields are used for the cultivation of drug plants instead. Here, too, local markets must be supported, however this may be possible. Neither the local mafia nor the power of global corporations should disrupt the necessary infrastructure. Profits should remain in the local market, which is why the tax should also be paid there. This can be achieved by abolishing business taxes and all other taxes not linked to the place of profit. If only profit taxes are levied, however, these must be divided between the political levels according to a distribution key.

If it were possible to make the tax on profits, with its obligation to provide proof, worthy of imitation and thus establish a stable source of income in the poorer countries, which can also ensure better conditions at workplaces, a great deal would already have been gained. If improved working conditions have a tax-reducing effect, they will also be more likely to prevail. Goods that are only cheap because the people working in production are neither adequately paid nor the necessary safety measures are observed should be made more expensive via the cost factor, so that the profit and thus also the profit tax is higher. This must be just as comprehensible for the import of goods produced abroad as for domestic products. That goods can survive in global competition is best achieved with the profit tax to be levied locally with true attribution of costs. Even the services that are only functionally offered, such as those of the large internet corporations, can thus be subject to a profit tax that is to be levied in the local market. We must also work internationally to ensure that in the long term all states abolish substantial taxes and introduce the functional profit tax instead, so as not to cut off the branch on which one is sitting.

8. Communities and their assets

In my book: "Sustainable Growth", reference is made to the need to distinguish clearly between private wealth, private property and the commons. Unfortunately, communities with common property is not sufficiently considered. If this is to be made up for here, then with a reference to the principles according to which a distinction is to be made between common and private property. First, it should be noted that private property can in any case be transferred to a community with clear statutes on ownership and management. This property of cooperatives and other communities with common property can be managed by these communities, or commons in Rifkin's parlance, as if it were private property, if the board of directors can act like a natural person according to the statutes and private law transfers to the board members. On the other hand, the objective of an association, a cooperative, if decidedly laid down in the statutes, can also acquire, after a basal land reform, the ownership of a plot of land normally reserved thereafter only for the public sector, if the public interests are thereby adequately secured accordingly. For example, a cooperative could be allowed to acquire land even in an area where otherwise only the public sector owns land. All that needs to be ensured in the statutes is that, firstly, the common interests are sufficiently considered and, secondly, in the event of the dissolution of the cooperative, the smooth transfer of the property owed to the common good into the possession of the public sector is ensured if no successor community can be found to take over the property. Here, as with properties from an expired hereditary lease, these are to be offered primarily to the previous users and their relatives and partners before a sale of the rights of use to outside interested parties is to be considered.

The ownership of commons, like the commons itself, stands between political communities with their special properties and the task of managing them for a community in its sense, and private owners who use and manage their private property for themselves and their family. Communities are not only cooperatives and sports clubs, but also the various religious communities with their property holdings. The same applies to the ownership of cultural property in the case of cultural associations and, where appropriate, private libraries and literary circles, insofar as they obtain a corresponding status with notarised and verified entries. Companies, on the other hand, should not be landowners, in contrast to cooperatives or corresponding organisations (commons) that are demonstrably locally anchored with at least 55% of the contributed capital and demonstrably represent community interests. Provided that they take over secured, non-profit tasks, the tax rate (in the system proposed here, the profit tax) can be reduced by 10%. It is sometimes not possible to completely prevent non-profit associations and cooperatives from being founded only to conduct the business of a company as an association, manufactory or trade organisation; even then the public interest principle applies, it should take precedence, as otherwise no ownership of common property should be permitted. Whenever public interests are affected, the 55% rule should be applied. Public interests are also addressed when it comes to preserving and managing technical inventions, works of art, literature and music with indigenous copyrights. If possible, these should be administered by communities that also help authors to obtain their rights and represent them beyond death. Patents should not be automatically transferred to the buyer through the purchase of a company. Similarly, works of art belong where they originated, where the artist created them. A collector should only be able to acquire them on loan for a limited period, patents should only be used by the company on loan for a limited period of time. The paintings of August Macke, for example, belong to Bonn, but are rightly in various museums in other cities because of their importance for art, but should only be held on loan outside Bonn. A sale, especially to private collectors, should be prevented; instead, it should be borrowed for a limited period of time for a fee.

The property of associations, cooperatives and other societies and commons, as private property, is in principle to be attributed to each co-owner with his or her percentage share of the total deposits, likewise with equal percentage shares. If, for example, the association XY owns a club house on its own property and equipment as well as bicycles and motorised means of transport with a total value of 300,000 euros, then with 300 members, each member has a co-ownership share of 1000 euros.

Cooperatives have had a special position in German law for a long time; they occupy a very specific legal position. For the future, free real estate cooperatives should increasingly be founded alongside the already existing cooperatives. If one brings one's property into a real estate cooperative, this can be worthwhile even if one rents back, one's own house, one's original condominium. In addition, further shares could be acquired, which could then also be used to expand the cooperative's real estate holdings. In addition to better professional management, the simpler inheritance and transfer of shares to children and grandchildren could also be a sensible reason for founding a real estate cooperative or becoming a member. Neither do you have to deal with tenants yourself, nor with craftsmen and the accounts, nor do you have to take into account rental income in your private tax return, but you do have to consider the dividends from the cooperative shares, if these are distributed and accounted for. owning real estate within the framework of a cooperative also does not reduce mobility in private and professional life like owning a house does. If there are partner cooperatives at the new place of residence, a change to the partner cooperative can also be planned and carried out in the long term if there is a change of residence due to work.

Membership in a real estate cooperative or building cooperative can be linked to a contribution with a property, but instead can also be a contribution with a sum that establishes a share in properties that already exist or are yet to be built or constructed. If the contributed real estate and payments are converted to working time values based on an appraisal in the current value, an equivalent business contribution can be sought or a division of profits can be calculated according to the business shares, whereby it is not important whether this calculation is made in the new currency or one of the old currencies. In the self-interest of all members, the cooperative can maintain the real estate holdings at a value-preserving and value-increasing level and sometimes also expand them, thus promoting real growth. Markus Miller's proposal to found a family cooperative is also interesting in this context. In the sense of the public service condition suggested here, corresponding the statutes, which are to guarantee control in the commons in accordance with the law, are to be included in state control via these laws.

The statutes, which are supposed to guarantee lawful control in the communities (commons), are to be included in state control via these very laws. How the use of a property from the housing cooperative's stock is to be accounted for must be adapted to local conditions. Whether a cooperative or a foundation or only an association is chosen as the legal form must also be decided locally. Completely different problems arise from joint-stock companies listed on the stock exchange and those not listed on the stock exchange. The size and number of shareholders alone can cause problems. Small shareholders can easily fall behind, even do nothing, if the managers of a public limited company decide to delist, to take the shares off the stock exchange so that they will no longer be freely traded in the future. This raises the question of whether such holdings are still desirable at all and whether they are even possible in a money system with safe money. In principle, in such a system, one should strive for conversion into cooperatively organised forms of company. Those who still want to invest in shares should be able to do so in the old currencies in the longer term. If the low-interest phase persists, delisting will become more frequent anyway, since the new large investors can more easily serve themselves via the bond market when interest rates are low than by issuing new shares. As a result, the share could even become a discontinued model by the end of the current century. If today's small shareholders are forced to invest in highly speculative corporate bonds in the future, then it is foreseeable when regulated securities trading will collapse, if by then participation in commons such as cooperatives have not largely prevailed, and today's dominant corporations have moved into the background.

9. Tax assessment: substantial or functional?

A substantial tax taxes the tangible asset. This tax is preceded by a valuation, while the functional tax is preceded by the determination of actions in which money is earned. The value of a good can be determined by experts, if necessary, if the trading parties cannot agree. How much money flows between the partners in a sale does not require an expert, but only a fixed way of fixing exactly this fact through corresponding regulations and laws. If it is stipulated that for every sale, every economic act, the money flowing in the process must be recorded in an invoice or receipt with date, amount and indication of the goods or service, once as a receipt for the buyer and as a receipt for the tax office, then every economic act can also be controlled and taxed with regard to the functional processes. The decisive factor is not the paper receipt, but that both the seller and the buyer can confirm the purchase with a receipt in case of controls. The seller can usually do this with the electronic booking in his cash register system, the customer with the receipt, which is currently only printed out in paper form, but could also be sent to the customer on his mobile phone as a receipt. The mobile phone receipt, like the paper receipt, could be presented to the inspecting officer during spot checks. If the functional process is taxed, due to the money flowing through it, the sometimes very contentious evaluation of the services rendered becomes unnecessary. Fortunately, the rather value-based view of the activities of the past centuries has recently been steadily giving way to a view that pays more attention to the functional processes.

Therefore the idea of taxing wealth is no longer in keeping with the times. This is supported by factual reasons, since the taxation of assets, not only of business assets, can be a good idea, inflict damage on these assets that restricts the possibility of making a profit with these assets, or even makes it impossible. This deprives the national economy of important growth opportunities. If, on the other hand, the profits made in trade are taxed, this will not inhibit real growth. Therefore, the demand here is that taxation should no longer be substantial, but only functional.

In addition to property tax, inheritance tax is also a substantial tax in its basic nature, since it can destroy inherited assets instead of leaving them to the heir in full and to the full extent for the realisation of profits. Land tax is another tax that taxes substantially, since the taxed land must sometimes be sold in whole or in part because of the tax due. In the case of land transfer tax, there is also the fact that this means that the wrong person has to bear the tax. It is not the buyer but the seller who should pay this tax; assessed as a profit tax, however, the costs would then also have to be imputed and the tax burden would only occur when revenue has been booked and the actual profit from it has been established. In the case of turnover tax, the name, which was originally VAT, has already been changed to a functional approach, without, however, drawing the factual consequences. As always, it is the increase in value that is taxed, which is clearly a substantial tax. Only for this reason can it happen that in Germany in the hospitality industry only 7% is charged on input taxes, but the tax authorities demand 19% on revenues. This VAT is due immediately upon sale, even if losses are being made. With the profit tax proposed here, these taxes would only be due when profits are made. Therefore, here is the proposal to integrate the turnover tax with the income tax as a basic pillar in the general profit tax. In practice, this would mean that instead of the turnover tax, 19% profit tax A would be paid on the sale, a tax that is not offset against an input tax, but instead is to be added to the total profit tax to be settled at the end of the year or even monthly, which is made up of profit tax A and profit tax B. The profit tax A corresponds to the previous profit tax. The profit tax B corresponds to the previous income tax, so that it should also be permissible, in the case of a discontinuation of turnover tax and income tax, to combine the previous taxes in the middle percentages for comparison and for the basic calculation, in order to obtain a profit tax that neither increases nor decreases the previous tax revenue. If we assume 19% VAT and 25% income tax, we obtain a combined value of 44% of the taxes to be replaced by the elimination of these taxes.

Since inheritance tax and property tax should also be abolished, a profit tax set at 50% will still be below the previous combined substantial tax burden. In the case of income tax, however, another principle must be observed. After all, this tax does not require a reversal of meaning as in the case of value-added tax; income is composed of a profit share and a function determining the substance of the service. The work necessary to survive is not profit, it serves to maintain the substance of the person who earns his living with it.

The elimination of an input tax simplifies the tax calculation for the trader, but also for the tax office; after all, only the costs must be deducted from the proceeds, and that for all market participants. Despite this general simplification, the individual case can still be just as complex as before. Equal calculations and equal treatment of trading partners are fundamentally necessary and important, can even help tax law and commercial law, which is certainly desirable and should be striven for. Some types of taxes could also be eliminated because there can be no taxation of general property and corresponding licence fees, leases and rents that accrue instead are simply not taxes. The advantage of leasing land, for example, is that the leases are negotiated individually and can thus be better adapted to local conditions than would be possible with a tax. Of course, motor vehicle tax is also a substantial tax, although this revenue for the state can be dropped in favour of profit tax on fuel and road tolls. If, in a land reform, land is withdrawn from private ownership, there can also no longer be a tax based on it. Many of the problems of current taxation could thus vanish into thin air, paving the way for leaner and simpler tax legislation that is easier to understand. Only the private sale of real estate would indeed not become easier for the seller, but more complicated, if a general profit tax were to apply here without exceptions. But offsetting the costs of renovation and repair also offers the chance of a fairer tax and would lead to houses no longer being sent to the market as speculative objects with a renovation backlog.

Another idea, namely to tax machine labour, is downright tempting, as it suggests relieving the burden on the worker by taxing all labour, not just his one. If you assume that labour is not to be taxed in principle, but only the profit from the result of this labour, then further discussion about which labour should be taxed and how becomes superfluous. Labour should not be taxed because this not only does not promote the willingness of individual citizens to perform, but even suppresses it. If the demand for a functional tax in the sense of growth-oriented control is based on the assumption that a tax on work performance is dysfunctional because it inhibits the growth of economic values, then work performance should no longer be taxed! The clear implication is that dysfunctional taxes should be eliminated just as substantial taxes are.

Without dysfunctional and substantial taxes, the tax system would be more transparent, fairer and easier to manage. For theoretical clarification, it should be considered whether the substantial tax is not even a kind of dysfunctional tax, since the growth of the economy is slowed down by this kind of tax, it does not serve the positive economic function for an economy with sustainable growth.

One could now say that it is functional to regard the house and the land as a single unit in the case of existing real estate, but that in the case of new buildings it is the land purchased before the start of construction and only this that should be taxed, as long as it is still privately owned, since this promotes the construction of new housing, but it remains a substantial tax. However, the positive function here does not come from the tax itself, but from the pragmatic boundary conditions. Functionally more sustainable is sometimes a cost crediting by the tax offices that promotes new construction when calculating personal profit after tax.

Abolishing property tax would not only eliminate a substantial tax, but also make some inconsistencies disappear at the same time. In the case of income tax, a distinction must be made between the profit share and the taxation of work performance as such; in principle, only the profit and not the work is taxable; the costs of living and the expense of labour input are not taken into account in the calculation of the profit share from the income, a pragmatic approach to tax decoupling on income. A sometimes well-intentioned tax progression makes no sense in principle, especially not in the case of profit tax. It can neither be wanted that the main contributors to society lose the desire to contribute further, nor that they migrate abroad with their activities and register their residence in another country. Achievement should be rewarded for everyone, the low-paid citizen as well as the multi-billionaire. In the same way, the property rights of all citizens should be preserved, and it should be made easier for the dispossessed to acquire property. Every citizen should be able to move into his or her own four walls in the course of his or her life, or to expand, renovate or even beautify them. I can't think of a better way to stabilise the market than to have every citizen in their own four walls, which is why achieving this should be the primary goal and not the destruction of private residential property for the benefit of large housing associations.

The method in current tax law, which is mainly related to substantial taxation, the deductibility of larger expenses, be it for a car or a production machine, can no longer be applied as AfA in the previous procedure in the case of functional taxation, but it can be applied in a modified way via cost imputation. If the costs are higher than the income, the excess cost share can also be offset in later accounting periods, thereby also accounting for the costs progressively or degressively, comparable to the current progressive or degressive depreciation procedures, probably not related to economic values, but to economic expenses. Expenses are, this is definitely different, not to be validated in terms of acquisition values, but to be judged on the question of necessity within an economic cycle. If it is plausible that a machine in production needs to be replaced after 10 years, the costs can also be deducted from income spread over 10 years, even if they are incurred later. Functional taxation can thus adopt many tried and tested features of substantive taxation in a modified form, without running the risk of changing only the choice of words. There is also no danger of the gap between rich and poor widening even more quickly; on the contrary, it is more likely to close again, albeit probably with a time lag. It is probably true that if all substantial taxes such as wealth tax, property tax and inheritance tax are abolished, rich families will still be able to safely transfer their wealth to the next generation but one. If assets are not used, they will dwindle away over time even without wealth tax, unless the assets increase even without use via speculative profits. In the case of such profits, which have not arisen linked to any work performance, the procedures for determining profits could be adjusted separately. A special speculation tax derived from this could certainly have a dampening effect here. A functional tax could consider the speculative profit as no longer functional for the economy and therefore try to reduce it. If the speculative profit were skimmed off with a 90% profit tax, this could curb speculative sales, although not completely prevent them, which is not necessary either. However, costs that are not considered, because they are classified as speculative costs, could have a much greater impact on profits than a tax could. Let's take the example of the sugar tax, which has recently been introduced in many countries and is also being discussed here in order to increase the price of sugary foods in the expectation of reducing sugar consumption. It is having an effect, but is there no other way? Products with a sugar content of more than 20%, the chargeable costs can be completely excluded from the cost calculation for the tax and only 50% of the costs can be charged for products with a share between 10% and 20%, so that a more differentiated influence is possible than with the flat-rate tax on sugar or sugary foods. In general, not all costs have to be fully accepted, one can fully credit transport costs from the area close to the local market and only partially accept them in the case of transport costs from distant countries. Guidelines for the acceptance of submitted costs are also easier to change than is the case with taxes once they have been decided.

However, the different perspectives on functional, dysfunctional and substantial taxation should now be briefly touched upon before concluding the basic considerations on societal control. With any societal control and steering, care must be taken to ensure that society with its institutions only intervenes here if private control and community control cannot achieve the desired results. Here, too, it is important to distinguish between social and community control and steering, whereby the tax must always be understood as a social phenomenon.

A substantial tax is based on an assessment, whereby the assessment criteria can change over time and thus no planning certainty can be guaranteed. The functional tax, on the other hand, is not dependent on a material value, but on the function of an economic action that promises a profit over and above a performance, which does not inhibit growth, but promotes it. Dysfunctional are actions and profits that inhibit growth and should therefore be restricted as much as possible. Here, a dysfunctional tax, in our example the speculation tax, or a dysfunctional imputation of costs when determining profits can help. With the dysfunctional tax or the dysfunctional imputation of costs, one can try to limit dysfunctional actions for the benefit of the respective society.

Now, not every dysfunctional action requires a dysfunctional counter-tax. The decision to relocate the company headquarters from Germany to the Caribbean would also be dysfunctional. However, it helps to point out that there is no longer a trade tax in Germany, should one actually abolish it. This makes sense, because if a general profit tax is introduced, the trade tax no longer makes sense. It also makes sense and is desirable for various reasons if production moves to the consumer and the consumer is not asked to move to the production site. This is also part of a functional concept, namely that not only production costs should be kept low, but also logistics costs (travel and transport costs).

The renunciation of substantial taxation is not necessarily also a renunciation of all valuation, since valuations will also be made for the costs, but also for the values belonging to the community and society. If one wants to calculate the fees, rents and compensation for use levied by social institutions, one cannot avoid valuations here either, but must then make them comprehensible to the citizen and the different communities. However, a different valuation of cost approaches is more comprehensible than the valuation of assets to be assessed for tax purposes. That, for example, the transport costs for apples from New Zealand are not to be assessed to the same extent as the transport costs from the farmer in the Eifel to the local market in Cologne, should be sufficiently understandable. After all, it is not necessary to include such high transport costs in the sales price if sufficient supplies can be organised locally. In the case of not yet healthy or even unhealthy food, even if only unhealthy admixtures, the entire income may well be regarded as profit from which no deduction of costs is accepted.

XI. Community control

Before going into the question of the task and emergence of, for example, cooperatives as a prime example of communities with a social and economic function, it should be clarified what communitarisation is as opposed to socialisation.

Private wealth, when used for the misguided exercise of power, can create a great deal of suffering and misery. It is easy to come up with the idea of communitarising these private assets to remove power from the private individual and transfer it to a political body that brings about majority decisions and hopefully acts better in the interest of the community than individual decisions can be expected to do. Unfortunately, just as with individual decision-making, one can hardly plan ahead for the balance of power in the future; even in the short term, majority decisions can change quickly and may even be in favour of individuals alone and not promote the community as originally intended.

In contrast to socialisation, where capital is left to the political power structures, in communitarisation the capital under consideration should be made available to a community to which one belongs as a member and which uses these funds for very specific purposes based on the statutes and, in addition, on the basis of contractual ties, as intended by the members. These are communities with the same interests, so that already due to the equality of interests there is a certain guarantee that the funds are also used in one's own interest for a community in which one feels at home.

The cooperative is now also such a community, which is founded, for example, in order to jointly raise money and capital for the means of production that are too expensive for the individual, or in order to be able to store private money in a secured environment, or also in order to organise purchasing in general through the cooperative in a sustainable way in the sense of a community between producers and consumers in a spirit of partnership. What is important here is that there is no socialisation of the means of production as in communism; the means of production remain in private hands, even if it is not a matter of a single capital owner, but of many capital owners who have pooled their capital, for example in a cooperative, in order to work together with this capital. Cooperatives can be set up to jointly run an agricultural business, or a bank, a grocery shop, a library, a clothing shop, a hotel and a catering business, but in principle also a technology company. Co-operatives could also be the vehicle for privately organised social model experiments, for example in housing construction, in the coexistence of different generations, or also in the establishment of a new kind of monetary economy.

As a historically developed form of communal economic activity, cooperatives already carry within them much of the thinking that can give the new commons the necessary legal support. It is astonishing that despite sometimes adverse circumstances, especially in the financial sector, the ideas of cooperatives have survived quite well through the turmoil of time until today.

Today, cooperatives are mainly known in the banking sector as cooperative banks, in the agricultural sector as agricultural cooperatives and more recently in the construction sector as building cooperatives. Especially in social housing, the idea of forming cooperatives should be supported more strongly, as this could steer housing construction in a more desirable direction than is possible with today's large housing associations. Social housing should not create a tenant proletariat, but rather make citizens with lower incomes long-term homeowners through favourable rental contracts and subordinate purchase options, whether as individual owners of a condominium or also as co-owners in a building cooperative, that should be left to local conditions. This would also prevent only profitable rentable mass-produced housing from determining social housing construction by housing associations, thus promoting the formation of social hotspots. The goal of social housing should be to help more citizens own their own homes.

Every socially recognised community needs a legal form that sets out the rights of the individual members, and their obligations, as precisely as possible. However, this alone is not enough; the community must also set out in its statutes the rights and duties vis-à-vis society just as clearly and unambiguously for all members and society. Clear regulations and laws can help avoid disputes and ensure peaceful coexistence.

A building cooperative with the aim of providing affordable housing for its members could demand a building cost contribution, a building site contribution and a self-help contribution in addition to the membership fee. If communities are granted ownership of jointly managed plots of land and thus land ownership, it must be regulated how the use of individual plots of land by the members is made possible. The self-help contribution of a craftsman would sensibly be made with the craftsman's work possible for him, that of a merchant with corresponding commercial work in the office of the cooperative. If an architect is found who can develop the building plans with the future residents on an individualised basis using simple basic elements, it should also be possible to save costs here and still guarantee a good quality of living. Joint planning will sometimes require more time from the individual, time that he or she sacrifices for the community, but in return can expect a better quality of life with less capital investment.

1. Legal forms of communitarisation

Whether cooperative, foundation, association or church, all these social institutions are institutions that form communities, albeit with different goals and legal safeguards. Beyond the specific objectives, each community must also finance itself, either through membership fees or also through contributions with which the member becomes a co-owner. If a community not only finances its current costs through membership fees, but also acquires property, it must be determined to what extent this leads to a property claim of individual members, which is then equivalent to a contribution. For each member of a community, the co-ownership share should be determinable at any time. Upon leaving, a member should receive between 10 and 100% of the current co-ownership share, if possible, immediately, depending on the current financial situation of the community. It must be clear how high the individual contributions of the members are in each case and what of the total assets of the community is to be attributed to the individual members as capitalisable assets. In particular, the intellectual capital, described here in general terms as educational capital, must be examined in terms of its transferability into financial capital that can be accounted for in money, and must be re-evaluated from time to time. Particularly in communities that sometimes last for centuries, intangible capital in the form of knowledge accumulates in patents and books, among other things, but also in the organisational structures, knowledge that can be traced back to a shift in assets. Not only in the communities, but also in the market, more and more knowledge is accumulating, knowledge that is gradually displacing the monetary capital input of earlier times. Both the definition of goals and the handling of community capital must be fixed in the statutes in a legally flawless way. Religious communities, building cooperatives, sports clubs and cultural associations are very different, which also justifies different legal forms, from the rather loose socialisation in sports clubs to very close ties in religious communities. Ownership of land and capital should be granted to all communities, but without thereby elevating them to legal persons as in the current legal space. Legal transactions of these communities, however different, should be carried out with the legitimation and written mandate of all members. Powers of attorney with factual and time limits, usually for one, two or 10 years, could in principle guarantee the ability of the board, management and executive to act, although liability requires separate consideration. Communities can entrust their money to a bank, but they can also set up a bank themselves and run their own money management internally. Most communities are designed hierarchically, which also corresponds to a hierarchical monetary policy, but does not have to be so. The hierarchies of religious communities are particularly pronounced. The situation is different for cooperatives with rather flat hierarchies. However, communities can theoretically also establish themselves as public limited companies or limited partnerships. The simplest form of socialisation is through registered associations, be it the gardening association, the motor sports association, the neighbourhood aid association, the advertising association, the football club or even the church.

2. Sports club and religious community

The sports club, a football club for example, usually carries out its activities on rented premises owned by the town, the municipality. Only a few sports clubs own real estate and land. In the current legal system, the club, the municipality, is a legal person as an actor. In the new legal system without legal persons, the members, adding up the individual natural persons, should ensure this power to act by clearly formulated partial powers of attorney to elected representatives and, in the case of more extensive legal transactions, issue this power of attorney to the executive board with their majority vote in the main or annual meeting. Only in the case of land purchases should the unanimous decision of the board be sufficient, this in order to give communities preferential ownership of land. Religious communities should also be granted separate rights without deriving a legal person from this, even if the legal concept of a community of natural persons with delegated legal rights might not be unproblematic, especially in the case of religious communities. Churches acquire land not only for their purposes as a religious community, but also in order to have private buildings constructed on it, by making the land available in a heritable building procedure. In these communities there is usually no community control, but rather the control bodies are arranged in different hierarchical levels, without the individual members having any insight into the processes and decision-making. Whether or not communities also allow community control down to the lowest levels must be left to the communities themselves. Society can make community control palatable to communities with special legal freedoms, if one wants to do so at all.

3. Local markets and the new money economy

In a local market, the citizen can still understand all the decisions of the bodies exercising power and should therefore be able to support and co-decide them precisely there. Who is allowed to offer their goods in the local market and under what conditions should be decided by the local market participants. That is one side of the coin of an open and transparent democracy. Electing representatives who are usually not even known and who quickly lose touch with their base, this is how democracy loses ground over the years, especially when the corporations and globally active companies become more and more powerful and effectively co-determine the legislative process through lobbyists. Monetary policy and the process of money creation also largely escape the citizen's field of vision. What we need are local self-governing markets with their own market rights and locally anchored free banks in the hands of the citizens, a local jurisdiction and locally controlled and supported institutions of financial management. This will require the intensive efforts of all citizens in the local market. As far as the local market exists only in thought and in the cloud dependent on it, it will also be necessary to build up the local market step by step until it is a powerful reality. Initial approaches could be based on bringing together local businesspeople in a market community with the aim of building a market in which customers are actively involved in order to be able to build stable and lasting business relationships. The aim is to establish joint control in a market council, which can also enforce demands on politicians, considering the interests of both customers and traders for the benefit of both sides. Once established, the market council can then form an official market association in which all those operating in the local market become members. Membership must of course bring a benefit to all, which in some respects is self-evident, but must be explicitly formulated with special offers to back it up. As a registered association, the market association can appoint a managing director and fix the market council more precisely as the official body of the market association. Whether the market council then takes over the board of directors in the market association or is transformed into a kind of legislative institution for the local market, that is to be decided by the members in the local market association. It is important that there are regular meetings where decisions are made about the structure and further developments of the local market. If a market structure is built up in this way that is adapted to the needs of the local participants, it will also be easier to survive in the global economic world with a local market that has grown in this way, if, in addition, the national parliaments and institutions give their backing.

This is also important for a healthy identity formation of the citizens. It will help to weld regions together by bringing local trade markets, local production facilities and local politics together in a democratic consensus for the benefit of the local citizenry, thus bringing global markets down into the horizon of individual citizens and adapting them to the competence of its citizens and their wishes. The global economic activities must be reflected in the local market so that the refractive power of local institutions is clearly visible, as this is the only way that the necessary diversification in the economic sector can guarantee growth in the long run. This also includes sovereignty over funds in the local area and their control by non-profit banks owned by customers and anchored in the respective region. Nevertheless, there is nothing to be said against organising the local organisations and banks in corresponding supra-regional associations for the benefit of the customers in such a way that a movement of goods and money across borders does not pose any problems.

In the local market, as it is understood here, however, banks and insurance companies with international debt interconnections would have a disruptive effect, as they escape community control. A banking union, as planned in the euro area and already partly in place, also escapes local control and should therefore be rejected. Control within the social communities and their integration into society also includes, and this is clearly stated once again, control of the local market as control within a local community of citizens. Regulated processes are ensured by statutes that every member should accept, which does not mean that they cannot be changed over time by the majority of members. The statutes are formulated accordingly, the framework for a market right in the local market.

What is important is the division of power between the economic and political power blocs. Politicians have to ensure that national tax laws harmonise with local tax codes and that the management of communal land ownership does not clash with the ideas of separate communities with land ownership. On the one hand, the rights of the communities should be preserved, and on the other hand, the rights of state organisations and institutions should not be curtailed.

In a newly built city, the local market can be arranged as a ring around the political administrative centre with educational institutions. In established cities, businesses that have moved to the countryside will want to return to the city centre. This can be achieved through the building permits to be granted, i.e., no more building permits for supermarkets outside the city. It will also be helpful if the land is municipally owned. An interesting possibility, to return to the main concern in this volume, is to create a currency of one's own in the local market. In a restricted environment such as the local market, a cash only valid in that market can be beneficial in many ways. In addition to a membership in the market association, own market money would be the second pillar of a close connection of the customers to this and preferably only this market. The exchange into the market currency should be free of charge and most easily done via debit or credit cards in market-owned exchange offices. With the market's own cash, children can still experience the tactile handling of money and learn to calculate with money. Moreover, the customer does not disclose his bank details when making a purchase in the shop. Only during the exchange process in the exchange office are the bank details revealed. Through the exchange, on the other hand, every buyer in the market is registered with his bank details, even if not directly when buying the goods. In this way, a certain anonymity is maintained.

4. Employment for all citizens?

Ensuring full employment is generally the task of politicians, at least that is how it often appears during election campaigns. However, the control over the labour market that is envisaged in this way is usually only moderately successful, so the question here is whether it cannot be better achieved with the help of the various communities.

Money can be used to buy labour, but also the necessary resources or education quotas for employees, as well as the urgently needed energy. Of course, this does not change the fact that each factor must be available in sufficient quantities in order not to become a limiting factor, which, by the way, applies to all levels of control.

Since money can be used to compensate for a lack of capacity regarding the other factors, we must ask ourselves how quickly the monetary resources can be made available here. Thus, with money and financial capital, availability seems to be a crucial aspect for the growth that depends on it.

Not only the procurement of missing funds, but also the slow-moving mills of bureaucracy can hamper growth processes. Losses of time that cannot be planned for can bring entire projects to a crashing halt.

Secure money can be created relatively quickly for members of a free bank through a loan agreement and thus be available quickly, since all the necessary formalities have usually been taken care of long beforehand, for example when opening an account or a change in financial circumstances.

Once available, financial capital, no matter in which currency, can also vagabond around the world due to its easy transferability, since the global markets greedily absorb capital, not always in the desirable way, but also repel it just as quickly. The exchange rate plays a role that should not be underestimated. Exchange rate differences can bring in high profits in volatile times but can also make the purchase of larger acquisitions extremely cheap.

If one's own currency depreciates and it becomes cheaper for the buyer abroad, in most cases this has a direct corresponding impact on exports and imports and can thus influence the trade volume and the trade balance of the countries concerned. If more money is put into circulation to compensate for the devaluation, this also influences the measures expressed in monetary terms, such as GDP. A trade surplus that can be measured in this way can become a problem, but sometimes only on paper. If you look at longer periods and not just at the balance sheets between two trading partners, it usually evens out again. Not to be forgotten is inflation, which counteracts demonetization through higher prices, but also promotes it. A community like the agricultural cooperative has no influence on this at first, but it can look for partners who enable an exchange of goods that is independent of the classic currencies and thus achieve relative independence from the general fluctuations on the market. Co-operations with co-operatives from the handicraft and consumer sectors should have an additional stabilising effect. In this way, jobs can also be secured, and more sustainably than would be possible through state control. Within a community, jobs can be better adapted to changing market conditions even without job losses. In a craftsmen's cooperative, it will be relatively easy to divide up jobs in such a way that the customer is served on time despite absences due to illness. Younger colleagues can familiarise themselves with the new techniques and the older ones can maintain the older equipment that is still available, so that reliable customer service with maintenance is also ensured for years to come. The office can also keep the books and accounts correctly according to current requirements and relieve or prepare the individual craftsman of the bureaucratic, very time-consuming control and paperwork. A company with several employees will handle this in the same way but will not be able to involve all of them in equal cooperation on the common goals, unless the company is organised according to the principles of a cooperative community. In this case, control should not be exercised by a boss and the business should be managed by the board or the managing director; rather, the rules and the current solutions to problems should be discussed again and again at business meetings and readjusted according to changes in the market.

In the process, it will then also be possible to rearrange the tasks of the individual members of the community in the course of time in joint consultation and thus to give everyone in the community his or her Job. This is not only to secure one's work, one's job, but also to prevent the feeling of being controlled by others from arising in the first place.

XII. Private control

The craftsman who works alone and organises his business as a family business from a tax point of view, admittedly has everything under his control in his field, and external control can only occur through the state-initiated laws and rules. Unfortunately, those who have no one to interfere with them, at least no colleague and no managing director, often cannot avoid the impression that they feel more and more controlled by the decrees and regulations from the state and that their freedom of decision is actually restricted by more and more environmental protection laws. Yes, we need regulations for environmental protection and laws that can prevent a climate catastrophe. However, the social control bodies that establish, enforce and control such rules should consider that these controlling laws can only be implemented with the help of individual citizens and their control in the private sphere. Individual citizens must be involved in the control function of society as well as that of the associated community through their private control, which can only work if education and training provide the framework for this and, in addition, enough freedom is left for citizens to have their own unrestricted space of control.

Private capital and private debt should primarily be subject to the control of the individual, secured by the laws that are supposed to safeguard this private control. Through questions in parliament, it should also be possible to explain government spending to the citizen in more detail, if necessary.

Private capital and private debt should in any case be left to the control of the individual and should only be able to be withdrawn from him by order of a court after due process. In everyday life, the popular assumption is that the interest rate should control the behaviour of citizens in money matters. If the interest rate is high, people are more likely to delay taking out a loan, and if the interest rate is low, they are more likely to go into debt. In the case of building loans, for example, the fixed interest rate is not normally granted for the entire term and, despite ever new regulations on advice from bank advisors, it is not sufficiently pointed out that if a 5% unscheduled repayment right is exercised for a fixed interest rate of 10 years, 50% of the debt will have been paid off by the unscheduled repayment alone and, with 2% regular repayment, only less than 30% of the amount borrowed will still have to be repaid after 10 years, and if the repayment is insufficient, the financial burden is quickly too high due to the sharp rise in interest rates. Here it is not enough to oblige the banks to provide more advice, since honest advice will undermine the bank's interests. In order for private control to function on a broad scale, general education in financial matters urgently needs to be included in the educational canon. As a rule, loans that are offered to young families at conditions that are appropriate to their situation in life exceed their capacity to bear the burden after the fixed-interest period has expired due to an increase in interest rates and can thus also lead to financial ruin, at least in many cases preventing any financial mobility for this family after the fixed-interest period. The state must ensure that this cannot happen. On the other hand, the saver in The government persuades people to engage in risky financial transactions during periods of low interest rates, as this is the only way they can earn money or at least compensate for inflation. Here, too, the citizen's control over his money is being taken out of his hands. We need a monetary system in which saving is worthwhile, as this is the only way for citizens to plan their finances sensibly and sustainably. The pressure to invest in risky assets leads to losses that do not serve the national economy, but only fill the wallets of irresponsible traders. In an interest-based system, transparent, honest interest rates could guarantee rationally justifiable planning and thus successful private control; unfortunately, intransparency belongs to interest rates like clouds to rain. In a system without interest, on the other hand, even saving without interest can be attractive because of the transparency and thus the control of private control, of private finances, can run better. Especially in the case of larger purchases such as a car or home ownership, it must be possible to carry out sustainable planning of private finances without immediately having received the higher consecrations of financial mathematics. Most people are probably already overburdened with the calculation of the compound interest effect, and thus control over total expenditure is no longer really given in the case of a long-term loan. Better is the control over working time accounts and the accounting on a solidarity basis as with the Safe Money NIM.

Private capital and private debts should be subject to the control of the individual, secured by the laws that ensure this private control. State bodies at all levels must ensure that their citizens' control over private finances is not made difficult or impossible by opaque contracts and inadequate or faulty advice.

It is precisely the accumulation of capital out of debt that quickly gets out of hand for the non-merchant because of inadequate information, especially when interest payments are involved. The view that interest is necessary to be able to borrow and lend money is wrong and only serves as a good argument for unscrupulous money collectors not to torpedo their business. The control of capital flows, it is also argued, is not possible without interest. It is true that without interest, money would always head for the safe haven, with an interest rate differential then tends to follow the interest rate, even if the higher interest rate is associated with a higher risk. Of course, in the private sphere, emotional motives also play an important role that should not be underestimated when it comes to investing or spending one's money. The local company is more likely to be able to activate the emotional motives than the company from a distant country (the low price then counteracts this again). The local market also has rational reasons why personal control works better here, namely because of the short distances and direct insight into production, distribution and logistics.

In general, private control can be seen as a regulator of community and societal control, helping to ensure that the control functions in the economy are sustainable. Better private control can be expected in the secure system, since here, sometimes supported by blockchain technology, capital is built up continuously from work performance, even without interest, without the danger of falling prey to speculative rapid money multiplication strategies.

Private control also includes private liability! In the case of local family businesses this is basically not a problem, since here the owner always must assume full liability with all his assets, not so with the large supra-regionally operating companies and businesses. Due to the legal construction of "limited liability", an imbalance is created here to the detriment of local markets. That the investor is only liable to the extent of the capital he has contributed may still be plausible, but not that the managers of the company do not assume corresponding liability for their decisions. This could be changed by fundamental changes in company law! It should be stipulated that the managers assume the residual liability that is not assumed by the owners of the capital. It will also be possible to involve customers and the rest of the workforce to a small extent in the residual liability. Investors should determine the type and level of managers' salaries, while they are largely responsible for the salaries of the workforce. Investors could also contractually include their managers in the liability obligation, but a statutory regulation is preferable to private law regulations.

Without a liability obligation for managers anchored in company law, it is not surprising that in many places they only marginally live and work with the company and the risks for the company, and instead only think about their own wallets.

Money creation is different; in principle, it should be subject to private control, if only because state control of the market cannot function in a globalised market without private ties. Improvements can only be achieved by protecting the local market within the framework of international free trade agreements and by accepting private money creation. It should also be noted here that private money creation naturally transcends national borders and thus takes account of globalisation in finance, because private currency no longer needs a nationally dominated reserve currency. This could also make a dream of the largely still misunderstood economist Hayek come true, although free competition between any number of currencies is rather unrealistic. More than three currencies should not be allowed, if only to avoid overburdening all the citizens who are currently only familiar with one national currency.

1. Private capital and tax justice

As long as capital is scarce, one can also assume sufficient capital income, which is neither to be condemned, nor to be taxed lower or higher than other income. If one assumes a profit tax, then either 50% or 60% of the profit must also be paid as tax on capital income. Since the cost of living and the special professional costs are to be deducted from the income in advance when the profit is calculated for the individual citizen, even 60% profit tax is fully justified and reasonable, if necessary. In the normal case, it is to be expected that even in the case of medium incomes, a good 80% of the income is to be regarded as costs, which are deducted from the income in the first instance. If 50% of 20% is then deducted as tax, this amounts to 10% of the total income in the conventional system. The costs incurred by attending the general meeting of a partnership or a public limited company should also be counted as costs. On the other hand, the costs of maintaining a luxury car or the costs of the last holiday trip are not deductible costs, but sometimes the costs of a stay at a health resort are.

With the accumulation of capital, there should also be reduced profits from the capital. Once capital can no longer find anyone willing to pay interest on borrowed capital, then, one might assume, the end of capitalism has come. To me this seems, if somehow plausible, nevertheless a short-circuit, and even if it were so, what follows from it? Why not create an artificial scarcity? Besides, even if the trade in money disappears, there will be rich and poor. The important question is therefore whether we will succeed in defeating poverty, which demands an inhumane life from people, whether through better control of the money markets or with appropriate tax laws. Therefore, we will continue to be concerned with the question of what the state can do to reduce poverty and how this can be reflected in tax legislation. Promoting private engagement in the social sector through donations or foundations transfers tasks of the state to private control and strengthens the social conscience in the process. Relieving the tax burden on low-income earners by not taxing money that is needed to survive and maintain the labour force, this promotes self-control down to the wage earner. As far as possible, everyone should be able to list his or her costs and calculate the monthly burden; this is part of the private control that should also be expected of every citizen. Help for self-help would be quite appropriate here, if the school should have failed to teach it. It is not enough to enact individual laws for the benefit of the poor, these laws should also harmonise with each other and with other laws. Taxing the small jobs of basic income recipients or other types of social benefits in an insubordinate way only encourages a hammock mentality instead of promoting self-reliance. Preventing poverty and old-age poverty in particular will be achieved if at least 80 to 90 percent of citizens can be housed in their own properties. A low income is more bearable if at least accommodation in one's own flat, in one's own house, is secured. Tax legislation should also take this into account. It is not financial equalisation that should be striven for, but prosperity for all, a prosperity that should be based on the needs that can be fulfilled and not on the money available.

The question of a tax on the rich, which is also raised again and again in this context, is usually based on a progressive tax and the demand that everyone should also pay their possible share of public costs according to their means. The fact that the strong shoulder should bear more than the weak is already taken into account when 50% of the profit is to be paid as tax, since 50% of 50 million is considerably more than the 50% of 100,000. In this case, the aim is not a redistribution of wealth, as would be possible with a wealth tax or a tax on the rich, but neither is the substance taxed in an unjust way. Inheritance tax could also be helpful in the effort to redistribute wealth. However, there is the possibility of structural destruction that could be detrimental to the economy, as already mentioned regarding the wealth tax. If these types of taxation are therefore dispensed with, the top tax rate can be increased in the case of progressive taxation, the progression can be allowed to continue or a special capital tax can be levied, possibly the global capital tax called for by Piketty.

But with the capital tax, strictly speaking, one comes back to the wealth tax, which cannot really be the solution, for the reasons already mentioned. The difficulties begin with the valuation of securities and real estate and end with the valuation of paintings and jewellery, which may have little or no market value, but are assessed by the tax office according to their purchase value. With pure profit tax, on the other hand, there are other possibilities. The profit is not subject to any assessment criteria but is merely based on the objective payment receipts available. Receipts provide information on both income and costs. Although investments are also to be deducted from the income as costs, it is important to look closely at whether the investments are necessary or whether they only serve to reduce the profit. In order to deduct investments as necessary costs, conditions must be fulfilled, for example, that these costs must be spread over wear and tear and can be reversed if there is a suspicion of profit reduction. In addition, when calculating profits, care must be taken to ensure that possible profits, for example in the case of owner-occupied real estate, are also considered. If, in the case of assets amounting to several billion, only a few million in the single-digit range are declared as income, this may be because owner-occupied property has not been sufficiently reduced by the luxury portion and this is then considered in a tax-relevant manner. Similarly, a house that is not rented out should be offset against a potential rent if it is vacant for an above-average period of time and cannot be explained. A similar approach can also be taken with other properties. If a family with two household members owns five cars, one can assume that two cars are also completely sufficient, since five cars are probably not used permanently. If investments are made in securities or commodities, the profit is sometimes not so easy to determine, but it can be estimated if necessary, but will be determined at the latest when the investment is sold. If, for example, gold jewellery is treated as an accumulating investment that only makes the money saved available again in the proceeds when it is sold, one can either do without interim taxation here or, in the case of accumulating investments, generally demand a value adjustment after 10 years and calculate an anticipated profit on this. Sales proceeds, interest and dividends should be assessed at the usual profit tax rates. Especially in the case of very large accumulations of assets, the calculation of realisable but unrealised profits can achieve the same effect as a global capital tax, but avoid the negative effects of an unjust, equalising global capital tax and, moreover, in responsibility before the common good, thus strengthen it in every respect. Transparency, which can be achieved through a uniform profit tax, is also important, because what use is the global capital tax if it is undermined by other national taxes or leads to less transparent tax returns?

In principle, it can be assumed that money and especially financial capital can compensate for the deficiency in the other factors. In this respect, capitalisation and money play the role of a superfactor. As a superfactor I would like to describe here a factor that can be transformed very quickly and without detours into one of the other important factors of growth. Of course, this presupposes that such a transformation is fundamentally possible at all in the concrete case. If, for example, certain resources are missing because they have been completely consumed, sometimes even all the money in the world cannot conjure up the missing resources. In such a case, it is quite justified that unused capital as well as unused assets are temporarily not used to generate profits. Only if the non-use is excessively long or even without plausible reason is a separate tax justified. If the non-use is justified by a higher profit expectation in the future, this is speculation, which can justify a corresponding special tax.

2. Basic income for all citizens!

The basic income should not be understood as a handout, but rather as a benefit provided by society to the citizen who, with his identity as a citizen of the community from which he receives the citizen's income as a basic income, contributes to and promotes the preservation of the community. Therefore, it can only be granted to citizens and not to everyone who resides in the respective national territory.

If it is decided to pay a basic income to all citizens in communities that work with the Safe Money, this can be realised by the citizen then, if the basic income cannot be offset against the tax debt, taking out a loan with his house bank, in the Free Bank Safe System, in the amount of the basic income, and the tax office repaying this loan with offset tax debts and adding it to a debt account as a temporary loss. In this case, both the loan and the repayment must ideally be made in the currency of the "safe money", for example in NIM. If, due to illness or other acceptable reasons, the cost of living is higher than provided for in the lump sum, this must be additionally credited upon receipt. This could also be seen as a negative tax! By ensuring that every citizen has at least the basic income, the turnover in the area of necessities will increase, thus stabilising the market in the long run and promoting growth. The danger of this basic income becoming a social hammock for individuals cannot be ruled out in principle, but it is most likely less than in the previous social system! If the taxpayers do not pay enough taxes, it can happen that at the end of life a tax debt remains unpaid, a tax debt that is then part of the inheritance. In this case, the payment of the last tax debt from the inheritance should replace the inheritance tax. To ensure that the basic income can be paid out without any problems and can also be used directly by the beneficiary, a bank card of a state-owned bank should be handed out and only transferred to another bank upon request.

For the markets and with them the economic systems to remain stable in the long run, it must be ensured, among other measures, that the basic income remains exactly within the framework that reflects the basic needs of employees in the lower third of the population on the cost side. Basic needs should be determined from the costs of housing, mobility, insurance, food and clothing, as well as a basic need for cultural goods and costs for further education. If the cost of living can be deducted as a cost from income when calculating personal income, corresponding statistics on this also accrue at the tax office, which one can fall back on in order to be able to recalculate the basic need again and again and adjust the basic income accordingly.

It is important that a basic income as a citizen's income must be available to all citizens, the simple worker as well as the millionaire. In order for this to work, the basic income must in principle be offset against the tax debt, so that a basic income or even only a part of it is only paid out if there are no corresponding tax debts; those who have no tax debts receive the full basic income, and those who have only minor tax debts are paid this basic income minus the tax debt. The basic income is also regarded as a lump sum for basic survival needs. If costs can be proven that exceed the amount of the fixed basic income, these should also be taken into account, as long as all costs are disclosed, in any case if the higher costs arise from the fact that these costs in a broader sense only make the work activity possible, for example if a car is needed to get to work. Thus, if costs of 1,500 euros arise instead of the 1,000 euros to be imputed as a lump sum (insofar as this is taken as a lump sum basic salary), this is to be imputed as follows: Assuming a foreman or foreman earns 2,500 euros a month and needs a car because of the constantly changing places of work in order to always be at the place of work on time, this could result in a calculable profit of 1,000 euros plus the 1,000 euros from the basic income if these 1,500 euros are deducted as costs from 2,500 euros. If the total profit of 2,000 euros is taxable at 50%, this results in a tax liability of 1,000 euros in our example. If the tax liability is offset against the basic salary at the end, no more payments should be due with a tax liability of 1,000 euros and a basic salary of

1,000 euros. Another case is that 1,000 euros are paid for help in the household, the domestic help, to which another 1,000 euros from the basic income are to be added.

With living costs at the flat rate of 1,000 euros, a profit of 1,000 euros remains for the domestic help, which, taxed at 50%, results in a tax liability of 500 euros. If the basic income is still offset, a credit balance of 500 euros remains to be paid out and thus a total net income of 1,500 euros.

Any monthly payments from insurances or also from health insurances should not affect the payment of the basic income up to an amount of 1,000 euros in the total costs, according to the example above. On the other hand, a deduction could justifiably be made for shared flats, whether with or without a marriage certificate. It could make sense to grant only the first adult a citizen's allowance or basic salary of 1,000 euros and the other adults in the shared apartment 750 euros, as well as underage children 500 euros! A family with 2 children would therefore be entitled to 2,750 euros in basic income. With family earnings of 5,750 euros including basic income (3,000 plus 2,750), this results in a profit of 3,000 euros after deducting 2,750 euros in living expenses and thus a tax liability of 1,500 euros before offsetting. After offsetting against the basic income of 2,750 Euros, this would result in a negative tax liability of 1,250 Euros. If this money were now paid out, the family would have a net salary of 4250 euros at its disposal.

If in a family with two children the father and mother together earn 12,750 Euros per month, the deduction of the lump sum of 2,750 Euros results in a profit of 10,000 Euros, to which, however, the 2,750 Euros from the basic salary must be added. These 12,750 euros are then taxed at 50%, which results in a tax liability of 6,537 euros. After offsetting this with the basic salary of 2,750 euros, a tax liability of 3,625 euros remains, which in the current classical tax system amounts to approx. 30%. The family thus has 9,125 euros at its disposal in the month after tax. This corresponds to a tax of approx. 30% in the classical progression table.

The last case study now assumes an elderly woman who can no longer work and thus has no income of her own until she retires; if costs of 1,000 euros are considered in this example, no tax is payable, but 1,000 euros are paid out, a kind of negative tax. It should also be discussed whether, in the case of accommodation in a nursing home and costs of 2,300 euros in the home, these 2,300 euros are also paid out. Here, of course, private insurance could also make up the difference, possibly the pension accruing at retirement age. In a Safe Money system, the 1,300 euros in excess of the basic salary could also be paid out of the business balance, which must be paid in when one comes of age in order to have an account with the bank that generates the Safe Money. In the event of long-term care and old age, the business assets can also be used to top up. In this respect, the business assets additionally take on a kind of insurance benefit both in an emergency and at the end of life. As in the case of the familiar life insurance policies, the paid-in credit balance can be used at the end, depending on the conditions, either to cover the need for long-term care or, if sufficient private insurance has been taken out for this purpose, to cover the need for long-term care. The insurance policy may also be partially paid out in the event of death. In the case of a depleting insurance policy, the entire remaining amount in the event of death can then be considered as a payment into this joint insurance policy. Private insurance and assets can also be taken into account but should in any case lead to a better position, since otherwise no one would take out private insurance.

Basic income and secure money probably require carefully planned and scientifically accompanied model experiments. Important variables are the amount of the basic income, the determination of the beneficiaries and the integration into a local market. The starting point is a basic principle that preserves human dignity: every citizen should have the opportunity to manage his or her own personal affairs and receive the necessary assistance to be able to do so, if possible, until the end of his or her life.

Beneficiaries of a basic income can only be citizens, not guest workers from another country with a different citizenship. Every non-citizen should be treated in social matters according to the corresponding jurisdiction in his or her country of origin but should be given the opportunity to apply for naturalisation on a preferential basis after several years of work as guest. Be it a Briton, an American or a Romanian, for all these foreign workers or guest workers it must apply that they can only claim a basic salary in the host country once they have accepted the citizenship of their host country. Those who do not have a German passport, for example, should be allowed to continue working in Germany when a basic salary is introduced, but should be able to claim the social security cover of their home country and must be able to cover higher costs through private insurance if necessary. In this way, the individual national social systems could be protected and yet freedom of movement in the choice of employment, as in the EU, could be maintained. There is also no reason to do away with insurance-based benefits with the introduction of a basic salary. Health insurance benefits should of course be paid out in addition if there is an entitlement to them.

3. Money in private hands

Money as a credit or deposit of the citizen, one might think, is best kept in every citizen's own home in the private safe, just like the other private values and possessions. In the age of zero interest rates, why not keep one's own money in one's own safe? Cash in the safe is the official means of payment that can be used at any time, which is not necessarily the case with deposits at the bank. Only cash can be sensed and counted. If cash is abolished, this possibility will disappear, children will no longer be able to learn how to handle money by counting the coins. Also, without cash, there is no more money that must be accepted by state bodies and institutions in any case. One can only say, "nip things in the bud" and ask with what aims cash is to be abolished. But how could cash be introduced and secured in the system of free banks with the new Safe Money? Even if initially only a digital currency is launched, it is worth considering whether, as soon as possible after the cashless introduction of NIM coins, a new system could be created. are to be minted, if necessary, only for the local market. With a bank's card, one could then perhaps obtain the coins in the local market by debiting the equivalent amount from one's account. Moreover, an alternative to cash could be the cash card. A cash card does not require new technology, only new rules. One of these rules: Each statement on the bill should first show the amount still usable at the top. Further, goods, cost of goods and total amount as well as remaining amount should be shown on the bill too. The cards of the future should be able to manage at least two currencies. Cards with one euro and one local currency could even become mandatory for the EU. Simplification of private control is also important in the purchase of real estate, when the land is omitted from the purchase price and land transfer tax no longer must be paid either! Without interest on the financial capital required, it is also easier to include the purchase of real estate in future planning.

The use of private capital in companies that serve the common good, as well as such in public institutions, should certainly be understood as a way of exercising private control in these areas. However, private capital in the public sector should not destroy the public character and should therefore be limited to 40% of the total capital. Wealth confers power, which can be dangerous for individual citizens, but also for public institutions. Therefore, the influence of individual citizens in the public sphere should be limited, as should the accumulation of power among individual citizens and companies. In principle, it should be enough to prevent cartels and pave the way for small firms to be able to compete in the market. Since financial capital will no longer play its current role in the future, because more and more intangible values will determine economic activity, financial capital will also lose influence, an influence that will be absorbed by educational capital and human capital.

XIII. Investments with and without capital!

Nowadays, investments are made in different currencies. Whether in euros or in pounds, or in dollars, the stake is always one with only limited safe money. Even the expected investments using safe money, i.e., in NIM, cannot eliminate the entrepreneurial risk despite safe money. The prohibition of using money or capital from legal entities may well lead to changes in investments. With the use of NIM, the investment is personalised and can thus only be made by natural persons. This limits the amount of capital that can be invested, since with NIM each person can only invest as much as he or she can offer as collateral in terms of working life. The resulting limit in the safe currency replaces the interest in the old currencies, but we still remain in a monetary system that, conceived as a capitalist system, invests with existing capital. But what is investment without capital supposed to look like? The fact is that more and more companies are getting by with only a very small amount of capital. In addition, the valuation of most large corporations, especially those related to IT, can no longer be substantiated with tangible values. In many cases, these intangible assets do not even appear on the balance sheet and can only appear there under very specific conditions. Only when a company is sold does one obtain a value for the intangible values of this company by attributing the rest of the remaining value to the intangible values after deducting all tangibly determinable values. Nevertheless, these values already exist before the sale, but only after the change of ownership can the new owner clearly and unambiguously identify the intangible values with a value that can be expressed in money. Patents and licences, as well as the organisational structure, bind knowledge that, as part of an educational capital, makes the company more valuable than could be determined by the pure capital investment before the sale. This also allows new firms, so-called fintech firms, to get started with only a small amount of capital, as their founders usually bring extensive knowledge with them, which they have usually previously acquired within a university degree.

C. LEGAL CERTAINTY – MAINSTAY OF THE SYSTEM

XIV. Security and equitable distribution

The various currency reforms throughout history have shown that money and the investment in money only provide security to a limited extent. If a new currency is introduced because the old currency is no longer sufficiently valuable, this is certainly only the end point of a longer development in which money continually loses value through inflation and the printing press of the central bank. Nevertheless, the general assumption that the loss of value of money must be accompanied by inflation does not seem to be entirely correct. For the internal economic cycle, it should indeed not matter how much the money used is worth in external circulation. Also, value adjustments of the same kind in the most important partner currencies can weaken or even cancel out the effect of an impairment. Even if the money pumped into the market does not reach the customer, inflation cannot easily occur. The money from the central bank's printing press must first reach the ordinary citizen before higher demand follows with the result of higher revenues and the possibility of raising prices. If the money pumped into the market does not end up in normal circulation, it cannot lead to higher inflation. If money is hoarded or sent abroad, the expected inflation may not occur. Investments in real estate, gold and foreign securities can lead to a second-order hoarding effect. If gold is hoarded to secure money, this will also have a negative impact on inflation. Friedman's calls for the expansion of a free gold and foreign exchange market may have contributed to leaving the gold standard. In principle, this was supposed to strengthen the market, since only the freely operating market also guarantees pricing in line with the market. Since then, however, there has been a lack of a fixed reference value to which the currency can align itself and which also sets the necessary limits that convey security. Of course, the realisation that gold cannot be hoarded and held in arbitrary quantities in order to be able to satisfy the growing activities with it, moreover, permanently rising population figures, was also decisive; even the partial hedging of the currency is not a solution in the long run. After the abolition of gold cover, central bank credit becomes a pure question of trust, as does private bank credit with commercial banks, although here a part is covered by the collateral objects over which every bank customer must assure his bank as security the power of disposal in the event of insolvency. As a rule, however, full coverage is not achieved. Only the security via work performance accounts, as proposed, can lead to full coverage and thus to money secured in real terms. Secure financing is becoming increasingly important for all time-sensitive projects, especially construction projects. Sustainable and lasting growth is hardly conceivable without secure financing. Therefore, sustainable financing is absolutely part of the sustainable economy.

Securing through working capital accounts is more secure than through gold, but has the disadvantage of the necessary contractual security, whereas with gold only physical ownership plays a role. Since the gold standard no longer plays a role worldwide, hedging through working time and performance is an excellent solution in the search for a new standard. Such a standard would above all also have the advantage of automatic adjustment to population growth and shrinkage in the economies to be observed.

Working time accounts, it should be explicitly noted, are not the basis for wages and salaries to be negotiated, they can at most be a guideline for this. Working time accounts are only essential for the granting of loans, but they can also be used in other areas for the assessment of value. The salary of the managing director may well be higher than expected according to the working time account. Above all, the safe currency offers security in lending as well as in the investment and savings behaviour that depends on it. Of course, high standards must also be set and maintained for the secure storage and data protection of clients' data. If, on the other hand, we look at the cryptocurrencies that have emerged in recent years, especially the best known, Bitcoin, alongside Ethereum and Ripple, it is noticeable that these are becoming increasingly popular, although they offer no hedging, either through gold or any other substantial value. Nevertheless, Bitcoin has emerged from the past 5 years up 30,000 per cent and has further potential. All cryptocurrencies combined are said to have circulated billions of dollars to date (as of 2018). One might think that the smooth handling and speed of money transfer are more important than security. However, that would be too simple, because Bitcoin also offers security with the blockchain, namely in the transfer of money, not in the preservation of value. Since the value of cryptocurrencies has risen enormously in recent years, maintaining their value is less of a focus now. The dependence on state monetary systems due to the exchange value may not yet deter anyone in view of the enormous increases in value. The introduction of a new protocol has now made Bitcoin more secure again for the next few years, but for how long, and what is this security really worth? The warnings against Bitcoin are getting louder and louder, up to the view that it is a Ponzi scheme scam; others nevertheless see Bitcoin as an alternative. Miller even shows how Bitcoin is becoming an everyday means of payment with a credit card designed for Bitcoin.

The growing number of card payments overall means that less and less cash is needed and thus less cash is held by banks. This and the ever-improving security technology also led to a drastic reduction in the number of bank robberies. On the other hand, criminal activities on the internet are on the rise. Money as such is still exposed to the attack of criminal activities. The fact that bank robberies have not been consistently condemned in the past, no, even glorified in various films, shows that criminality aimed at the pure acquisition of money is even socially accepted to a certain extent.

A redistribution of unjustly acquired money is propagated, which also accepts criminal acts, if the objective is good. There is an absolute need for a discussion here about the value of work on the one hand and an outlawing of any kind of criminality and carelessness that not only allows assets and money to be stolen but also looks the other way when people are still working like slaves. There is no question of work performance being paid fairly in general, and this will hardly be realisable even in the conventional classical money system, except for small successes. The Safe Money NIM offers more hope here, because if it is realised as proposed, there should be working time accounts based on which the services and their remuneration become more comprehensible.

1. Growth in freedom and security

The regulated market, even the closed financial market, can also provide impulses for growth. Whether centralised regulation with plan specifications is the worse alternative in every case also depends on the general circumstances. In the case of finance, the optimal supply of sufficient funds will be important; Friedman proposes continuous expansion with a certain percentage. In any case, the volume of money in circulation must increase with the population and its activities but should also decrease again with the decrease in population density, should be in relative proportion to the population size in which it is valid. In the case of non-national currencies, the reference point can also be fixed towards the people who use this money to carry out their economic activities. In a highly diversified economy, an economy with a high division of labour, only money can make smooth rapid exchange possible and, as the saying goes, "time is money". The temporal component, with which money can act as an accelerator, is in many cases only able to set growth in motion and maintain it. In these considerations, we always assume that money is scarce, i.e., not available in abundance. As with every factor that can promote growth, we must also assume with money that after saturation there will be more growth, factor input will not cause increased growth. The question of whether there is saturation or a shortage of the factor in question, which thus becomes the limiting factor, is important to know if one wants to correctly assess the influence on growth processes and incorporate it into planning. Since different growth processes and decay processes always run side by side in time, the right assessment can only be made for individual processes, so that central planning in the individual economies can only be successful to a limited extent. Free financial markets seem to focus more successfully on the different projects.

With Safe Money "NIM", the amount of money in circulation should be oriented towards the needs of the citizens, since it is they who are responsible for the creation of money. However, it would also be wrong to imagine that everyone can borrow money in the NIM currency without limits at any time. The limits, however, are not state guidelines or arbitrary state decrees, but limits set on the basis of contractual rules and agreements. In the case of a money-creating credit contract, it must be determined how many of the total working hours to be used in a lifetime are to be used as collateral, the term and then the amount of the instalment to be repaid, the repayment. It must be ensured that the agreed instalment can be paid without any problems based on the current employment situation and living conditions.

It must be emphasised that the freedom of the financial markets and their stability can only result from contractual arrangements and their transparent enforceable agreements. Free financial markets therefore also need a free judiciary that obeys only the law.

Clear contractual regulations provide the security without which growth in a modern economy cannot take place undisturbed.

2. Gamblers, gamblers, fraudsters and the grey money market

"The very sight of banknotes makes different people out of us: we become greedy, stingy and selfish."

(Beck, 2018)

The question of security does not apply to the gambler, he only has the thrill and the guaranteed "safe bet" in mind. The question is whether gambling winnings promote economic growth. Since many a company has ended up in ruin due to the gambling addiction of owners and members of the management, it is probably more likely to have a positive influence on decay. Even if gambling losses tend to have a destructive effect, positive effects through gambling gains cannot be ruled out. However, the destructive share is to be rated higher, if only because playing for money can generate antipathies and positive effects from gambling winnings occur rather rarely and are due to chance. Funds can also have a very negative effect on the activities of a company, which in recent years has been blamed on hedge funds. Individual private majority owners can also negatively influence the management of a company with their vote; however, the possibility of a positive influence should not be concealed.

It is also questionable whether money used to purchase bonds and certificates is beneficial to the growth of the economy in question or whether, on the contrary, it inhibits growth. Insofar as money does not end up directly in real investments or consumption, no direct effect on growth can be expected. The situation is different for corporate bonds and capital increases, regardless of the type of company. If outside capital is taken in, this is always associated with a reduction in the value of the company, but it can also generate new growth impulses through new investments, which bring in further revenues and thus increase the value of the company again. In many cases it is also important to raise money as quickly as possible to be able to transfer money. Fintechs and new types of financial institutions in general offer excellent services in this segment, so that money can be transferred around the world in a matter of seconds. These include companies that specialise in the rapid transfer of funds to the remotest parts of the world, so that it is no longer necessary to wait several days for the money to arrive. In the process, even changing into another currency becomes child's play. Internationally active institutions in particular are predestined for this, which also includes the new internet currencies. Payments in Bitcoin can be made worldwide in seconds. One problem that should not be underestimated, however, is the way in which money is created in Bitcoin through mining, whereby the Bitcoins created in this way are also to be regarded as profit, just as winning the lottery or a lottery is, and should therefore also be subject to profit tax.

In the meantime, there are also voices that do not ascribe a long life to the new cryptocurrencies on the internet. The cause for the assumed collapse of the internet currencies is seen in the dubiousness of most cryptocurrencies. In particular, the meteoric rise in the value of cryptocurrencies can be seen as an indication that there are no real values to back this up. Since national currencies also fundamentally no longer reflect real values, the lack of a link to real values does not equate to a lack of seriousness either, perhaps the approach taken by the internet currencies OneCoin and Swisscoin, which according to Miller are to be classified as pseudo currencies!

Money, however, it is created, should benefit society and the individual. In order to avert dangers to society, it needs social control, just as state institutions need private control. The control should point out negative effects so that in reaction the causes can be eliminated.

Money is too important for stable growth and for maintaining a state of equilibrium in the societal context to leave the creation of money uncontrolled to individuals who sometimes put their personal interests so far in the foreground that the well-being of all is thereby endangered. This does not speak against private money creation, but it does speak against uncontrolled money creation without regulations and legally secured contracts. Securities, such as those in closed-end funds and joint-stock companies, which cannot show an orderly and transparent record of capital ownership and, moreover, are not freely traded on a controlled capital market, should be banned. If the registration of all money transactions involving longer-term commitments becomes compulsory, this could dry up the money market, known as the grey market, very quickly in the longer term, to the benefit of honest citizens. The maxim must be that money must not become a plaything for criminals. This does not rule out the use of money with criminal intent in principle, but only curbs it in a hitherto non-transparent sub-area through a new transparency. If speculative financial instruments are developed, this is sometimes only opaque to the layman and, above all, gambling addiction is activated in the process, where any caution is quickly put aside. Here, only regulations can limit the possible damage.

If, on the other hand, money is used to pay for criminal acts, this can never be ruled out. Strategies to curb this nevertheless remain the task of a free and independent judiciary. Furthermore, it is the task of the judiciary to also curb tax evasion and social fraud with legally binding judgements. However, there is a grey area between fraud and honesty. Especially when there is insufficient or no transparency, mistakes can occur that are avoidable. Avoidable is also social fraud, which is not fraud, because "only" a legal loophole is being exploited, the article by Brigitta Beeger is worth reading.

As I said, there is a grey area between fraud and the honest handling of money, a grey area that does not always make it clear whether it is a matter of criminal activity or a lack of transparency and insight.

It is also interesting that the way money is handled even depends on whether it is clean or heavily polluted. Those who pay with clean money are more likely to count on the seller's honesty than those who do not, who pays with dirty money. The psyche plays a role here in very different facets. In purely cognitive-rational terms, the money economy is much easier to analyse than is actually the case. Money is not only the printed value to be used according to a current psychological state, but also the cause of changed behaviour. Money can change the psyche, just as the use of money also changes social relationships. In the field of action between social dependencies, emotional drives and rational thinking, both egoistic and altruistic patterns of action can develop when dealing with money, even if the sight of money and especially bundles of money tends to produce egoistic behaviour. The greed for more and more money in one's own possession, irrespective of services rendered, produces all the gamblers, gamblers and fraudsters who make us worry about the security of our money, whether in the wallet or in the account. The acceptance of a fair distribution would be a step towards more security, the fair distribution itself the next step, help to learn the right way to handle money, another important step to be able to guarantee more security. If money becomes a secure image for work performance, as in the case of safe money, this can also bring about positive changes in consciousness.

XV. Money Creation, Distribution and Safekeeping!

If money is stolen, the thief can sometimes be identified via the registration code, and metal stripes and watermarks should also help prevent the counterfeiting of banknotes. However, this does not mean that storage at the bank is safe. Storing banknotes in one's own safe may offer a certain degree of security in times of crisis, but it does not protect against theft with burglary and certainly not against devaluation due to inflation and currency reform. Safekeeping would have to guarantee two things: firstly, safekeeping of the money, just as I could put it in the safe, and secondly, security that preserves value, i.e., no devaluation through inflation. In the current currencies, the preservation of value cannot be ensured with a savings account, but with safe money savings accounts. The citizen can only obtain security from the beginning if he accompanies the money creation process responsibly from the beginning. Only then can a fair distribution be made, especially if the performance criteria of a working time account based on performance are considered. A separate control of all private value creation chains can be dispensed with if the legal framework that has been set allows for this control to be carried out in a legal dispute, ordered by a court, in a specific case even after the fact.

1. Private money creation versus central bank money

The Safe Money presented in this book is a purely private form of money creation, whereas the procedure of commercial banks to create money through loans, which is common in the euro area, is not a purely private, but also not a purely state form of money creation, even if the private share is relatively high; it is a kind of mixed form. Currently, there are already various purely private currencies, but strictly speaking they do not create new money, but exist only on the trust of the users that after an exchange from another currency this money can be used and utilised in the same way as the different national currencies. Examples are the many internet currencies, most famously Bitcoin, which do not exist independently, but only in an exchange rate to central bank currencies. These currencies take over the security of the central bank currencies, if these securities still exist at all. As international currencies, they offer the following: Transactions worldwide within this currency have the advantage that exchange rate losses across continents are excluded within the system and, in addition, extremely fast transactions can take place without inconvenient checks, for example on the origin of the money, but the necessary exchange of money into a national currency can quickly turn the advantages into disadvantages. If the Secure Money NIM is transferred worldwide in the administration of Free Banks, which control currency and transfer for their members with or without a blockchain technology in a corresponding IT network, NIM could come up with comparable advantages as with current internet currencies, but with the difference that NIM is not only exchangeable into other currencies, but as an independent private full currency it offers a security that cryptocurrencies like Bitcoin cannot offer. The link to working time accounts is both an advantage and a disadvantage. The advantage is the full security provided by working time accounts, the disadvantage is the link to the bank where the working time accounts are held, which also causes a somewhat higher effort when changing residence than with other accounts, regardless of whether you want to take the account with you or move completely to another bank. However, with a worldwide network of free banks with the NIM currency, the disadvantage of being tied to a free bank should become more and more negligible with the spread of the safe currency system. Especially in the first few years, acceptance is likely to be a problem. In contrast, the full money of the central bank offers acceptance guaranteed by law or decree, or at least immediate acceptance by government agencies and institutions. One disadvantage is the limited scope of central bank money within a nationally defined framework. Moreover, central bank money is also at the mercy of the non-democratically controlled influences of the central bankers. If the central bank did not create money, but only controlled the creation of money of whatever kind, this could also facilitate the introduction of democratic structures at the state central bank. Other alternatives are proposed by international IT corporations, first and foremost Facebook with Libra, a new creation that, in contrast to previous cryptocurrencies, provides for a fixed link to internationally important trading currencies. With this and the possibility of generating a high number of users worldwide, it could be achieved that a currency emerges here that in the long term also becomes a serious alternative to the existing currencies. Due to the large number of users, it could even come to the point where work services are no longer paid in euros or dollars, but in this new currency. However, this currency, like other private currencies, is still a long way from achieving the acceptance of central bank money. The central bank can still force a change into the money issued by the central bank, generally for payments to the public sector, be it taxes, levies, licence fees or rents, if the new currency is not accepted for such payments.

2. The fair distribution of the proceeds!

There will hardly ever be a distribution of money and assets that is fair in the eyes of all, whereby the question of what is to be understood by "fair" still has to be answered! In this respect, the distribution problem could also be seen as a pseudo-problem. However, we must neither regard equitable distribution as solved nor equate it with an equalising distribution. It should be made clear at the outset that the gap between rich and poor cannot be closed so easily with redistribution. Wealth must take on social responsibility, and no one should be above the interest rate, and certainly not via the compound interest effect, existing wealth can continue to increase without work, because precisely with this, the responsibility for the use of money is already relinquished, or not assumed, as is to be expected! Now, distribution problems may hardly be solvable rationally at the end of a chain; rather, the question of fair distribution must always and at every place be asked in order to be able to lead the problems to acceptable solutions. If the profits from production are not directly distributed equitably, then a subordinate redistribution can perhaps mitigate some peaks of an unjust distribution of wealth, but only at an increased cost, and that without being able to extinguish the negative emotions in the case of unjust distribution at the point of origin. The evils must be eliminated where they originate. Looking back at history, the will to stop distributing profits so unjustly from now on, as has happened in the past, will not simply sweep the existing injustices off the table. The realisation of the need for fair distribution among the haves will sometimes be able to lead to voluntary redistributions, as this increases the stability of the system, which also increases the security in the system and thus also the personal security of the rich and super-rich. On the other hand, a natural inequality must also be accepted by everyone, which is the only way to build and stabilise solidarity. After all, not everyone is born with the same abilities, but should begin life with the same solidarity-based demands on themselves and society. For this reason, every citizen should be provided with the necessary money to survive in solidarity. All that is required is the solidary obligation that everyone also does something with his or her assets for the community that offers him or her this security. It is irrelevant whether social benefits or basic income dominate! The introduction of a solidarity-based basic income and a corresponding solidarity-based basic benefit could, however, bring many problems to a level where a solution is feasible.

If every citizen is now made to contribute 2.5 hours a week in solidarity, this could also considerably reduce the necessary tax burden, which would be entirely desirable. However desirable this may be, it will not be the most important result of such a measure. More important are the changes in consciousness to be brought about by it and the expectation of a higher commitment to the community!

It is therefore important that everyone makes this time available to society with their own skills, the teacher by using these 2.5 hours to help pupils understand the material better, the craftsman by taking on minor repairs for the town free of charge, and the policeman by organising and running training courses and taster sessions for pupils, the manager by helping with planning in the public sector. Those who are unable to contribute this time to society should, despite reservations, be able to compensate for this with a monetary payment, for the unskilled worker perhaps 20 euros per week and for the manager 1250 euros per week (8 euros or 500 euros per hour). A basic salary paid out or offset against tax should also be sufficient to live a decent life within society. Services not rendered to society could be claimed by the tax office, just like tax. This should also be enough to satisfy the needs of the public purse in purely mathematical terms. If we do not try to distribute wealth, but the results of productivity, i.e. also those of the increase in productivity, we are moving towards the real distribution problems, which consist in enforcing the claim to social work, participation and the satisfaction of basic needs, demands which, similarly, the rich and super-rich do not only regard as. The government must not only accept the fact that taxation is justified, but also that it is necessary for peaceful coexistence.

3. Tax justice and tax simplification

Fair taxation starts with the problem of distribution, since many politicians assume that all injustices in taxation, especially income tax, are to be compensated for by a correspondingly different tax legislation. However, tax legislation is becoming more and more complex and complicated, so that only experts can keep track of it all. If, as a result, I am no longer able to understand the demands of the tax office without a tax advisor and experts in my own office, then this already leads to injustice and inequality in favour of the rich in this society. Therefore, the first demand should be to make tax laws understandable for all citizens. Outdated tax laws should be reviewed to see if they make any sense at all and, if necessary, abolished. Subsequently, it should be examined whether the individual taxes are substantial or whether they are functional or dysfunctional. In the case of substantial taxes, a conversion into functional taxes should be considered and, if possible, all these substantial taxes should be abolished. Dysfunctional taxes, on the other hand, must be justified very precisely with their objective of restricting consumption. The introduction of a general profit tax with the abolition of turnover and income tax would be the best immediately feasible simplification in the tax code. Another simplification would be the abandonment of progressive taxation. If the profit tax is set at a uniform 50% or even 60%, everyone can quickly work out their tax liability. Only the offsetting of costs can become more complicated but should also help the citizen to have a better overview and perspective of his finances. To relieve the burden on the average citizen, however, flat rates can be introduced, such as a living allowance of about 1,000 euros and a work allowance of 500 euros if a car is necessary to get to the place of work; if possible, kilometre invoices should be dispensed with unless the taxpayer expressly requests this.

However, the tax office should be allowed to verify the necessity of a car in order to deny, if necessary, the granting of an increased deductibility and that of the lump sum. Special flat rates are also conceivable for different occupational groups. If, for example, teachers are granted a lump-sum allowance of 250 euros for their profession, then a lump-sum of 1,250 euros could be applied!

The teacher who earns 3,400 euros could thus deduct a flat rate of 1,250 euros if he lives around the corner, would thus have to declare 2,150 euros as profit and would then have to pay 1,075 euros in taxes on 50% of that. If he has to go to school by car, the profit is reduced to 1,650 euros, so that only 825 euros in taxes have to be paid. If the basic income of 1,000 euros is offset, a negative tax of 175 euros could even arise in individual cases. If the flat rate for the car is reduced to 200 euros, there is no longer a negative tax. Over the years, it will be possible to determine more precisely which flat rates are appropriate.

Likewise, flat rates for travel, entertainment and hospitality can be applied. If one sets the lump sums in such a way that they cover 75% of the possible individual settlements, then fair taxation is also achieved with this. High rents in the city could also be considered as a lump sum, but here one can also use the demand individual billing and thereby possibly save taxes with higher deductibility.

A simplification for the tax offices could be achieved by having the taxes for all purchases on the net and for digital services go through a central tax office or customs office, i.e., a national institution and, in the case of the EU, perhaps also through an EU tax office or customs office. If the European Union agrees on a common profit tax, it might even be possible to dispense with separate taxation of international internet corporations.

However, special attention must also be paid to hidden profits, which sometimes make up the main profit, especially in the case of internet groups. Even with free services, the real profit margin per customer contact can be determined via the hidden profit. If customer data are collected and evaluated, this is a profit per customer who makes his data available. The profit is easier to determine when selling a tangible good. In any case, however, the hidden profit is better and easier to determine than the hidden value, which is why the hidden profits cannot be determined via evaluations. Any company that generates profits through customer information also generates revenues, if not directly from all the customers whose information is collected and stored, then through advertising, sharing information for money and generating sales profits. If, from the total profits without the hidden profits, these are also included according to an agreed procedure, one could arrive at the real, the genuine, profits. One possibility would be to classify a certain percentage of the total profits as hidden profits, depending on the costs deducted from the profit before taking the hidden profits into account. If one knows that for most products on average 40% as costs determine the final consumer price, one can assume an average profit of 60%. A company that, after deducting all deductible costs, has a profit of 80%, according to this logic, has a hidden profit of 20%, which should be relevant for tax purposes. If corresponding winnings are paid out in the case of competitions serving the purpose of advertising and are also recognised accordingly as costs, the information received in the process is to be additionally reported as hidden profits. However, hidden winnings are also the unpaid winnings from prize games in the various media, insofar as they were announced but only the actual payouts are assessed as costs.

XVI. Identity and money, activators in the space of action

> *"Before we can understand contemporary identity politics, we need to step back and develop a deeper and richer understanding of human motivation and behaviour. We need, in other words, a better theory of the human soul".*

In the modern diversified society, the citizen acts with his own and others' money in his own space of action. In this space, he has developed his identity and lives it as a member of a society, a group with its own group identities, which also determine his relationship to money and especially his buying behaviour. This becomes understandable if we see the human being as being formed and educated, formed being in its social and psychological as well as physical conditions. The dimensional subspaces that determine the space of action correspond to this: a) the physical time space, b) the relational time space and c) the emotional time space. Every action has a physical, a relational and an emotional component. As dimensional components, they can form and shape the spatial-temporal identity. But how are these time spaces to be scaled? In physical space, we know three dimensions that can be scaled in metres: length, width and height. Relations, on the other hand, are scalable via the intensity of the relation, namely in the sub-dimensions "competition", "cooperation" and "feedback". We know the scalability of intensities from the realm of sounds, where you can scale the volume. Comparable to this would be a scaling of relational intensities as well as emotional intensities. The emotional space could then be describable with the scaled dimensions "I", "You" and "We". Let's take the example of a sales talk when buying a car: The emotional component is determined from the buyer's point of view by sympathy towards the salesperson (You), the effort to stand out from the neighbours, the family, for example the one in the street who can afford the new BMW. (We) and towards myself, who manages to buy a car in his favourite colour (I). The relational component may be determined by competition, as the larger car offers more space for goods to be delivered. It may then be that cooperative and feedback moments do not play a role. But always, of course, all three dimensions of the physical time-space are addressed; when buying a car, the car should perhaps fit into small parking spaces, so it must not be too long, nor must the fixed budget be exceeded. The money for the purchase must either be available in the stock market or in the bank account, or it must be possible to obtain it through a loan, and that here and now at the time of purchase. If the money can only be in the account in 2 months, a loan must also be available for today's purchase, otherwise the purchase cannot be completed. Even if all identity criteria have been positively decided, if the money is missing, the purchase cannot take place. If, on the other hand, the money is sufficient, but the identity criteria are not sufficiently fulfilled, the purchase will not take place either. For this reason, the identity criteria should be examined more closely based on the assigned dimensions and subspaces in the action space. A surcharge may possibly help to subsequently improve an inadequately fulfilled criterion, missing money can only be replaced by a loan if creditworthy. The top salesman may be able to draw conclusions about preferred car types by means of the affiliation to a sports club, a leisure club, with more precise indications of the customer's identity, he may even be able to advise him to the point what the right product, the right car, is for him. Maybe the customer is looking for a status symbol, or maybe just the best working machine for his business. Quite a few people want to be noticed with what they buy, to stand out from the sea of the invisible. The greed for more and more money is certainly also a way of confirming one's success, of standing out from the masses of others with a reference to one's own account and thus being noticed. This can be described as an individual phenomenon or also systematically in the various dependencies in the space of action with physical, emotional and relational references. Perhaps it is not the decay of liberalism or democracy that is the real problem in these times, perhaps it is the invisible person who finally wants to be seen.

1. The rational (physical) time space

In the physical space we find money as real objective and usable material value, we can touch the coins and the banknotes and, with some practice, quickly determine the value of the present amounts of money by stacking the coins or banknotes. The human being who defines his value and thus his identity through the possession of this money will consider it the highest maxim to collect and hoard money in all situations.

Money, like tangible assets, now exists both real in the now and virtual in the dimensions of the past and the future. The creation of money by commercial banks in the 21st century via credit agreements is a good example of how the past and the future affect the present based on agreements and contracts. Money is created here as necessary for the exchange of services not only in the present, but also between past services and future services with the current services again and again. With credit, money is created in order to be able to mediate between the present and the future, money is thereby brought from the future into the present.

For economic activity to be possible in the modern sense, it must be made possible not only to exchange values in the present, but also to fetch them from the future. In the process, shifts and imponderables can change the fixed value in the dimensions of space and time. Just as inflation lowers the value of money, innovations can also raise the value. Although we speak of the value of money, today's money generally has no intrinsic value, no material value. The intrinsic value can be fixed in the money of a currency, but it can also be fixed in other ways. Material values will be lower in the future for depreciating material assets and usually even higher for non-depreciating assets, even though equivalence is initially promised. A gold coin also has an appreciable material value, whereas a banknote only has a material value approaching zero. On the other hand, money has an ascribed Janus-faced exchange value. Money is Janus-faced because it has two sides, that of the creditor and that of the debtor. In general, the value attributions in the common currencies diverge between creditor and debtor. The future value for the creditor is higher than what he gives away, and the current value for the debtor is lower than what he must pay back. Via interest, the value of money changes, and surprisingly for most of us, in the negative direction. Money lent at interest must be repaid with more money in the future, which increases the money supply in the future perspective. In a pure credit-based money system, increasing the money supply also means increasing the amount of credit. Whether we have to take out higher loans to pay for the increased prices of goods due to inflation or to pay the interest on repayment, in either case the exchange value will be lower. If the exchange value becomes lower in the future, this can be compensated for by an increase in the circulation of money. In addition, there is also what the banks siphon off for money creation before they pay out the credit money. If one thinks this process further, monetary reform is pre-programmed in the foreseeable future. But one can also conclude from this that with low inflation or even 0 – inflation and 0 – interest, money remains stable in value.

Another idea is to stimulate investment by lowering the interest rate. Translated, this means that lowering costs induces the entrepreneur to borrow money for new investments. But what if this does not seem to make sense, because neither the sales market for the additional products is available nor the old machines to be replaced? If there is an expectation that the interest rate will remain this low in the future, then the low interest rate will not stimulate purchasing behaviour to the extent expected. An increase in the money supply will therefore not automatically lead to an increase in the volume of investment.

If one now wants to record the loss in value of money over time, one can use the inflation rate for this purpose. But how is the inflation rate calculated? Without questioning this, the loss of value presented in this way is just as questionable as with another possible reference, the relationship to other currencies! One definition of inflation on the internet assumes that the value of money falls and the price level rises. Inflation is measured by comparing a basket of goods from the previous year with the current basket of goods, and the difference then represents inflation. Central bankers usually refer to core inflation, which is inflation adjusted for food and energy prices. Since the basket of goods on which the calculations are based is also adjusted over time, the data from the Federal Statistical Office can only be used to a limited extent for long-term studies without being asked. However, rough tendencies can be observed everywhere with these data. On the basis of these data, one can say, for example, that with an average inflation of 2%, money will only be worth half as much in 35 years. This may reassure some, worry others. However, changes in the inflation rate will certainly change the flow of money as well. If one wants to capture basic needs, it would be advisable not to use the official basket of goods, but to create a special basket of goods that is only geared to food, energy needs, housing and mobility costs.

The devaluation of money in space and time is fundamentally socially conditioned and has no reason hidden in physics, but it is not otherwise explained with the description of the devaluation of money, but only described. Even the reference to inflation is not an explanation, but only a description. The explanation only begins when we consider and interpret the accompanying shifts in the social fields. The statement that the rich are getting richer, and the poor are getting poorer is also not an explanation; we must already fathom the causes. Should cooperation make the rich richer and richer, or is it rather the ego-relatedness of the rich?

2. The relational time space

The relations, these are the relations that exist, for example, between the producer and the consumer, or between two competing producers, or between two producers who are in a cooperative relationship with each other. What role does money play here? Well, money is used to buy up competitors, money is used to buy into the cooperative partner, or to initiate cooperation or stabilise feedback.

The competition strives for a change, to beat the competitor out of the field, to destroy him, to push him into another niche or even to conquer a new niche itself! A competition can only survive time if it is stabilised by other relations; through cooperation and feedback, a competition that by itself would mean the end can be maintained because the company stabilises itself through other partners. In ecology, such relations are described in. For economics, the arrow from competitor A to competitor B can be formulated in such a way that an increase in sales revenue for competitor A leads to a decrease in sales revenue for B. This assumes that the market only has limited capacity to absorb the competitor's products. It must be assumed that the market only has a limited capacity to absorb the competitor's products. If the market is far from saturated, the success of the competitors can be recognised by the relative expansion of business in a comparison period. The arrow here stands for "the more, the less", but equally for "the less, the more". This indicates that relations always initially have reciprocal effects, which is why they can also be depicted as cycles, since the effect of A on B always has a counter-effect from B on A. In the case of competitors, it is always a matter of counteracting effects (-) as described above; in the case of cooperation, on the other hand, it can be assumed that it is a matter of concurrent effects (+), the partners mutually reinforce their effect so that, by definition, they continue to grow exponentially in substance on a permanent basis. In the real market, however, we are dealing with a networked relativity structure in which the cooperation cycle can become a superordinate competition cycle through coupling with a competition cycle. We only obtain regulated cycles in the coupling with feedback cycles, which are therefore also so important in order to establish and stabilise equilibrium positions. As in ecological systems, it can also be assumed in economic systems that the multitude of subsystems, in this case special relations, is important for stability and makes the effect on the next and next-but-one interlinked relations calculable.

In economics, relations are, for example, what makes the relationship between two producers enter into cooperation, or what makes two producers act as competitors in the market. With money, competitors can be bought up and cooperation can be initiated. Whether the costs are worthwhile, i.e., whether the hoped-for profits will be made, is not always something that can be planned in advance with certainty. In the case of cooperations, synergy effects can push down costs so that the money initially invested can be saved again later. In competitive situations, one will sometimes sell goods below the production costs in order not to be ousted. However, it may be cheaper to improve the quality or to occupy a new niche with different products. The money spent on new product development may be more profitable than price dumping.

Whether competition, cooperation or a typical control loop, the identities that operate in the current sphere of action are formed through the feedback between the relations. The fan of a football club, the group identity in the club itself, the identity in a nation state, for example as a Frenchman or as a German, in the future also increasingly as a European, are evolving classifications in a social community. The social relationships that develop in the community form the identity of the members, the citizens, of everyone. The developments and the results can be quite different, one person defines himself by his house, which is the most beautiful, another by his car, which is the fastest, another by his body, his position, his money. It is not money alone that determines the formation of identity here, but as a rule it is also not insignificantly involved.

Just as the value of money can change over time in the physical space of time, it will also change in the structure of relations, in relational space. On closer examination, the change in the valuations in the spatial and temporal space is not a matter of time. time depends on the changes in the relations, even if we do not directly perceive it that way. Only in relational space can the social fields also be viewed in their contexts. For example, if the price of a loaf of bread becomes 10% cheaper in a competitive cycle, the monetary value increases, which of course also influences the shopping basket. For the customer, who must get by with a certain budget per month, the issue here is how he can and must position himself between competing and cooperating suppliers and in determinable control loops. Since competition cannot depress prices in the long run, it makes sense to observe pricing over time, keeping a particularly thorough eye on the large corporations and their pricing policies. Since competitors are also eliminated through price, pricing should be kept on record until after the event. The citizen must be able to influence pricing on the spot and not just as a virtual world customer. In addition, the often-missing transparency regarding warranty claims and sustainability must be established in order to be able to carry out personal financial planning in a secure manner in the long term. This becomes possible in local markets with separate market rights, which, for example, can also force international corporations to be represented in the market by market law.

Special attention should be paid to the control loop with its feedbacks. Producer-consumer communities could build up their own protected space with guaranteed purchase obligations and guaranteed prices that follow the laws of a control loop. Money also plays a role here, but is usually less important in such relations than in the other possible relations between producers and consumers and between suppliers and customers.

Of course, relational space is also a space that changes over time, as we know it from physical space. The basic dimensions of relational space are as follows

1) competition, 2) cooperation and 3) feedback, i.e., three dimensions comparable to the three dimensions length, width and depth in physical space. The scaling in the relational space is possible via the strength of the mutual relationship or also dependencies on a scale from 0 to 100, as the percentage connections are immediately recognisable in this way.

3. The emotional time space

Every human being lives in a limited time space that belongs only to him and in a relation space that is affective to him with a special emotional space structure of his own, which builds up each person's own emotional time space, in his own psyche. In the emotional space we find, in addition to the monetary evaluation of the things and relationships around us, through our psyche also non-monetary evaluations. The emotional evaluations can be congruent with the rational ones but are more often strongly divergent from each other than taken into account in the economic calculation. If the emotional value exceeds the purely rational one, one is also prepared to spend more than what would result based on pure work performance. This explains why a painting is valued differently by different customers. The exaggerated prices of paintings by well-known artists at auctions are not yet adequately explained by this alone, but expectations still arise that do not affect the artistic value in any way. This is where the market comes into play with its own dynamics. The market not only generates preferences and a sense of well-being in our psyche, but it also generates expectations that, with a dynamic of their own, do not merely have an effect in the psychic space. The expectation of being able to achieve significantly higher prices in later years can catapult the price here and now many times over. Especially at art auctions, the price is usually determined by the hope of being able to achieve a higher price in later years, and not so much by the intrinsic value of the painting. In the case of a car, one would rather expect a loss of value projected into the future. Decreases in value are normal and typical for all depreciable goods, while increases in value are typical for non-depreciable goods from the ideal realm or also from the natural realm for goods that are not the result of labour and thus cannot be adapted to demand. A landscape can evoke strong emotions, for example in the case of the landscape in which one grew up, one then also speaks of home, just as a picture that reflects an emotional experience, perhaps even that of being close to home. The picture can be destroyed, can also be changed, but after the sale of the picture it has found a conclusion that transports the picture's message over centuries without losing its expressiveness. This picture is unique and therefore cannot lose value in this respect, but only gain. Strictly speaking, because of its uniqueness, there can be no true market value; it therefore belongs to all citizens who have something to do with this artist; like air, water and soil, it should be common property. Stored in a museum, such paintings can be a strong identity builder for a landscape, for a region, for a nation. The cultural landscape can strongly influence the identity and thus also the activity of an individual in the space of action. The emotional space, like the other subspaces of the space of action, is always carried by a projection into the future and an equal projection into the past. The present is always a time window between the past and the future. Those who donate to a good cause may do so out of a sense of guilt, an emotion that reaches into the past, but the donor may also be concerned with standing up for a better future in general, so that his grandchildren can still live in a world worth living in.

As coordinates in the psychic space, we could introduce the I as a basic dimension, next to it the You as another basic dimension and the We as the third basic dimension. All basic dimensions in emotional space can be scaled according to the emotional strength of an action, from 0% emotional involvement in an executed action to 100% emotionally conditioned action, in each case relating either to the I-dimension, the You-dimension or the We-dimension. The "we" is strongly influenced by social norms and values, as formed in the parental home, school and education. The "we", which can also be described as the superego in the Freudian sense, provides us with moral guidelines, whereas the "you" is the direct emotional attachment to another person, which is also expressed by the word "love". When buying a car, you might go for the black leather upholstery because your partner likes it so much. The sleekness, on the other hand, may satisfy one's own ego. The dimensions in emotional space seem less complex than those in relational space, more like physical dimensions. Just as we can determine a point in physical space by its coordinates, we could also determine the position in emotional space and thus obtain an emotional coordinate that has higher values for the ego dimension in strongly egocentric people and highest values for the we dimension in very socially minded people. Altruistic action could thus be described in the same scale as egoistic action. The time dimension here, as with the relational dimensions, is the same as in the physical time space; there is only one time in which we move physically, psychologically and as social beings, a time that we as human beings can, however, anticipate into the future and recapitulate into the past. We can trace time, and not only in physical space, as stored information in our cognitive cosmos, in which we can also cognitively anticipate the future.

4. The space of action in the structure of time

Although the current action in the market, be it buying or selling, is not only rationally conditioned, but is always accompanied by feelings and social relationships also play a role, as a rule only the rationally acting human being is seen in physical space and subjected to analysis. In fact, our actions take place in an action space composed of the three subspaces with a time dimension belonging to all spaces. The time axis only knows the past and the future. The present is a time window between the past and the future, superimposed on the last past and the next future. We conceive of our space of action from the past while we plan the future. In relation to a certain point in time, this space can be further defined by the dimensions and the coordinates resulting from the dimensional values, in physical space with for example P (2.00; 2.00; 3.00), in emotional space with for example E (0.5; 0.4; 0.4); in relational space R (0.5; 0.4; 0.6). In words, this could be described as follows: 50% ego-orientation, 40% you-orientation, 40% we-orientation as well as 50% competitive pressure, 40% cooperation and 60% feedback, all this in a room of 2x2x3 metres, perhaps a small sales room or with reference to an object, perhaps a digger. This kind of scaling will probably initially represent more of a virtual reality that springs from the describer but can certainly be empirically substantiated with the methods of sociology. Money, like the object offered for sale, is part of the space of action in which, in the simplest case, two people act with each other, people who are in competitive relationships, react partly in an ego-related way and negotiate the price for a digger. Money and the object of purchase thereby change position in the time line. Feedback can play a role if there are also permanent business relations in the process, in the way that, due to the contract, if the stock of goods is lower than what is to be sold in a week, the new order automatically provides for replenishment. This means that competitors are no longer taken into account and a regulated business relationship is created, at least as long as the contract runs. However, the empirical description in the action space is always preceded by an exploration, which is carried out by questioning or also finds out the possible cornerstones of a contractual relationship in a hermeneutic style. Hermeneutic interpretation is also able to grasp the interrelationships quite well for the time being, so that empiricism is rightly dispensed with for the time being. If we want to think and act in humanistic time horizons, then we have to reckon with more complex goal setting than with a more one-dimensional egoistic way of acting. Building and maintaining local, socially functioning regulatory circuits is certainly more demanding than competition geared only to private success. The actions of the participants in a space of action are always time-related and take place in a precisely definable place. The concert-goer experiences positive or also negative effects with the music at exactly one specific place at a very specific time that will never return. The following day, Beethoven's 9th Symphony will be played in the same way, if this is on the programme, but it will still be a new experience for the visitor, who will find himself in a different spatial constellation, even if the concert hall is the same and the neighbour is also the same; the day with all its experiences is different, and even the performance will not be exactly the same as the performance on the previous day. The market is also constantly changing; originally, people took the goods with them to exchange, but nowadays they just take their wallets to make purchases, pay with cash or a card, and sometimes even with their mobile phones via a payment app. This also has an impact on the identity of the individual, since one can still impress with the platinum card, less with the payment service used, more with the professional position, the car, the house, the position in the city parliament.

But how will the individual citizen with his or her identity defy the factors in the interaction on the market? Many things will become easier if, for example, we no longer have to activate the payment process separately in the future, since this is done automatically when we take out the goods, and we leave the shop with the purchased goods after shopping, without a wallet and without paying by card, even without checking at the door. We will then be controlled and directed via sensors and cameras just as we have been up to now, and the factors of growth will also continue to be effective in their interplay.

Losses of reality that can arise from a not fully developed identity and cause the process of radicalisation of people, that could also be attributed to a misguided identity. In this process, the factors of growth can become imbalanced and not growth, but destruction can be the result. The longing for the ideal identity, which is grasped as lost, also makes people run after the messages of salvation, no matter how well-founded the statements may be. We must always recognise and analyse the dimensions in their historical context.

Even new situations can be better managed if the experiences from history help to recognise and change contexts. Only if the next generation understands the interaction of economic factors from history and uses this to stabilise its own identity will it be possible to cope with the future. Money is the factor that can both stabilise and destabilise an identity. An identity that is not derived from the possession of money is therefore also able to survive a lack of money, at least in the short term. Last but not least, education and training in a good education system are important here. The knowledge extracted and activated from educational capital is becoming increasingly important and can in the future almost completely replace financial capital in many areas, i.e., cancel out the hitherto very dominant position of money.

D. THE GROWTH-PROMOTING INTERRELATIONSHIPS

XVII. The Interaction of the Factors

Assuming that 5 factors have to work together in the best possible way to produce optimal economic growth, we should first examine each of the factors to see how they perform under the possible variations from suboptimal to optimal when the remaining factors all act optimally on growth. In our case, labour (3), information (2), resources (4), and energy (5) should act in an optimal way in order to be able to bring the variation in the influence of money (1) to the examination. If the construction plan is exactly planned down to the smallest detail (2) and the employees are available in sufficient numbers with the necessary qualifications (3), there is no lack of resources (4) and the necessary energy (5) is also available, then it can only be due to the lack of capital (1). Thus, growth can only fail because of the presence or absence of money, money being the factor that promises security in the field of financial capital, a security that promises all-embracing help in the event of sudden problems. If we assume that there is only a lack of capital, it can be the capital needed for permits, fees and charges, as well as taxes. The use of capital to compensate for non-optimal non-capital factors must be considered separately but excluded here for the time being!

If, for example, there is a lack of money to purchase sufficient resources due to miscalculations, this will restrict, slow down or, in extreme cases, even prevent growth, no matter where we look at it. Money has the advantage over all other factors of being able to be used quite quickly and to quickly replace the lack of use of other factors. Of course, the other factors can also be exchanged for another factor in transit via the money factor. The individual factors of growth can be exchanged for each other, in a way comparable to the change from one type of energy to another. However, since each factor exchange is also associated with losses, this should only be used to a limited extent, i.e., not without taking the additional costs into account. Another aspect is that of expectation or information on future conditions and future availability.

In order to be able to look into the future, one often uses statistics that derive a trend from past data, a trend that, interpolated into the future, allows statements about future developments. In principle, such forecasts can be made for all factors; an echo (retroactive effect) is to be expected above all for factors that can be shifted and transformed quickly, such as money. For this reason, statements on developments to be expected in the future by economic leaders and money experts very quickly influence the liquidity and tradable goods available on the market.

1. Regulated growth, with and without money

If we now ask how growth is kept in balance in a regulated way, we approach the question of regulated growth from the opposite side as in one of the last chapters. Instead of regulated, we could also use the term steered and thus think of the steersman and the target to be steered towards. In the control loop, this is the target value. If these values are to be scaled, a scalable value must be specified, for example, one that has been agreed upon. In economics, the most common, though not necessarily the best, value is the gross domestic product (GDP), but one could also refer to productivity in hours worked, as well as unemployment or turnover. If we assume, for example, that the target is to increase GDP by 5% per year, the target value is equal to the value of the previous year plus 5% of that. If we then find a deviation of 2%, we can try to increase growth by 2% via the control path through the actuators. Changes in the control value could be, in relation to the factors, their increased use. If, as here with the factor money, the increased use of money is made possible by increasing the money supply in circulation, so growth, measured in GDP, can be stimulated. This need not succeed, but disruptive factors can work against it. It can be regarded as a disturbance if the money thrown onto the market is hoarded and thus does not arrive in circulation, i.e., does not reach the marketplace. If a certain GDP value is set as the target value, one can try to achieve this value; whether this succeeds is sometimes questionable, and it is also questionable whether this should succeed at all! If different data are collected with a relation to growth, these can also be used as indicators to obtain better target values. An indicator for growth can be the decline in unemployment, or also the increase in the amount of total goods sold.

In the case of safe money, it can be assumed that the money supply is regulated in the market without the need for intervention by the national central bank. Both the money supply and the value of money are regulated by demand in the case of pure credit-based money supply and private hedging via labour supply. If, nevertheless, an imbalance should arise, the central bank can still provide a short-term remedy with one-off limited money supply and limited-value money. In the case of Safe Money, we can start from a notional target value that is correlated with the corresponding population size multiplied by average activity in the market, the market quantity activity. Since borrowing should also rise with the increase, we can expect a corresponding correlative relationship and thus also an automatic regulation of the money supply. The scarcity of available labour and the scarcity of supply possibilities also provide the absolutely necessary limits, which are realised with almost all other currencies via the interest rate, according to the motto, the higher the scarcity of money, the higher the interest rate. If money is no longer scarce, the interest rate must run towards zero and thus loses the possibility of having a limiting effect. In a purely credit-based money system, as with NIM, the amount of credit taken out is controlled by the contractually stipulated rules; with NIM, it is controlled by the hedging stipulated therein through the deposited working hours.

Regardless of whether the regulation of growth is managed by a set of rules or is in the hands of experts, for example the managers of the national central bank, it is worthwhile to compare the interlocking feedbacks that can regulate themselves in the rule-based system. There is no harm in gaining insights into the basic mechanisms of control loops, here of course regarding theoretical modelling as an aid to reconstructing complex interrelationships in economic growth.

If growth in an economy is no longer seen solely in terms of the gross national product achieved but more in terms of the balance between growing units (for example factories) and decaying units (disposal and dismantling of production units that are no longer needed), it may also become possible to see the growth of an economy in a new light. The increase in growth in the circular system is always associated with an increase in decay processes, which is why a positive circular coefficient is to be aimed for, not only absolute growth is important. Money always plays a role in modern economies, both in the processes that build up and in the processes that break down. In principle, however, growth can of course also be achieved without money. Money is thus the only factor that can be dispensed with if all other factors are sufficiently applicable. Work in the family as well as neighbourly help are examples that contribute to growth even in modern economies without the use of money. If economic growth is defined only in terms of money flows, this does not reflect the whole picture; essential shares that are involved are missing

2. Decay – Destruction – Growth

When we think of growth, we must not forget decay, because without decay, sustainable management, a sustainable economy, is inconceivable. Long-lasting products can even disrupt or inhibit progress. Whereas in past centuries we tended to focus only on new products and left decay and destruction to chance, in future the targeted destruction of obsolete and worn-out consumer goods should already be factored into the planning of growth. Instead of letting cars rust away in the scrap yard, one could plan for the recyclability of individual parts after wear and tear in order to be able to carry out effective recycling for a sustainable economy. In the case of modular construction, perhaps individual modules can be remanufactured and still be used in the second-hand goods segment, for example. A systematic trade-in of old cars could also serve sustainability. Leasing offers for batteries in electric cars and used cars from the 1st leasing cycle could support this. The development of e-mobility could be accelerated by tax incentives for leasing contracts for batteries, rather than a premium for the cars. With the industrial revolution and the use of machines, in the future increased using robots, manual labour is disappearing and so is the repair shop. If we want to get away from the modern throwaway society, we must also plan for the refurbishment of technical equipment and old furniture. For the repair, the companies that produce all the goods we are familiar with must be included in the responsibility, either through their own repair workshops or through appropriate cooperation with specialised workshops approved by the manufacturers. Those who help in this way to prevent waste generation and to promote the longevity of products should be rewarded with generous cost credits in terms of taxation, since this also saves CO_2 in terms of climate protection. On the other hand, waste disposal can also be made more expensive, but above all the penalties for improperly deposited waste should be drastically increased. It would also make sense to demand that manufacturers take back their waste, so that no one gets the idea of disposing of rubbish in an uncontrolled rubbish dump. Also, many valuable items ends up in the rubbish instead of being reused. This is only one of the negative results, however, as production is also targeted at short lifetimes, thus stimulating new purchases. Moreover, the producer does not feel responsible for the waste. It is easier to burn the waste and then buy CO2 certificates. The decay and destruction of industrial products must be dragged out of the back room and onto the stage of the growth strategists. It is not a matter of demonising industrialisation and the ever-increasing transfer of human labour to machines, as might first be assumed; we just must finally see that decay and destruction are part of the cycle of becoming and passing away. Those who earn money from new products must also bear the costs of later disposal. Modern industrial society only plans for new development and new production, but not for the preservation and targeted destruction, as well as the recycling of worn-out goods and parts of them. From the monetary politician's point of view, money is thrown out the window here, and moreover, potential jobs are not only not created, but even destroyed. In a sustainable economy, durability and wear and tear must be included in the calculation. Produced goods must always be taken back by the trader when they can no longer be used. The costs of disposal must be included in the sales price, as this is the only way that even long-lasting products have a chance. Without legislation, machines and robots will continue to produce only new goods, with a short lifespan and no repair service.

We cannot simply tick off the finiteness of all existence, our lives, the products of our labour, after growth has ended and then consign them to the rubbish. Those who want growth should also aim to catch the inexorable decay in a circular system and thus advocate a sustainable growth strategy that buys longevity with delayed growth processes and uses all resources sustainably through intensive recycling. However, growth in such circular processes does not become cheaper, at least not at first glance. In the long term, there are indeed savings effects, resources are also conserved, and people can be better integrated into newly created jobs in machine-oriented production processes. Since dismantling, recycling and the use of strategies to promote longevity in all areas also require money and capital in a modern economic structure, strategies must be promoted that do just that. However, such a circular system can only work if all factors and conditions work together optimally.

No matter how high or how low the production costs are, the disposal costs must be included in the calculation as a mark-up before the goods are sold in the local market. For example, for the kitchen appliance that lasts twice as long as the competitors, only half of the disposal charge should be included for sustainability reasons. Waste disposal charges can be levied like taxes, if at the same time the non-property-related business taxes are reduced and ultimately abolished. The costs of disposal and compulsory recycling can be included in the sales price not only for machines, but also for clothing, buildings and food. Those who can prove the longevity of their products can thus save a lot of money and offer their durable products at a competitive price.

If one wants to capture the functional relationships mathematically, one will also have to take wear and tear into account in the equations used. The decay is there from the beginning, already in the growth phase. A growth curve does not normally take this into account directly. One possibility would be to plot the decay simultaneously in a decay curve, with an opposite scale. It would then also become clear that sustainable economic growth, which must reckon with the longevity of products, has to reckon with lower increases in terms of overall productivity in the new goods sector, but that the general public has to bear lower costs in return. The cost of waste disposal will fall considerably, and efficiency will be increased as a result. An efficient circular economy will also take care to be as energy-saving and resource-conserving as possible. However, companies that want to grow sustainably must also reckon with the fact that outdated products and product lines will be less and less in demand over time. Without innovations and new products, economic growth will stagnate, and the downturn will approach, become a reality, and the recession can thus no longer be averted. With innovations, companies can even occupy new niches and thus initiate the new upswing; price dumping, on the other hand, only has the effect of a flash in the pan, is not sustainable.

3. Disturbances in the concert of factors

When we talk about disruptions and want to take a closer look at them, we must consider the direct effects, but also the frictional losses in actions that are otherwise apparently free of disruptions. So much in advance. If we distinguish between usable and unusable energy in the energy sector, we should distinguish between usable and unusable capital in the financial sector, and we should not lose sight of the origin of capital. Capital can also have a destructive effect and, like the untamed energetic forces, must be tamed and directed in the right directions. Blood money and money from illegal sources are also not so easily used without problems. If we distinguish between usable and non-usable capital, analogous to energy, then in the context of a circular economy, attention must be paid to the flow of money. Capital flows should not be blocked and must be continuously controlled. The production of goods and money therefore does not belong in the hands of the public sector if it does not want to control itself. Disruptions in the control functions should not be underestimated. Only flawless control can detect and eliminate disturbances in the entire system in time.

The individual disruptions that can be uncovered by controls basically concern 6 areas in the case of finances.

One disturbance in finance is certainly 1. the use of capital and money for speculative purposes instead of using it for productive purposes.

Another disturbance is 2. the use of money for criminal purposes.

Moreover, money is always subject to 3. predatory attacks.

However, money and capital can equally 4. facilitate the abuse of power.

Money and thus financial capital can 5. also lose the value attributed to it, which then also influences on the money in circulation, whether through general devaluation or through a population growth. 6. a shortage of money can arise, a conditional shortage of money, which can then only be remedied ad hoc by an expansion of the money supply.

The circulation of money and capital is not kept in balance if the money in circulation is used for purposes other than those that stabilise the circulation. Only in the case of private credit-financed money can one assume that self-regulation is possible if the corresponding framework conditions do not stand in the way. In any case, more money is needed in circulation when the population is growing and less when, on the contrary, the number of people in the economic area under consideration is decreasing. In any case, the amount of money in circulation must also adapt to the activities of the people in this society, otherwise disruptions in growth and in the processing of decay processes are pre-programmed. It is not only a question of how much money is in the market, but above all of how much money actively determines the flow of money; hoarded money is not part of this. This is why the unequal distribution of money in a society strongly inhibits growth beyond a critical point. Hoarded money cannot actively cause new growth, and missing money cannot spur consumption. The resulting slowdown in growth also has a negative effect on the rich and the super-rich; a general basic income could certainly have positive effects on the growth market.

Taxes levied on substantial values can also have a disruptive effect. An example of this is inheritance tax; if, in the case of inheritance, the family home and the parents' car are subject to inheritance tax, this is in any case a substantial tax, as is wealth tax. Since the taxed value is not in the form of money, the tax levied can only be paid out of the inherited cash assets, one's own assets or the sale of the inherited property. The sale of parental real estate from the inheritance then eliminates the possibility of renting it out and thus making a profit. Moreover, errors in the valuation of tangible assets cannot occur if they do not have to be valued in the first place, but this is not the case with the substantial tax, because then it is unavoidable. Furthermore, valuations will also no longer be able to be made in line with the market if the tangible assets in question cannot be reproduced; after all, land, for example, cannot be multiplied in line with the market in the event of increased demand and thus a fair price between supply and demand cannot be expected. If, nevertheless, the price is determined by supply and demand, this can lead to wrong prices in the market; therefore, in such cases, licence agreements, leases and rental agreements for a limited period of time are the right means to avoid undesirable developments. If goods that cannot be multiplied at will are valued and offered on the market in the same way as those goods whose scarcity can be easily eliminated, this leads to disruptions that can lead the entire economic area into a recession. To avoid such disturbances, non-reproducible goods such as air, water and land should be declared common property. Necessary expropriations can certainly be initiated in a socially acceptable way, for example by converting taxes into rents, thus hardly changing the existing conditions on the outside. However, corresponding disruptions also arise in the case of exorbitant price increases for spiritual, non-depreciable values such as those of a novel or a painting. In the case of paintings, this problem regularly arises when the painter has died and thus no more paintings by this artist can be expected. Sometimes, only the destruction of the painting can stop the exponential price pressure, or the declaration of the painting as national cultural heritage with immediate expropriation in favour of museums, where these paintings are then accessible to the citizen. Written intellectual property, a novel for example, can be copied and reprinted as often as desired, as long as a complete copy is still available, and copyrights are not violated. In the case of a book, a distinction must be made between the reproducible book print and the non-material value resulting from the unique content. This is also to be applied to companies that have obtained the rights to patents and also non-patented plans and structures through their employees. If such a company is sold, all rights and patents are usually sold along with it. This usually happens over the heads of the authors. However, the law should protect the rights of these authors, which is only possible if substantial and non-material values are treated separately. In the case of non-material values, the clarification of authorship is important; in the case of substantial values, the costs in the event of a loss for the work to be protected regarding restoration. Intangible values can only be determined with regard to authorship, substantial values regarding the original work effort and the use value. In the case of intellectual property, however, the agreed non-use or the prevention of use could also lead to interference, as could unhindered use in disregard of copyright, not to mention the effects of product piracy and unhindered copying without naming the true author of the thoughts. If the author does not receive the necessary financial support to develop his or her ideas further, this can have serious consequences for the community, as important ideas are sometimes lost or never developed. When companies are sold, all the intellectual property that has accumulated there should sometimes fall to the community where that company has its headquarters and production facilities. The justification for this is that this municipality provides and pays for the necessary infrastructure and educational facilities, if this justifies a claim!

A particular problem is the new form of information exchange on the internet, on noticeboards and generally the unregulated exchange of ideas within social media. If filters are used to protect intellectual property, filtering out as much as possible to avoid legal problems, this may well be interpreted as censorship by those who just want to discuss something with others and are stuck in the filter for safety's sake. In a conversation among friends, it is very well not possible to check every term, every sentence for copyright, which is why protected spaces must be possible in which things may also be said in a non-filtered way without being directly sorted out by a filter. However, this will only be possible if such chat rooms have blocking filters to the outside. Misdirected information can quickly become the worst troublemakers, which is why special attention is needed here, a problem that is also particularly relevant for the Internet of Things and in the AI sector will still cause a lot of headaches.

4. Profit tax, a tax that does not prevent growth

Taxes that are applied to substantial values can disrupt and even stop economic growth because they do not target the factors of growth. If, for example, assets are taxed, this can lead to assets being sold in order to be able to pay the taxes. As a result, the remaining assets are associated with lower revenues and, if necessary, this can drive a business, a company, into insolvency. This then disturbs a functioning equilibrium. It is therefore better to dispense with substantial taxation altogether and to tax only profits earned, i.e., functionally. A basic problem of substantial taxation is the valuation with constantly changing value allocations. Even at the same point on the time scale, different valuers will come to different valuations. This is different with profits, because once a profit has been made, it does not change in terms of amount unless the calculation of profit is changed, but this usually only changes future profits. The profit is always what remains of the proceeds at a certain point in time after deducting the costs, i.e. the value attributed to an object or service as profit at a certain point in time. In this context, profit does not only include the profit of the trader, the merchant or the entrepreneur who deducts his production costs from the turnover in order to calculate his profit, but also the profit of the employee who deducts his living costs from his income in order to calculate his very individual profit. For many citizens, there will be no profit left, but then they should consequently not have to pay taxes. Those who are only able to finance their modest livelihood with their income should in principle not have to pay any tax, as they contribute enough to the profits of companies and corporations through their consumption, which make profits from sales that far exceed what is absolutely necessary to live on and which is taxable according to historical jurisprudence.

Profits, no matter from what business and because of what work they have arisen, should always be taxed at the place of their origin. In this sense, the profit from goods should always be taxed where the goods are sold, the profit from an employment relationship where the workplace is located, the profit of a provider of easements on the internet where the easements are used, and the profit from a lottery where the lottery is held. If money is created not by private credit commitments secured by working time accounts and not by money distributed by the state, but by private money creation without adequate security, from real assets or from algorithms in a computer, this is money created without labour, which should be fully subject to profit tax. Credit based on labour, on the other hand, is not profit, since the labour register is not settled according to wages actually paid, but according to mutual labour before profit. Similarly, the overdraft and the savings credit are not profit-based credits, since only mutual services are charged here.

Whether the winnings from a lottery are to be compared with the winnings from a business activity and an activity from an employment relationship, this can at best be touched upon here, but is nevertheless to be addressed here in the essential points. If the lottery ticket is drawn in Cologne, for example, then Cologne is the venue where the tax is also due. Since in a lottery no counter-value is offered for the money paid in, the prize is after all no counter-value, the prize paid out is not a normal prize from a barter transaction or an easement like all other prizes, but a payout from a pot of collected money. For the lucky winner it is nevertheless a profit, but not an exchange profit, but a random profit, comparable to the random winnings from a found object. In principle, no costs are incurred in the case of chance winnings, so that no costs can be offset. This justifies the measure of only having to pay half of the profit tax otherwise due, if one wants to take this into account. But who is to pay this tax on random profits? Accidental winnings must be declared, as otherwise it can be assumed that it is not an accidental win, with the consequence of a 50% tax assessment on the full proceeds. The person who declares or must declare the winnings has to pay the tax. In the case of lotteries, the organiser of the lottery must declare these winnings and thus also pay the winnings tax due on them. Whoever finds a lost object or a valuable stone, for example, must locate the possible owner and, after a search deemed sufficient, may keep the found object, but must pay the tax on these chance winnings, deducting the costs of establishing the value and searching for the owner. If a lottery declares 50,000 euros as a prize, it must pay 12,500 euros in tax on this, if it is classified as a chance prize; this prize must be paid out to the lottery winner as a net prize of 50,000 euros, and the lottery operator has expenses of 1,500 euros plus the costs of administration and advertising with an estimated 1,500 euros, i.e. a total of 15,500, tax included. However, costs incurred, for example administrative costs, can only be deducted for tax purposes if the winnings were not declared as random winnings. For the fact that a profit tax is paid, no trade tax and no turnover tax should be levied. The requirement of a profit tax should also apply to prize games that are only intended as advertising. The winnings declared in the advertisement must also be declared to the tax office and the corresponding tax paid on them.

As a tax that virtually combines income tax, trade tax, corporate income tax and turnover tax into one tax, the profit tax is a considerable simplification in tax law, even though the deductions entitled to be deducted can be just as complex. Simplifications due to the simpler calculation with the basic salary as a kind of negative tax should be noted, whereby the child benefit should be eliminated, since it is more functional and sensible to provide children with a lower basic salary (approx. 50%), but without child benefit and otherwise to treat them fiscally like adults. A basic income for children should also be based on a flat rate for living expenses, at 50% of the flat rate applied to adults. If a child who is entitled to receive a basic income does not grow up in Germany, the maintenance costs are to be offset in the country in which the child actually lives; a flat rate is only to be applied for persons living in Germany.

The profit tax is a functional tax which, figuratively speaking, demands only a portion of the harvested fruit, but not a portion from the fruit-bearing tree, as revenue for the state. Income tax and sales tax are as primarily substantive taxes, figuratively demanding the fruit-bearing branch with fruit, so that less revenue (fruit) can be expected in the coming year. A moderate profit tax promotes growth in contrast to most other types of tax and is also fairer, as can be seen when comparing it with child benefit. Overall, the profit tax is the fairest and, in combination with a basic salary, the only tax that does justice to human dignity in all facets. In contrast to the progressive tax with top tax rates of 75%, a profit tax of 50% leaves enough, even at 60%, not to scare away even the highest earner's enjoyment of earning money and not to give him a reason to leave his home country. In order to strengthen and promote the education system, our millionaires and billionaires should probably also be prepared to voluntarily grant the state a surcharge, to be levied at varying intervals as a one-off tax related to the subject matter.

A central problem with the introduction of a general profit tax is becoming apparent in foreign trade, and the actions of the EU authorities with regard to a digital tax for internet corporations are certainly leading us in the right direction. When switching to a profit tax, however, it is important to bear in mind that profit is only what remains after deducting costs from revenues. The profit always arises where the provider can book money as revenue for his goods, his service, i.e., with the user who pays for it, and not at the place of production or even the company headquarters. The goods are paid for in the department stores', at the house bank or in the restaurant, and that is also where the profit arises, which is taxable at the local tax office. At the production site and in the administration, only the profit of the employees who work there arises. Only these profits can be taxed at the company location. Letterbox companies no longer stand a chance. It is not the letterhead that should be decisive, but the place where something actually happens, where money is exchanged for performance. In addition to the profits of those who work there, the profits of the suppliers who deliver the necessary resources and provide the required energy also arise at the production site. In return, labour itself and production itself should remain untaxed. For goods that have already been burdened by corporate taxes abroad, these expenses can be recognised as costs that are deducted from the proceeds when determining profits; moreover, it should also be possible to reach international agreements on this so that world trade is not disrupted by corresponding changes in tax law. The introduction of a general profit tax should also make land tax and land acquisition tax overdue. Lease income and the normal profit tax on sold real estate should certainly make up for the loss of revenue from trade tax for the municipalities. If corporate income tax and trade tax are abolished, the profit tax shares to which the municipality is entitled should be precisely circumscribed for the municipalities as a substitute. For the merchant, it is important that this means that only goods that have been sold are taxed and not, as has been the case up to now, also partly the goods waiting to be sold in the warehouse. Only in this way can the various factors at work in growth interact freely without the disruptive braking effect of substantial taxes.

5. Growth at the different levels

Sometimes there are worlds in between, and something different is meant when growth is mentioned, be it in nature, in the laboratory, in the market on the global, communal or private stage.

First, growth can be clearly defined in terms of individuals. As an individual or generalised entity, we know the concrete plant in the flowerpot in front of us, our pet dog, our cat, the bakery around the corner, the grocery shop or even the factory in the parallel street. If we first take a plant as an example, we can observe how a seedling stretches out from the seed with its cotyledons into the light above the earth. Three important factors are involved in this process, firstly water, because without water seeds would not be able to swell and activate the nutrients in the prepared cotyledons. The second factor, light, makes the plant grow towards the sunlight and activates photosynthesis; the third factor, resources, which here are the nutrients available in the cotyledon, and only when these are used up, in addition to water, the nutrient salts from the soil, the energy of the sunlight and the CO_2 from the air. If we now take the bakery around the corner for comparison, we have the flour and the yeast as resources, but also the various additives and for a cake also fruit for the topping. Without the energy that powers the ovens, neither bread nor cake could be baked. Money is also needed to buy the ovens and to equip the shop, and of course the workers in the bakery and in the salesroom must be paid. Without the skills acquired by the employees and the master craftsman in an apprenticeship, the bakery that has just opened would not be able to establish itself and grow. What is needed to even get started can be compared to the nutrients in a seedling. Of course, expenses are also necessary for the ongoing operation, without which the business cannot be sustained. If the price-performance ratio is right, it will soon be the word gets around that you can buy fresh bread and delicious cakes there. If more and new customers come to the shop over time, this can be understood as growth and can be seen in the increasing turnover. With growth, the need for resources also becomes greater, expenses increase, and the question soon arises whether income is increasing at the same pace as expenses. The first problem arises with the choice of indicator for growth. Do we take the increase in profit as an indicator, or absolute turnover, or productivity, that should be clarified in advance? At the lower level, that of the individual business, both the measure of profit and the measure of productivity are of interest. Profit can be expressed in absolute terms in euros or NIM or dollars, or in a relative measure such as profit per capital employed or profit per hour of labour employed. If the labour hour is calculated with its monetary input as capital input, one can better compare financial capital and human capital, which in my view is preferable to other types of calculation. On the other hand, machinery with its time input could also be converted to labour hours, and thus the comparison would be possible via labour input. It would probably be easier to use capital as a reference value, but not without taking labour into account.

If we now switch to another level, the municipal level, which I would like to show using the example of a city, other perspectives also arise. The city can grow simply because the population is growing. A city that has 1,000 more people within its "walls" after one year also needs more food, more clothes, more living space. To accomplish this, it also needs more money in circulation in this city. Accordingly, total productivity should increase, even if productivity per capita remains the same. Here, too, the capital employed per hour worked can be used as an indicator. It should also be easier to calculate the profit per capital employed if relative comparisons are required, or simply the profits if absolute comparisons are needed. Of course, absolute turnover can also be used for comparison. If we compare economic growth in larger regions, it is easy to calculate capital input per hour worked, but we are more likely to find a figure based on turnover, the so-called gross domestic product (GDP). A questionable aspect of GDP is the fact that not all labour input is taken into account.

If statistical values are used at the global level, it must be asked whether precisely these statistical growth increases are to be seen in connection with, for example, the actually serious global climate problems. The more CO_2 is released into the atmosphere by cars, industrial production and domestic exhaust fumes, the more our affluent society is exposed to the danger that our global gas equilibrium will collapse. Now we can consider how to reduce CO_2 emissions by curbing growth in all areas. Strangely enough, no effort is made at the political level to immediately capture the emitted CO_2 gases at the point of origin, if possible, and thus rid the air of this gas. When fossil fuels are burned, whether for electricity generation or for heat, CO_2 emissions can relatively easily be used to speed up plant growth, since CO_2 is generally a limiting factor for plant growth; in this respect, the destruction of large areas of forest is a particular problem for the global gas balance. At industrial sites, CO_2 from the air can also be used to produce new purely synthetic hydrocarbons, which subsequently do not produce any additional nitrogen oxides when burnt, as the synthetic hydrocarbons do not contain any compounds with nitrogen. In the competition with fossil fuels, however, the price that can be achieved by the customer in relation to the costs of production will not be unimportant. If we want to move towards electric cars, we will have to promote synthetic fuels to a limited extent in the meantime, until the necessary infrastructure for electromobility also enables problem-free driving with electric cars everywhere. Growth in future economic systems can certainly contribute to getting a grip on our climate problems through the increased use of green electricity and the abandonment of technologies that emit CO_2. to get. If we succeed in balancing CO_2 consumption and CO_2 emissions in a globally understood cycle on our planet, we will not only solve the climate problem, but we will also be able to promote plant growth in greenhouses and provide the necessary synthetic fuel that will secure the electromobility of the future. Electromobility that is geared towards the use of environmental energies can promote growth everywhere on this planet in the future and thus trigger the Green Revolution. It is precisely such revolutions that will be able to get off to a better start and initiate green growth with sufficient capital and sufficient sources of information, whereas without sufficient capital they will sometimes not get off to a good start at all.

In a circular economy with planned reprocessing of degradation products from recycling, capital will also be needed to finance the regulated degradation and processing of degradation products for new growth. In the process, new jobs can be created along the way, providing work for those who have lost their jobs in the rationalisation of the production process.

An essential aspect that must not be missing in sustainable management is not only sustainable commodity management but also sustainable management of jobs and sustainable financial management.

6. Models of economic management

Interrelationships are best understood in terms of models. It is not exactly new to see the economy, the economic process, as a system in equilibrium or striving towards equilibrium, as a model based on the well-known equilibria in physics and chemistry. In economics, however, we are not dealing with static or dynamic equilibria, but with steady-state equilibria, in some respects comparable to the steady-state equilibria in biology.

Starting from the factors that we can understand as inflows in the system of the steady state, we still must represent the outflow with the reaction products, the generated products. Let us first take a bowl with an outflow in the middle and 5 different inflows placed around it, which flow onto the bowl from above. If the inflows are placed at the same distance from the drain and each brings the same amount of liquid into the bowl, this corresponds to a model in which the factors act in the same way and accordingly produce the products that flow out in the centre of the model. If the rim of the dish is 50 cm high, it can hold twice as much of the factorially bundled output substances or effects (reactants) in the reaction space of the dish than if the rim were only 25 cm high. If the input is higher than the output, the excess input will run off unused over the edge of the shell; this can be money, this can be energy, but also information. If the bowl is now placed on an articulated sphere with an integrated drain, it will sit horizontally on the drain when the inflow of all factor channels is equal. As soon as one of the factors with lower or higher inflow unbalances the shell, it will tilt in the direction of the factor that disturbs the equilibrium position, for example, with additional inflow downwards, with lower inflow upwards. The bowl always tilts to the side with the greater inflow. The surplus inflow will then flow off over the edge, but also parts of the factors that are not present in abundance, which can no longer be used if the reaction partner is missing. The surplus can flow off until equilibrium is reached again, whereby the portion that is altogether superfluous is determined by the one factor of which there is too little, through it the total production process is pulled down. This is because the factor that is not sufficiently present acts as the limiting factor. For example, if energy is lacking, the entire production will have to be oriented towards the available energy. Accordingly, aluminium production, with its high energy demand, will choose the location with seek energy reserves that are easy and cheap to obtain. Similarly, one can simulate a shortage of labour. In the model with a bowl that can be tilted in different directions, this can be shown very clearly. If one now works with movable inflow pipes, one can also demonstrate the effect of the distance from the centre. If I now shift the money inflow from the centre to the periphery, this shift alone can lead to a tilt in this direction and thereby cause an unwanted outflow over the edge of the shell, i.e., ensure that money and energy flow away unused. As a model, this shell can now only be related to a limited area. For larger areas of influence, one will have to work with several shells in the model. If one works with different levels, several shells must be positioned on top of each other. If we take water for the factorial flows in the model, it is necessary to work with an inverted pyramid. The top level is the largest with the primary productions and below that smaller and smaller levels down to the state government level as the smallest of all. Products move from one level to the next through the central production channels. With different levels, one should use oval trays offset from each other, each to be supplied individually with the different factorial supplies. If the supply, in this case money, hits the plate close to the centre, I need more for the same effect than if it occurs in the periphery.

The economic shell model can also be used to demonstrate why innovations are more likely to emerge from imbalances than from equilibria. In the case of imbalances, movements are indicated with which the balance can be restored. It can also be shown that if the imbalances are too great, the whole thing tips over and only minimal production rates can be achieved, or even none at all.

If the money tap is turned off, the equilibrium is considerably disturbed. The bowl tilts in the direction with the highest counterweight. There, everything that has flowed into the shell, the illustrative reaction space, will spill over and thus not flow out properly, energy and resources will disappear unused just as information can no longer be used sensibly.

Money can sometimes be replaced by work that is not remunerated, or the balance can be readjusted to a lower level with less energy and less use of resources.

Just like the money tap, one can also turn off the resource tap in the model and see what the consequences can be.

The shell model can be used to illustrate some things simply and clearly, but by no means everything. Problems of avoiding competition to save money and capital, as well as the synergy effects of cooperation, are primarily not equilibrium problems, but relational problems. The representation in the relational space does not automatically take into account the subjective effects that are to be classified as behavioural economic variables in the overall construct. However, behavioural economic findings should find their place in the relational space. Just one example: cooperation can only succeed if the chemistry in the personal relationships is right. Let's conclude with an example that seems very abstract at first glance, but nevertheless has a real connection. If, for example, money is not available at a certain point in history, but the other factors are not lacking, the equilibrium will be disturbed in any case if differentiated monetary economies were the norm beforehand. However, with some effort, the other factors can then be shifted so that a new equilibrium can be established. Relationships in relational structures can prevent or promote precisely this.

The weight assigned to the individual factors is not dependent on laws as in the natural sciences. Here, social conventions interact internally, and system-theoretical limitations interact externally with those of the natural sciences.

The semantic narrative processing, as Yanis Varoufakis masterfully manages in the book "Time for Change", is also a didactic modelling of how the economy functions and has developed, but not in a pictorial, iconic way, but in a linguistically explanatory, narrative way.

A distinction must also be made between didactic and experimental models. Wörgl, for example, is a real experimental model. There is also the theoretical simulation model, a variant of the experimental models. In addition, there are the various approaches to derive laws with causal effects from correlative relationships. Such conclusions should be treated with particular caution, since all correlations in the field of economics depend on social agreements and are not natural. Moreover, one should only work with systems of equations if the axioms have first been clarified in their conditionality. Simulation models with the help of computers use probabilities and assume certain initial decisions as an axiomatic basis; in this way, developments can be predicted by recording them as probable from different decision-making situations; systems of equations will then also be used. If, on the other hand, reality is modelled on the basis of historical data sets, the axioms, as set by people in historical times, also play a role. They are just as variable and not set by nature as the variables in the simulation. Correlations derived from them do not represent irrefutable laws as in the natural sciences. Only by means of behavioural economics could one derive certain laws that are understandable from natural human behaviour. When Piketty attempts to derive general laws of capitalism from his historical correlations, this seems to me to be somewhat presumptuous, since other social arrangements than those historically handed down could also lead to other correlations. Viewed in a historical model, one can observe legal developments that are hypothesised, but one should not generalise them. Let us now go back a few steps in the modelling process in order to be able to model smaller areas. Equations are a good way to do this, even if they also describe relationships that can only be observed as equations in a more compact way.

For example, one could ask whether Cobb–Douglas productivity is suitable for describing productivity development in the EU. According to Cobb–Douglas, GDP divided by the weighted product of capital and income should be able to capture this demanded productivity by means of an equation. The weighting for capital with 0.35 and for income with 0.65 is not to be evaluated here; for the sake of simplicity, let us assume them to be 1 each, which, although simplifying, no longer corresponds to the proposed weighting, nevertheless clearly shows the present intentions. Let's take a rough look at the formula: TFP = Y/(K★L), which means that for a given Y(GDP), productivity (TFP) decreases when K★L increases and increases when K★L decreases. Translated, this means that productivity decreases with increased use of capital and labour, if GDP does not change as a result; clearly, if I must use more capital to get the same result (GDP), then productivity is lower. If, on the other hand, I use less capital and less labour, this means that productivity has increased while GDP remains the same.

In reality, however, it may also happen that productivity increases although all other variables remain the same, we get an inequality. This can be caused by innovations that are not included in the monetary calculation. If we add the information term to the inequality, then it becomes an equation again, i.e. TFP = Y★(1[I★K★L]), where probability values are to be used for I. A probability of 1 would then mean that the productivity of a company has increased. A probability of 1 would then mean that the information has 100% no influence on prod to introduce information as I simply by another multiplier below the fraction line is obvious in the derivation from the function at hand but cannot be fully satisfactory. Therefore, another variant is to be presented here, which promises a better coverage of reality. As an equation one could formulate

TPF = Y/(I★[n★K + m★L]), where "I" stands for the information coefficient, n and m for the respective weightings. TPF in this context would be the money-dependent component of productivity or also the productivity growth expressed in money. The formulation of possible correlations by mathematical means is, in a certain sense, always also a kind of modelling. The use of such equations in simulation experiments is an excellent way to explore and better understand the use of money. For the student in the middle school and also already in the lower school, the use of cash in a real model is better understandable than the simulation on the computer. School companies are already being used in various schools; the shielded school market with its own money, which is only valid there, is more costly, but promises better insights and learning effects.

From a didactic point of view, the shell model should be optimally applicable for upper grades and studies, the school market optimally for lower and middle grades. Here, rational, emotional and relational moments can be represented and conveyed quite well in the temporal amalgamation.

The money-dependent innovative power of productivity can be achieved with the model market and the simulation with the additional use of the relational components. Equations such as those used to calculate productivity can now be used to determine productivity increases precisely, but also to build an IT-based model of a city programmed for growth with such equations, to work out forecasts for the future and also to use them to prepare didactic models in the school sector. Dealing with money can certainly be practised best in a didactically prepared market with market cash.

XVIII. The digital future?

"It is true, then, that the modern world is replacing dark satanic mills with service business that invest in systems, information, and ideas?"
                                            (Jonathan Haskel and Stian Westlake, p. 30; 2018)

The digital future is not the digitised past, no, there we find less and less financial capital and more and more intellectual capital. It is ideas, systems and information that will determine the future growth trend! Digital information plays a significant role in several respects: it can be transferred more quickly, can be incorporated into any device and is thus also the basis for the further spread of artificial intelligence, which will soon conquer our everyday lives.

Let's follow J. Rifkin's historical classification and now recognise our economic system as such in an intermediate stage between the 3rd Industrial Revolution and the Industry 4 stage; after that, the 4th Industrial Revolution could come. By this I would like to understand the development towards a society that, using ecology as an example and also biology in general, develops a working world and a mode of production that takes up all the positive inventions of humanity and nature in order to integrate them into a self-controlling production process that promotes regulated circulation systems for the benefit of humanity and the environment and links this to the digital standards of Industry 4, best described by the term Economy 5.0. This would involve, in addition to the general use of environmental energies that are available everywhere (also known as regenerative energies under discussion) and the production of artificial fuels also include the use of artificial organelles such as chloroplast substitutes and mitochondrial substitutes. Thus, even in the smallest units, hydrocarbons and hydrogen can be produced on the one hand through the binding of CO_2 and the splitting of water, and on the other hand, energy can be produced on a small scale through the binding of O_2 on a molecular basis, without the predominant part of the energy being dissipated in space, as in the combustion we are familiar with. By using organelles and their substitutes, one can also assume that the general increase in entropy is reduced, especially in the immediate environment. It is obvious that research funds will play a decisive role here. In Rifkin's linguistic style, it is correct to speak of a revolution, although it would be more accurate to speak of an economic evolution. If electricity is produced in coal-fired power plants, this could be seen as counterproductive with the current power plants, since the climate-damaging CO_2 emissions are only shifted from the street to the factory site of the power plant. However, if the CO_2 emissions were not released uncontrollably into the air around us, this could certainly lead to a reduction in CO_2 emissions just as much as the use of environmental energies to generate electricity. What would be necessary is to consider all CO_2 produced by burning carbon as a raw material that is further processed or stored in the earth's soil by converting it into a mineral. The simplest use would be in greenhouses, using cyanobacteria in tanks, for example, to help produce oxygen and biological carbon compounds that could be further processed either into livestock feed (if toxins are eliminated) or into fuels.

For the aforementioned purposes, these should be oxyphotobacteria in the broader sense, and the nitrogen-fixing representatives should also be of interest. Of particular interest, of course, are the CO_2-binding variants without toxins. If feed or food supplements are to be produced from them in further processing, care must be taken, as already indicated, that no toxin-producing species are used.

In the long term, systematic afforestation will also have to be considered. The greening of urban areas to directly fix CO_2 in residential areas with interspersed greenhouses can also help to reduce the emission of excess CO_2. It makes sense to enrich the air in the greenhouses only until the level of CO_2 in the air is high enough to no longer be the limiting factor in growth. Parks in cities are another way of reducing CO_2 emissions into the atmosphere without already using newer processes such as binding in molecules that could be used as N-free fuels in conventional petrol engines.

If one takes the cycles in nature as a model, one could understand the use of money in such a way that one initiates and accompanies growth processes with it, in order to subsequently draw the profit from the fruits, which then also brings back the money invested. In the model, money would have a function comparable to water in ecosystems; it is needed for growth, especially for transport, and is also partly converted into products, but is not lost in the cycle between growth and decay if strict sustainability is observed.

Digitalisation may help to keep the individual processes better under control. The end of cash and the triumph of cards may also be seen as a way to better control the financial cycle and economic cycles in general. The better control is also accompanied by a simplification in the processes, since only virtual money stocks are shifted back and forth. The end of cash and the practical consequences are presented very clearly in an article in the Handelsblatt of 23 December 2018: "It's all happening very quickly. The customer of the supermarket on 7th Street in Seattle grabs a salad, a few muesli bars and sandwiches, lets everything disappear into his bag, walks out through the exit and disappears into the hectic after-work bustle. No alarm, no security stops him." What is not yet addressed here is payment by mobile phone and then receiving the receipt on the mobile phone display. Perhaps we can then even look at how climate-friendly our purchase was and how this affects the profit tax statement and how much of our budget we have spent if we immediately transfer the remaining money from the purchase back to the NIM account, as this way we always have an overview of our money.

1. Full employment as a goal!

Optimal management of investments by means of digital tools, including intangible capital stocks, should also be part of efforts to achieve full employment. Furthermore, so-called think tanks are important, which can more quickly manage and promote the necessary exchange of ideas through digital progress.

Among the most important state affairs that belong to the tasks of the public sector are, apart from waste disposal, the expansion and maintenance of the infrastructure, as well as the maintenance and further expansion of a top education system, the stabilisation of the monetary system and full employment. The view that the state must incur debt to finance job creation measures when the economy is limping is plausible at first, but in the long run it turns out not to be as positive as first thought. It is true that public-sector contracts can preserve jobs and sometimes even create new ones. However, even in such a case, credit financing by the state is nothing more than a shift of capital in favour of the rich and the haves. Since the loans, including the interest, ultimately must be paid by the taxpayer, the interest payment has the effect of a tax cut for those who can lend money to the state, since the interest hardly reaches the lower and middle incomes. On the other hand, as the proponents argue, more citizens are in work. What kind of work is at stake is not further inquired into, since it could be that citizens' money is also being used to promote unproductive work? Perhaps the citizens themselves could develop better alternatives!

So, here's the question: Is it possible for public authorities to intervene in the labour market with the aim of achieving full employment without taking out a loan? I think so, although credit financing is easier for the time being and can also be implemented immediately.

The following measures by the public authorities could help in the long run and should become the basis of a pilot project with accompanying research:

1. lowering the business tax by 50%, then abolishing it later,
2. offer land for lease as company premises
3. grant building permits only for leasehold land
4. abolish turnover tax completely
5. introduce profit taxes at 25–50
6. lower income tax, first at 50%, then to 0
7. put 50% of lease income from the public sector into the purchase of land
8. offset work for the community against current and future tax liabilities
9. introduce a tax-exempt basic salary to all citizens (with restricted immigration)
10. tax offsetting of basic salary and at the same time the abolition of exemption limits
11. possibilities of reducing basic salary benefits in accordance with a court order in the event of delinquency
12. discourse-driven measures to activate innovation and increase the acceptance of new types of employment. Workplaces adapted to the new digital goals
13. agreements on controlled working life with a labour register, so that pensions in old age still allow for dignified living spaces for the elderly in the future
14. debt relief for the public sector within the framework of a state insolvency procedure

Reduction by 50% should mean that all those who currently pay 30% will then only pay 15%, and for all those who currently pay 48%, the payment obligations will be reduced to 24%. For further explanation, leasehold land is land that is provided by the municipality with a heritable lease, just like the leasehold land that is provided in many places by church communities or also by housing cooperatives.

The basic salary should in principle be paid unconditionally, yet certain services must be rendered to the community in order to otherwise have this basic salary either paid or offset unconditionally. The community should insist that basic rights and duties are exercised. Also, every recipient of a basic salary should demonstrably not have committed a crime in the previous 2 years, i.e., be a blameless citizen. In addition, every citizen should be able to refuse to accept the basic salary.

Those who do not accept the basic salary cannot have it offset but are thus not fundamentally exempt from the duties of a citizen, which is why it is better to understand it as a solidary basic salary. In the case of guest workers who do not have citizen status and therefore do not receive a basic salary, social benefits are to be paid on application if they are in need, as before, although this is only to be approved for a period of 3 years according to the Social Code, the social benefits should in any case only amount to a total of up to 90 % of the basic salary, moreover they are also only to be paid as a repayable loan. This could result in a desired increase in the number of applications for naturalisation.

Extreme excesses of old-age poverty can certainly be eliminated by the age-independent payment of the basic salary from the age of 18 onwards but should be additionally secured by a pension that is commensurate with the total amount of work to be expected in a lifetime. For this, however, full employment in the actively working lifetime is important.

A question currently widely discussed in the media is also whether digitalisation will cause jobs to disappear and unemployment to rise as a result, or whether the robotisation associated with digitalisation will not also create new jobs. If this is only a matter of restructuring, then care must be taken that it is not carried out at the expense of the working population; in any case, great efforts will be needed to adequately expand the education system. A good education and good training in general are becoming increasingly important in the labour market. As a flanking measure, a reduction in weekly working hours should also be considered, the working hours that are sufficient for full employment. It should also be considered that the money accumulated during the active period is sufficient for a sufficient pension, whether as a supplement to a basic income that continues to be paid as a basic pension or as a retirement pension on its own. A uniform pension system for all citizens, into which the self-employed and civil servants also pay, could help to collect the necessary funds. Moreover, with a basic salary also for pensioners, the actual contributions could be taken as a basis, irrespective of the years of contribution. How high the pensions would then be would have to be calculated separately on the basis of the available figures. The basic prerequisite for a humane solution, however, is the will of a community to find a satisfactory solution. result.

2. Investment today and tomorrow

It is likely to make a difference whether investments are kept going with safe money, for example NIM, or with euros or with dollars, whether it is research money or also the use of capital, for example, for the digitalisation of work processes. Since less fluctuation is to be expected in a secure currency system, this means that planning can expect less disruption and is therefore more securely carried out. In an uncertain environment, on the other hand, less is invested and thus less growth is generated. In this respect, we must not only ask ourselves whether the new currency can provide stability and security, but also whether, in addition to the NIM, the euro or the dollar as a second currency would disrupt the security and stability of the NIM, a security that every growth-promoting investment needs.

In any case, a clear advantage of the euro over the originally different national currencies is the single currency area, in which exchange rate losses, as with the original national currencies, are eliminated. At present, however, the euro cannot clearly exploit this advantage because the social systems and the tax systems in the various national economies in the euro area are in no way at the same level. The necessity of aligning social systems and tax systems in a currency area was not overlooked during the construction, but it was obviously assumed that the desired alignment would be promoted by a common currency. In 2017, a decision was to be made to either abolish the euro altogether or at least to allow the euro as an official means of payment in all EU countries. Now, as I put these lines on paper, in 2020, this decision has not yet been taken. What is still missing after that are agreements to promote the necessary approximations. Of course, one could also question the necessity of alignment. If one could agree in the EU to allow all state currencies in the EU area, if they still exist, and possibly also one or two private currencies as official currencies in the EU, then one could approach the question of unification in the fiscal and social area in a much more relaxed way.

A central problem also remains if other currencies are officially permitted in addition to the euro. Japan has already led the way by allowing the cryptocurrency Bitcoin as a means of payment. The national currency with the yen is still weakening in Japan and the economy has not yet returned to the old growth. In the euro area, the euro has other problems to deal with besides the excessive government debt burden. The gap between North and South in debt is one of the problems. A stronger integration of the states in the Eurozone could provide a remedy, the communisation of state debts being the prerequisite for this. If this is seen as a first step towards a general debt relief of the euro states, this could succeed. However, sceptical observers suspect that this would only lead to a shift of debt from the South to the North. What is not addressed in all the discussions on this: It will be necessary to contractually fix the non-acceptance of further debts. However, as with private insolvencies, this will also require agreements between creditors and debtors that lead to a reduction in debt and interest payments through the cancellation of debts and interest claims. It simply cannot go on and on with new debts and new debts again, which are simply added on top in order to still be able to pay the old interest. A positive environment for investment is collateral that allows for long-term planning without taking major risks. Indebted State budgets offer just as little security as currencies that permanently lose value.

Therefore, the money saved through debt relief must be used to carry out the tasks of the state organs even without new debts. These are old problems, but problems that should be easier to solve in the age of digitalisation.

Of course, one could also achieve the goal of debt relief by the classical means of a currency reform, but at a high price, since then the great mass of citizens would have to reckon with great losses and economic growth with a depression. An insolvency regime would be the better solution for all.

In order not to burden the hard-working citizen with paying off the accumulated debts, while the owner of capital can count on lowered interest rates and tax rates, neither monetary reforms, nor inflation in combination with low interest rates, nor fee increases in cities and municipalities are the desirable means to get the public sector out of the debt trap and thus ensure a better investment climate. As with the insolvency of merchants and private insolvency, debt cuts with interest rate reductions for old loans are unavoidable within the EU and are also quite feasible by means of powerful computers. If the debt ratio exceeds 50% of economic revenues, the national debt should be cut by 50% and interest rates should also be reduced by 50%. In any case, a single currency area across different state jurisdictions needs an interstate insolvency law. To install precisely this insolvency law at the European level would be the demand of the first hour, but everyone seems to be shirking it. A rough proposal for determining the framework conditions could look like this: in the event of insolvency, all debts of a member state would be reduced by 50% and interest payments would be reduced to 75% for 1 year, after which they would also be reduced by 50%. An insolvent state should not be allowed to take on any more debt until the remaining debt has been repaid in full. Anyone who nevertheless lends money to an insolvent state should reckon with the fact that, from a legal point of view, this money is to be regarded as a gift.

Whether the insolvent state will ultimately stop taking on debt, also in order to be able to elevate the safe money system with

NIM to the official money system, remains to be seen. However, it should probably be possible in any currency to adequately meet all state transactions without debt, and without taking on new debt if no interest on debt and no repayments has to be made. Whether an investment makes sense or not should by no means be determined by the ups and downs of interest rates. It is more important to keep full employment in mind as a goal. With programmes for self-help and self-organisation in the non-employed groups of people, the goal of full employment should be more attainable.

A new problem in investment is the growing share of non-material investment in total investment. The stock market value of most global corporations in the IT sector is no longer fed by the value of buildings and machines, including the computers used, but by the knowledge of the new software developments used and the development of new organisational structures. In the process, capital accumulates that is not backed by financial capital. In terms of the balance sheets, this capital disappears and only appears in the balance sheet when the company is sold.

3. Growth factors in the digital age!

Let us not simply understand growth as a variable with which we can play and fill in statistics, but as a model of a functioning national economy in the new form, the new paradigm of sustainable growth in a sustainable circular economy, the factors in this model are important, and it is precisely these that need to be determined and balanced if we want to achieve presentable results. Also, and especially in the digital age, the semantically correct and clear definition of the terms we are working with is of utmost importance, because only in this way can all facets of a newly emerging paradigm be grasped and subsequently subjected to analysis. Let us first approach the term "growth";

under no circumstances should we equate growth with multiplication. In each generation, the knowledge of humanity is multiplied, but what is important is the conducive growth in the current society. The copying process in every multiplication is also necessary in growth, but not decisive for what we call growth. In principle, every growth creates something new, driven and controlled by information that is laid down at a certain point in time, using random environmental information and special resources to create a new entity by means of available energy, be it an animal, a plant or even a human being that has never existed in this constellation before, even cloned animals are not totally identical. It is also important to be able to use the term "sustainability" in the right way. Sustainability can only be what is built up again and again in a cycle system without requiring fundamentally new information and resources, owed solely to the renewed labour input. Even the labour input serves to maintain the entire cycle system, from which, if possible, the energy for the labour input in the system is also taken, so that sustainability can be realised as an output designed for the long term.

If we ask about the factors of growth, as they are taken into account in modern macroeconomics, we come across labour, resources and, more recently, information as a factor; money does not appear as a factor, but capital does. Since capital is to be understood as saved money or also frozen money, one can argue that it does not matter whether capital or money is a factor, after all, both are nothing other than the modern convertible promissory note. However, financial capital as pecuniary capital is to be distinguished from money, just as information and knowledge are to be distinguished from educational capital. With money in an account or as cash in one's pocket, one can buy the most diverse things and provided with the IBAN, transfer money almost in a flash in digital banking, pay with money. The digitalisation of all banks in recent years has accelerated processes enormously, not only in current accounts, but also in securities trading, where speed is often the decisive factor between profit and loss. The average citizen quickly falls behind when professionals with particularly fast computers step in. With digitalisation, stress can therefore also increase to an unbearable level. In principle, this should not play a role in Safe Money NIM, but the acceleration in trading will not stop there either. In their digitalised form, all factors can be better recorded in their fields and thus also replaced and supplemented in the event of a shortage by means of quickly procured funds from the field of financial capital. Digitalisation also allows us to better recognise and analyse structures, as in the case of energy in the field of regulatory capital. For background understanding, the individual factors in their fields are only briefly presented here. Just as money is collected (accumulated) in the field of financial capital, knowledge is accumulated and stored in educational capital, labour in human capital, energy in regulatory capital and resources in physical capital = tangible assets. Energy and order capital may seem somewhat surprising at first glance in this context. Although we know the counterpart to energy, entropy, and that entropy also represents a measure of order or disorder, we have not yet decidedly derived the field function as a capital of order from this. Insofar as the entropy decreases in a delimited area, this is no proof that the total entropy in space would not increase, nor is it proof that the energy in space would decrease, because in delimitable areas only the usable energy becomes smaller in terms of amount, since in all energy transformations a part always disappears in the non-usable heat energy. Interesting in this context are the possibilities of digitisation in the language area by deleting redundant information in order to reduce the storage requirement and thus to be able to use the storage more effectively. Digitised and compressed content is also easier to transport and easier to reconstruct than purely analogue and encrypted data.

By digitising all information available to humans, it can be accessed more quickly in the future and thus also be better searched for possible correlations. Sustainable growth based on nature's model is thus also more likely to be achieved than has been possible up to now.

4. Statistics as a planning aid?

When it is said that 60% of the population are poor or that 50% of the population together earn less than 1% of the super-rich, the question arises as to how these figures come about. Questioning such data and statistics is not the same as rejecting a fair distribution of earned profits. Rather, it should be a call for transparent social research and for a reappraisal that does not disregard the horizon of origin.

When comparing real net incomes, one finds very different statements and differences between the statistics of the Microcensus, EU, SILC and SOEP. Three statistical studies on the problem of poverty lead to at least three problems: the factual problem of the study, poverty itself, the methodological problem of the significance of a statistic and the problem of practical relevance. If we start with the practical relevance for the future, this should already be clear before the investigation, the design of a research project. If there is a high degree of practical relevance, people will be prepared to provide funds for appropriate research, although it is not unimportant whether there are falsifiable questions or whether the evidence is so compelling that it seems more sensible to channel the funds directly into aid measures. If falsifiable questions are present, the selection of the sample is very important in order to be able to make representative statements on the falsifiable questions. After all, one cannot speak of "the students" if only the students of Cologne University were included in the sample, to give an example. In order to be able to make representative statements, preliminary studies are often necessary. Of course, one can also include the entire population in the study, as was done years ago in a study on the social situation of students in the Faculty of Education at Cologne University. From a scientific point of view, the results then only apply to this population of pedagogy students in Cologne in the 1980s. A certain degree of transferability to other, comparable populations is certainly permissible if one is aware of the problems of such transfers. If one takes a random sample of education students from all over Germany or from the EU-wide, which correspond to the same origin grid as in the Cologne study, one obtains a representative comparable sample. What is more or less lacking in the studies mentioned in the FAZ is the lack of comparability due to different representation criteria in the time frame. These problems cannot be brushed aside with the significance of a statement. In the case of purely descriptive methods, the questions of significance and correlation should be secondary anyway. Comparisons with past years are sometimes very lopsided, as can be seen from an article in the FAZ. What do statements such as that the bottom 40% of employees in Germany had lower real wages in 2015 than in 1995 mean? "Behind this is primarily a positive development on the labour market," explains Judith Niehues, a distribution researcher at the employer-affiliated Institute of the German Economy (IMF). The populations examined are different because in 2015 people appear in the wage statistics who previously did not appear there because of unemployment. Let us now turn to a general problem: poverty can certainly be described in terms of the money available, which also works with percentages. In order to plan, such statistics, as mentioned above, are only of limited help with regard to the problem of distribution. If there are people in a society who live below the subsistence level, this is not simply a social problem in a democratic society, but a problem that can shake the pillars of the fundamental structure of freedom, a problem of the very structure of society, which can be grasped without large-scale statistical studies.

If we now ask how much money one needs in a certain social environment, this naturally also depends on the society in question, which is why purely money-based statements do not necessarily help. Neither the television nor the car is material goods that is reserved only for the rich in industrialised nations today. Wealth must be defined in terms of the means available to live a carefree life in moderate prosperity. This results in a basic problem of money; it cannot always correctly determine the real world in terms of value to the extent expected. If we then also ask about life values as distinct from exchange values, it becomes even more difficult to find a consensus on values. Among democrats, however, for the sake of the survival of democracy, a consensus acceptable to all should be found very quickly. Once this consensus has been found, it will also be possible to use it as a basis for transforming meaningful and further-reaching statistical statements into helpful activities. Data from the public sector can be taken from the census and the civil status data of the municipalities; data from the tax authorities can also be used to answer questions about current developments in society. Since there is no longer a wealth tax, however, there is a lack of corresponding data on assets. Surveys based on questionnaires can be helpful, but they involve considerable effort. A profit tax, where cost receipts must be presented, could be helpful, since statistics on cost developments can be derived from precisely these receipts, with which the need can also be determined more precisely. If the profit tax is levied in all business areas without exception, it will also be possible to present more precise studies on the development of construction costs and land costs in the real estate sector without having to conduct elaborate surveys. In any case, statistics require information, which can be obtained in various ways; in addition to surveys and documents from the public sector, there are also the data repositories of the retail chains and the records of banks and associations sources of information, insofar as these are only utilised anonymously, should only be utilised in this way. Continuous data collection, also with the help of increasingly usable AI systems, should be able to provide reliable data in all relevant fields. However, the consent of citizens to the use of this data must be available, in the case of anonymised data certainly in a weak form, i.e., not through individual declarations of consent. Private companies and international consortia should not have access to this data; only university institutions should be allowed to access anonymised data and statistical evaluations.

5. AI research and Industry 4!

Just as statistics depend on data, so do the intelligent systems built into the machines of Industry 4 depend on data with the help of which they can control the corresponding machines. The buzzword for this, which also refers to the decision-making level in machines that are also capable of learning, is "artificial intelligence". The machine of the future must be capable of learning, whether it is a car or a cooking robot. The use of AI requires interdisciplinary research activity of the highest complexity and people who can not only guide the machines, but also people who can live and work together with such intelligent machines. AI requires technicians, philosophers and linguists, but above all new ethical approaches. The research results must be protected, inhumane applications must be ruled out.

This is why state funds are particularly important here but should not be taken as unconditional funding from tax revenues, as has been the case so far with research funding, but should be understood as loans, funds that subsequently flow back to the state as an investment in a new technology or are available again through licence fees.

Above all, it is important to realise that progress towards systems with adaptive intelligence requires enormous efforts and funds in order to also have the people available who can handle these systems, develop them further and ward off dangers. The increased flow of funds into the education sector can, on the one hand, tie up the capital that is not needed, but on the other hand, also create new jobs, the jobs of the future. If new research results are licensed, this will have a lasting effect on the establishment and further development of AI research, and not only on that.

6. Model and paradigm

By combining individual research results and analyses in an effort to use them to rebuild and update the future, different models and theories emerge for understanding this world of ours. The time-dependent nature of such models and theories is shown by the discussion on the Phillips curves at the end of 2017. The correlation between inflation and unemployment in the last century obviously cannot be generalised but must be reassessed in conjunction with various other correlations. If one sees the succession of different theories in history as being in the context of evolution, the first economic models, starting with Adam Smith, can be understood as goods-oriented and thus postulate a first economic paradigm, the goods paradigm, which is substance-oriented. With Keynes' reflections on monetary policy, the more virtual view of a paradigm based on money is considered, the money paradigm. Since the boundaries and the transitions partly disappear when it comes to the ideological view, these two views should perhaps rather be understood as different models in a still rather uniform paradigm. According to this, it is a paradigm that starts from the observable phenomenon, here the created good, which has a value, and there from the created money, to which one assigns a value backed by material assets. It is always about values that manifest themselves differently, i.e., a value paradigm. What is paid less attention to, but what demands, should demand more and more relevance, is human performance, which in economic contexts is indeed remunerated with money, but also exists as unpaid performance.

Work performance depends on experience and training as well as on emotionally determined commitment. Labour performance is therefore not to be equated with work as described by Adam Smith. In future monetary systems and currencies, work performance is to be used as the basis for valuations, as in the case of the new money, since only the work performance that I have made available to my neighbour today can he easily demand back tomorrow as work performance, a paradigm related to performance. With the awareness that money is a debt instrument with which I reciprocally demand a service that I provide again somewhere else, or have already provided, money also becomes a universal standard of valuation independent of material assets. The value of an hour's work is on the one hand a socially determined agreement, and on the other hand also a private appreciation. In the context of valuing work performance, a different understanding of economic activity emerges it is about the human being who, in addition to the possibility of contributing human capital, also always contributes himself as a human being, and is sometimes only a human being. From a humane understanding, the human being is not just a functional part of the economic machinery. If we assume a basic salary for everyone that expresses responsible cooperation and see work as an achievement with which every citizen contributes to the community as a citizen, we could arrive at a model that fundamentally changes social cohesion and the common economy and, in this respect, need not fear comparison with the paradigm shift from the Ptolemaic world view. It is important that models, also and especially models of the monetary economy, become more accessible and comprehensible through digitalisation.

XIX. Sustainability in Finance

"So, a fierce competition for the best investment opportunities and returns has arisen among the major investors, even though they are themselves intertwined in many ways. Asset managers compete with pension funds, private equity firms with sovereign wealth funds. The demands on the financial system have become huge. The reality is overheating, which harbours dangers. But it is important to build up the real economy, to create new products and companies, to help start-ups and reform traditional businesses, in other words, to really strengthen growth in a sustainable way. This is the difficult but indispensable path. In the long run, 'easy money', the effortless profit from financial participation for all, is an illusion."

(Hans-Jürgen Jakobs, 2016, p. 639)

Sustainability in ecosystems is only possible through the existence of circular systems. There are various studies on this, which should also be of interest to economists in a basic discussion but are only mentioned here in passing. However, for reasons of plausibility alone, a well-planned energy- and resource-saving cycle should not only be possible in economic systems but should also be planned specifically. An economic cycle consists of the decay of economic structures and material assets on the one hand and the new growth of economic structures on the other. Everything that has grown at some point will also decay at some later point in time, will be subject to degradation. If the products of decay are fed back into the construction of new structures, we get an economic cycle that conserves resources and can also be considered sustainable. Often forgotten in planning is the use of the apparently free air, as well as water and soil. However, sustainable use can only be stated if, during a production process, the pollution of the air also becomes chargeable according to the polluter-pays principle and is taken into account in the calculation of costs. It is one thing to demand that the air, water and soil be kept clean and to punish non-compliance by law, but this does not necessarily lead to the elimination of the damage caused. The costs for this must not be imposed on the taxpayer. If the polluter does not remove the damage to air or water, for example, or cannot remove this damage, then at least a hefty compensation payment is due. From the point of view of the tax office, however, the benefit accrued by an environmental resource that belongs to the general public and can also be seen as profit, which is taken into account in the determination of profit with an appropriate tax assessment. In a sustainable economy, individual companies must compensate the society that provided these resources for the consumption of pure air as well as pure water. If, for example, pure water was permanently withdrawn from the sustainable cycle, then at some point in the future a collapse of the natural cycles and the circular economy is to be expected. A central problem for economic systems is the fact that money is not inherently recyclable, to put it bluntly. Society must agree on procedures by which money can be used again and again without destroying the otherwise intact cycle. In order to be sustainable, money must be created again and again if it is to adapt to new situations. But the newly created money must also disappear again regularly to make room for new money. Even if this may seem strange at first, the cycle requires all factors to disappear again and again in an act of decay and to reappear in an act of new growth. Since money cannot grow naturally, it needs a social agreement that reproduces or even cancels out precisely this in an artificial financial cycle. Although the invention of an interest rate goes in this direction, it does not lead to the actual goal of a stable and secure currency within a circular economy because of the market interest rates, which can only be controlled to a limited extent. There is a danger that the financial economy will decouple itself from the real economy. Therefore, the creation and decay of money must be contractually regulated in such a way that the money cycles do not become independent. Credit agreements offer an excellent opportunity to make the financial economy sustainable. For the sake of sustainability, these credit agreements should be designed in such a way that no contractual reduction of the agreed monetary value is stipulated in them, neither explicitly nor implicitly. In principle, each factor should work in such a way that it achieves an effect but does not consume itself in the process. When money from a credit agreement is repaid, this does not mean that it has been consumed, it rather means that it can only be reprocessed and returned to the cycle, just like rainwater in the water cycle. In the water cycle, the conditions are set by nature; in the financial cycle, it is the specific contractual conditions and the general statutes of the bank, the banking community, that set the framework for a sustainable financial economy with a sustainable money cycle.

Sustainability is now also conceivable with money systems that are not based on credit. It is worth recalling the distinction made at the beginning between passive and active money systems and the fact that a mixed system is currently the common practice. One might think that in the active money system, sustainability can be achieved simply by feeding the money collected via the tax office back into the cycle. Thus, the once printed 50 Euro note would perhaps enter circulation a hundred times before it must be replaced by a new one. At the same time, the new creation is only seen as a replacement creation. New money is only to be created when it becomes apparent that more money is needed in the market as a result of higher activity; this can be handled by an expert council or the board of a central bank. In the active money system, an expert or a committee of experts is necessary in any case. In an active money system, self-control in the market can only be an assisting factor; without the advice of experts, it will not work. Wrong decisions are more likely, unless the experts are all wise people who act only for the good of the community and who have no selfish motives. Even wise decisions need not be sustainable. However, without a regulator, the market will not steer itself in a sustainable way either. The laissez-faire style is not a desirable alternative, we already need a rule-based self-regulation with rules that have been fixed, frozen, in laws by a parliament. At the same time, some basic principles should not be disregarded. For example, money that has not emerged from a labour process, that is legitimised by it, can hardly produce positive growth. Nor can money that is not honestly acquired, money stolen from hard-working fellow citizens, be expected to produce sustainability-promoting feedback.

1. Financial cycle and humanity

Sustainable economic activity can help to feed even more people than before on this earth with the available resources and the usable energy reserves, and even help them not to slip below the regional subsistence level. What is sustainably humane is a financial cycle that helps to always avoid a life below the subsistence level, even into old age. This could be a basic income based on the subsistence level, but also a pension for all that is saved through an automatic accumulation of funds during an active working life. Whether this would make everyone happy is another matter. Since people's needs are not always the same in many respects and are also not always rational, the question in this respect is how we can build an economy that does justice to people. Here the results of behavioural economics are certainly also important pieces in our overall puzzle with which this could succeed. In an overall theory, the individual behavioural science approaches should be located in the relational space and assigned to an overall theory. The important question of trust arises both in the cooperative cycle of cooperation and in the competitive cycle of competition. Whether the citizen trusts the value of money or not is important for the existence of a monetary order and cannot be explained purely rationally. Similarly, the entry in the register of labour performance will only coincide with the current market value in exceptional cases. However, the reference to labour performance can strengthen trust and thus generate security and the resulting stability that is necessary to generate prosperity on a broad scale. In the case of cooperation, it is perhaps most apparent that performance and return are not always balanced. Inequality need not be inhumane, but people should work towards a balance. It is precisely the tension and the effort to eliminate an inequality that can have a positive effect, but unfortunately can also slide into the negative if poorly handled. However, the fact that inequalities can have a positive effect should not be an excuse for not wanting to eliminate them at all. Nevertheless, a humane goal is not necessarily the elimination of inequality, but the effort to keep existing inequalities within a positive range for society. In the simplest case, this can succeed due to an insight into the justification of inequality and its acceptance, for example due to a difference in the relevant level of knowledge and special skills. A humane economic order must above all grant unhindered access for all with the proven potential to educational opportunities as well as basic democratic rights and must not allow any citizen to languish in inhumane living conditions. To achieve this, the democratic penetration of the financial economy, the money economy, must also succeed, for example, by citizens taking back their money from the central banks and creating their own money secured by labour services with Free Banks. Why should citizens continue to work with money that is not their money, from money creation to devaluation? A humane democratic monetary economy is only conceivable if the citizen creates his money according to his needs and also determines the time of devaluation. Since money is not a natural product, there must be people who create it and those who devalue it. Why should these be bankers who are in no way subject to the directives of the citizens or of an institution elected by the citizens? One can only demand, citizens, that you take back the power over money that was granted to you in the natural society! A monetary cycle can be considered humane if it reflects the needs of the citizens as closely as possible. It should not be forgotten that monopolies are to be avoided in all respects, certainly a more important requirement than majority decisions. Several small firms cooperating and competing with each other are better than one big firm swallowing up all the small firms. Inequalities in small firms are also better to buffer than in large firms, since they are in any case more limited in their extent. The occupation of all the economic niches possible at any one time by different niche operators should be the goal, not the majority decision that restricts the activities of oligopolists and monopolists. If we want sustainable growth in sustainable financial spaces, then we must also realise that monopolies can only grow unilaterally and absolutely; a disintegration of individual segments can be temporarily absorbed, but innovation from positively developing competitive cycles usually disappears altogether. If the disintegration of the monopolists, the expected effects are devastating, since there is no competitor who could take over the business areas that would otherwise be abandoned to destruction. This also means that the decay products can no longer be used to build new structures and thus the financial capital contained in the structures cannot be preserved, at least in part. Changes of use and reprocessing are more humane than allowing senseless destruction, in which no value is then ascribed to individual human lives.

2. The cycle, the basis for sustainable economic activity

A cycle comparable to the ecological cycles will not be found for the financial economy any time soon, since money is not subject to natural wear and tear like all other economic goods. Money is not subject to natural decay and cannot grow. Money as an asset can be exchanged for other goods on the market, but it does not depreciate by itself. The material on which the banknote is printed and on which a value is written can be destroyed and wear out, but the value of the money does not decrease. Money as a virtual value is not depreciable, but money is also not a natural commodity. Money is perhaps to be understood as a virtual commodity with real value. Does this mean that money cannot be integrated into circulation systems, that money is inert against sustainable tendencies? No, we just need other cycles! In this context, one can demand that the missing decay process be virtually attributed to money. Such virtual attributions can certainly succeed in a constitutional state with contractual agreements. One possibility would be the direct time-sensitive attribution of value up to an agreed expiry date. However, this would quickly catapult the bureaucratic effort to dizzying heights, and would also, if practicable, surely have been tried out successfully long ago. Inflation targeting is another option, but one that has all too often ended in galloping inflation that can no longer be controlled. Inflation then heads for monetary reform in the short or long term, necessary when the value printed on it is not at all worth the paper it is printed on and is thus not sustainable at all. We must find a way that develops the existing system in the sense of evolutionary development, with an eye on sustainable systems. In the search for suitable cycles, one quickly comes across the gold currency. The gold coin, once minted, can be used again and again, but initially has no direct relation to the service that is paid for with it. Only when a value is assigned to the gold coin can it be used to pay for goods and services. Without a value assignment, the gold coin also has no currency value. A gold currency and the reference to precious metals that comes with it can create stability without also guaranteeing sustainability. If the assigned value loses its validity, the metal value may also be higher than the coin value. The stability of a currency based on tangible assets can quickly come to an end, namely when the corresponding tangible asset changes its value drastically, be it through losses or also through disproportionately high replenishment. Because gold reserves today would hardly suffice for a gold-based global currency, this is precisely why people have parted with this reference point, albeit without determining a new reference point. Cryptocurrencies also suffer from the fact that they lack a reference point. With the focus on human labour power, a reference can now be found that is always emerging and passing away, as with natural cycles, and in this respect provides a borrowed sustainability. If we combine the reference to labour power with the credit cycle, we come closer to the natural cycles, since every credit also has its individual life span, here through the agreements in the credit contract and not, as in nature, through the information on the DNA.

The creation of money by credit is currently the only existing monetary cycle in which the money created disappears from circulation again after a contractually fixed period of time, without devaluing money in principle. That is why credit is also a good way to build a sustainable monetary system. From the perspective of the It is irrelevant whether the credit cycle begins with legal entities or with natural persons. If stability and security are taken into account, legal persons are ruled out after careful consideration, as only natural persons can guarantee a work performance for the rest of their lives with their signature.

The money in the credit cycle enters circulation after the creation of money through the loan and is also withdrawn from circulation again with the redemption. If, in addition, it is stipulated that money is only newly created by means of credit, then, even with the appropriate safeguards, no money can enter circulation that does not originate from credit, and thus no money can enter circulation that is not withdrawn from it again after an agreed period of time in circulation. This would then also ensure that all money that enters the market also disappears again when the time comes. Money thus does not have a natural expiry date, but it does have a legally clearly fixed expiry date through the credit agreement. The important thing is that money can always be created anew, just as growth can always start anew. Money functions in the economic cycle in some ways comparable to the function of water in the biomass cycle. Just as the plant takes in water in order to be able to realise the metabolic processes in the body, the market takes in money in order to be able to realise the economic metabolism. Money, like water, is always already present, even if only virtually. As a reminder, even the gold of a gold currency is only virtually present as money, since only the allocation of a monetary value to a piece of gold turns it into the money we are talking about here. With all such allocations, be it gold, credit money, i.e., liability money or asset money, they may be pronounced for eternity, but in reality, this eternity will sometimes be shorter than the average contractual period of a credit agreement.

Money, whether in the asset account or the liability account, is always an allocation of value and not a value in itself. The allocation to a tangible asset, as in the case of gold, is also linked to the availability of corresponding tangible assets. The allocation to an easement, on the other hand, is linked to the availability of this easement. If this easement is the labour of the debtor, the potential loss of this labour becomes a risk, just as with the tangible asset the loss of the tangible asset is a risk. Both risks can be insured. However, tangible assets cannot be increased at will just because the population is growing exponentially. Gold, for example, is only available in limited quantities on earth. Since every borrower brings his labour power with him, the limitation in this potentially possible labour power in his lifetime can be seen here, apart from insurable sickness-related absences and equally insurable early deaths. If working time accounts are managed and secured in the same way everywhere according to strict criteria, this should be the best safeguard for a currency. This brings us to the safe money proposed here, with which a sustainable financial economy can be established because of contractually secured returns of the funds created. Relying on a financial economy that is bound by laws and rules, a sustainable monetary economy can be established in this way.

It is important that this kind of financial economy detaches itself from the directives and imponderables of the respective governments and, free from them, adapts itself in a purely private economy to the wishes of the market participants, but not to the wishes of the politicians who are currently in power. Only when citizens create their own money or "take it back" and only give the state what is due to the state, only then can democracy really succeed at all levels. A sustainable financial economy, it should be said here, can certainly also be successfully established and succeed in a dictatorship, but it fits perfectly with the principles of a democracy.

Money, no matter where it is in the world, must no longer be understood as the alms that the ruler gives to the people; it must rather finally be recognised as what it should be, the mutual promissory note with which we grant each other the help that we need in a highly differentiated world of work. need. This can also work practically if the individual labour services are recorded in a cadastre in order to secure money, and to be able to determine and compare the exchange value of labour services. Private credit agreements as the basis of a new free economy in the recognition of a necessary indebtedness for the good of the community can democratise the financial world with the recognition and commitment to a common economy. In the sense of a republican and democratic separation of powers, it is a matter of exchanging labour services for the benefit of all in a non-violent atmosphere that is legally secured. In order to promote a common economy based on reciprocity, the currently non-remunerated labour services must also be included in the register of labour services, as this is the only way to build up a generally just lending and old-age provision system. If one takes the non-salaried work as credit security for the state's basic security, or the basic salary, then the unemployed citizen can also become indebted to the state, since he is also contributing a service to society. A settlement at the end of life, if it is made, should not leave behind excessive debts as a rule. However, the deposit of potential work as collateral when granting loans must not lead to the enslavement of the debtors, which is why the 50% limit must be observed in any case. What is meant by this is that no one should provide more than 50% of his remaining life's work as collateral.

It must be prevented that the debtor is no longer able to meet his own living costs due to his debts. In this context, it should be assumed that the general cost of living should be set at twice the cost of survival.

3. Disruptive influences on sustainable financial cycles

If we assume that a sustainable financial system exists that is designed in such a way that it meets the criteria of sustainability and that speculative use is almost impossible, a money that repeatedly disappears from circulation due to its credit reference, but that is also repeatedly created, then this money in the economic cycle can support the sustainable cycle of material assets in the market. Such a cycle can be legitimised by the citizens who use it. The best legitimisation by the citizens is that they themselves can determine the target value. But how can imbalances occur in well legitimised financial systems and less well legitimised systems? One very easy-to-explain imbalance is the one that arises when there is no longer enough money in circulation during rapid population growth. Since every citizen needs money if he wants to buy in the market, additional money must be available with every new citizen. However, the existing money supply will not be sufficient even if the population remains constant, if the activities increase. It will also have a disruptive effect on the existing amount of money in circulation if larger amounts of money are stashed away, whether under the mattress or in the safe. Since stashed money is not used in circulation, it cannot be considered part of a sustainable circulation. This does not lead to the conclusion that savings cannot be made in a sustainable cycle, far from it. In the case of savings credits, the money saved is definitely used in the savings phase and not uselessly stashed away, so saving is definitely possible in a sustainable financial cycle, even if it is a credit-based currency. Serious disruptions often occur in classical monetary systems because a lot of money is spent that is not paid for by those who earned it, and liability as well as responsibility is passed on to people who have nothing to do with the original decision. In order to be able to avoid the grossest mistakes, it is advisable to legal persons cannot apply for a loan and assume no liability. Natural persons should always be liable for wrong decisions, which is why only natural persons can apply for credit. Decisions made in politics must also be sustainable, which means that they fit into the cycle and do not leave the sustainable cycle with resources, information and energy used. If the public sector finances its projects only with the money it receives from the citizens through levies and taxes and not with money owed, and if it burdens its managers with a share in the losses from wrong decisions, then a distressed situation in the finances of cities and municipalities will probably be a rarity, perhaps even only known from stories of what happened in earlier times. A major disruptive factor, therefore, are the many wrong decisions for which no one feels responsible and for which no one is held accountable. Of course, natural disasters are also sensitive disturbances that can bring a well-functioning society to the brink of the abyss. Surprisingly, such disruptions are usually cushioned quite well, as the willingness of neighbours, and even distant people, to help is sometimes quite high. On the other hand, we find far-reaching aberrations in the financial system, triggered by the greed for more and more possessions by individuals and groups of people, even when they themselves hardly lack any wealth.

In fact, in current financial systems, the imbalance is often caused by the greed of those who work in the financial system and by those who want to perpetuate their name with lofty plans at the expense of future generations. The paths to a debt-free national budget can be very different and will certainly not be enforced quickly with a majority decision. The best way is probably to enforce it in the radical way by declaring the state to be in a state of bankruptcy and repaying all government securities at only 50% of their imprinted value. A more moderate approach could be to gradually reduce the value of each security by 25%. In a transitional period, it could even make sense to issue zero-interest securities in order to initially reduce the interest burden without postponing the necessary investment expenditures for an unnecessarily long time. In the long term, however, only a structural change can provide a remedy. The necessary public investments in the education system and infrastructure must be financed by the beneficiaries, whereby the state sensibly advances the funds, but later recovers them in the sense of sustainable financing. The development of new structures also creates new capital that can help to cushion imbalances in the future in good time.

But technical innovations can also be the cause of imbalances, especially if the distribution problem at the origin of the innovation cannot be tackled immediately. Robbery and criminal activities, just like armed conflicts, can very quickly erode and destroy an economic structure. The drug cartels active in Europe alone drain several billion euros a year from the financial economy, money that is not used productively, but rather used to destroy human lives. Likewise, changing fashions can cause fluctuations, which, however, can only be classified as serious disruptions in extreme cases, since they promote economic activities, even if they are usually not exactly sustainable. Fashions in particular target the mental space, which is why purchase decisions in this area are particularly emotionally influenced, but also have a strong relational component. Strongly disruptive advertising can affect the sustainability. While advertising can influence purchasing behaviour, it is rather rare that advertising promotes sustainable products, rather the not-so-sustainable products and services. Moreover, advertising itself is hardly sustainable because it is not necessary in the economic cycle; an independent information platform would also be conceivable as a substitute for or even in competition with the current advertising campaigns. This could push back the rather egoistically motivated advertising in favour of rational considerations. Now, one might think that the self-interest-oriented goals of a capitalist economy are the main disruptive factor of sustainable management. Now, self-interest is not to be condemned in general, as it is a strong driving force that could also work in sustainable systems and positively inspire a free sustainable economy. The problem is not egoism per se, but excessive egoism, egoism without altruism as a countermeasure to maintain the necessary balance in the market. One should rather speak of self-interest here, which has rightly been described as a positive driving force since the beginnings of economics. Self-interest and social commitment belong together and can be called the balanced emotional driving forces in the economic sphere of action. There must be rules and laws that can guarantee and maintain a corresponding balance. An appeal to the necessary ethical attitude is less and less enough, it must be learned during education in the general education and training phase; no one is a moral person from birth, even if the foundations for it are already laid. The responsible manager is not born either, he must learn to recognise the connections and to make ethically justifiable decisions, all against the background of a code of communal social values.

If we ask where and how communities of values can be created and preserved, communities without which life and work in sustainable circles is not possible in the long run, we find them in the lived neighbourhood, in the sports club, in the carnival club. The sports club and probably even more so the carnival club are special examples of identity-building groups. We can justifiably claim that without identity formation, sustainability and ethics in human communities become paper shells. That is why disruptions to the life of associations in a city, a region, are major disruptive influences on sustainability and especially on sustainable finance; in this context, it is often precisely the economic importance of carnival that is still underestimated, an economic pillar that without the many carnival associations and the support in schools would hardly achieve the impact that it develops anew every year.

4. Sustainability and justice!

Without the responsible actions of the citizens in a society, there will be neither sustainability nor justice. A stable social system gains its stability primarily from the fact that every citizen considers himself or herself, overall, to be treated fairly. Injustices, including those of an unjust distribution of productive goods, can become explosive. Therefore, the demand for a just society must be subscribed to by everyone who desires a stable society that does everything possible to maintain external and internal peace.

Unfair remuneration, unjust participation in the achievements of society, these prevent a lasting peace of mind. sustainable economic growth. A sustainable monetary economy can only succeed if the money pulsating in the economic cycle, like the water in the ecosystem, is constantly reintegrated into the cycle of growth and decay through an existing system of order. Just as water is incorporated into organic substances when they are built up, money is incorporated into commodities, social institutions and organisations when they are built up and becomes part of the valuation of these entities, even if money itself is not incorporated like water in the entities of an ecosystem. Money determines valuation; without money, valuation is no longer conceivable. As a social function, the valuation of goods and social structures up to the valuation of entire company complexes is subject to expectations about the future and is part of a trust in the people who create these structures. This raises the question of whether this trust is justified and sustainable. Trust should also be sustainable, a requirement that is becoming increasingly important, especially in the financial sector. If the customer no longer trusts his bank, he will withdraw his money from the account in order to entrust it to another bank or even invest in tangible assets because he trusts their valuation and, above all, the sustainability of these valuations more. Of course, it is also a question of whether these valuations are fair, whether they correspond to the labour input involved or whether they go far beyond that, because a shortage of goods on the one hand and a glut of money on the other shift the valuation yardsticks. Let us take the purchase of real estate as an example, in advance, it can be the purchase of an existing property, or also the construction of a new one. If money is used in the construction of a house, the money and the work paid for with it can be used to advance the construction of a house.

If the house is rented out after completion, one can compare the rent with the fruit that a tree bears after fruiting. By selling it, one can either make a profit or a loss on the money invested. Only the profits and not the value should be tax-relevant; this is also how real estate can be managed sustainably.

An example of a community task that ensures cohesion through justice is the task of providing affordable housing for all citizens. This is not primarily about building enough social housing. As a matter of principle, housing built with municipal funds should not be made available to those who only build and rent out housing in order to make money with it, sometimes even on behalf of the shareholders supporting the housing association. Well, it cannot be wrong to make money by building houses and flats. But it is wrong to use taxpayers' money to finance housing through the private housing market, rent it out at a discount and then sell it to a corporation. The sale of social housing should generally only be permitted to the tenants. It would be fair to offer these flats to tenants who, over the years, are no longer in need and are thus also able to purchase the flat formerly occupied as a needy social tenant as a freehold flat after several years of subsidised renting, to be acquired by the municipality. It is absolutely correct to sell flats from social housing in order to obtain money for the construction of new social housing, as this is the only way to make sustainable management with a closed-loop system possible in this area as well. In the name of justice, those who are no longer in need should also no longer be able to enjoy a reduced rent but should be given the opportunity to purchase property. This would also prevent tenants from being forced out of their flats through luxury renovations. Gradually, tenants can be offered the possibility of owning their social housing. If the municipality is able to buy a house, it can also make more citizens homeowners than is possible with subsidies such as the "Baukindergeld" or the "Wohnungsbauprämie". If the land on which the houses are built remains in the possession of the municipality, then, on the one hand, with a price for the condominium that is reduced by the price of the land, it can also be offered to less well-off citizens at a justifiable and affordable price, and on the other hand, with a leasehold contract, the municipality can be helped to have a source of money that flows in the long term, which, as a substitute for land tax and land transfer tax, is also more flexible and can thus be better adapted to the needs of the people. It can be argued that some tenants will never get their property this way, as they will never earn enough for a purchase to ever come into question. It should not be forgotten here that the mere fact that the neighbour can afford to buy is an incentive to do the same, a better approach than also spending a lot of money on advertising so that premiums can be brought among the people. In the course of time, 50% or more of such social housing will certainly become owner-occupied housing by the next century, if the right direction is first taken here, that is to be expected.

The new monetary system proposed here can support this equitable sustainability insofar as it also makes credit-based financing of a condominium cheaper through interest-free loans and thus even makes it possible for many in the first place. This could even be an approach to defeating world hunger once and for all. Since this is an important approach in all major world religions, one could even get the idea of finding allies here. In this context, the idea that the leaders of the great religions could support a financial organisation to launch a new money economy without interest may seem totally crazy. Even if the new money without interest is only introduced in manageable circles for private use, it would be able to change sustainability in the financial sector noticeably in a good sense in other areas as well.

A completely different approach is offered by the cradle-to-cradle approach, which I would like to outline briefly here. Michael Baumgart's approach assumes that all products are used for a circular economy planned from birth to birth. In doing so, the idea of a sustainable circular economy for production is thought through to the basic approach. This approach will certainly take a broad scope in the consideration of material resources. The only question here is to what extent this principle can also be applied in the monetary economy. If every newborn citizen receives an account and a basic credit at birth, this money could be used to establish a monetary system for which "from the cradle to the cradle" can also apply, since every citizen receives money at the beginning of life, which he or she can increase and consume as well as repay through work in the course of life, and with the last repayment makes the money available for the next new citizen, places it in his or her cradle (Michael Baumgart, 2009).

SUMMARY

"And as there is no means, except complete autarky, of protecting a country against the folly or perversity of the monetary policy of others, the only hope of avoiding serious disturbance is to submit to some general rules, even if they are by no means ideal, in order to stimulate other countries to follow a similarly reasonable policy."
(Hayek, p.117; 2011)

To point out and denounce the perversity of monetary policy is not the task of this book, other authors have already done that enough. Here I would like to point out an alternative, perhaps a possible parallel world, a utopia that gives money and monetary policy a possible other reality, makes it possible in the first place.

The folly of others, which makes it impossible to recognise another possibility, is sometimes only the different attitude to life in a different cultural context. That money is independent of the cultural context is something one should definitely not believe. In a community with regionally different cultural backgrounds, the different identities could cause problems if a community identity is not formed in parallel. Not only the national affiliation, but also the affiliation to a certain religion can form different identities and thus also change the relationship to money, without the currency having to take on a different status. Money, on the other hand, is certainly not the basis of identity formation, for that is the available information and knowledge from which the educational capital of a region, of a company can become effective within an individual context. Nevertheless, the stable currency and the value-preserving currency area in which one lives are important for one's sense of life and a life of prosperity without disregarding the human dignity of others, an important approach for humane identity formation. An important basis for identity formation is created by clubs and the profession with its social environment, in the age of social networks also the network used and the blog that strongly influences one's own identity, the writing activity, all approaches to positively stand out from the sea of the unnoticed and undescribed masses in the big cities and thus no longer be just one of the many invisible people. Money is important in this, regardless of whether it is active money or passive money. This division of Mayer in the monetary economy is taken up in order to present a secure currency with a money that does not float in the air like crypto-money, but is given a secure point of reference by being tied to work performance. This direct reference to work performance is also more secure than Facebook's attempt to establish this security by tying it to existing currencies. The fact that turning away from the conventional national currencies is then connected to a monetary economy without interest and compound interest is worked out as necessary, since the Safe Money should not be devalued by interest. The security of Safe Money, presented here as NIM, is fed not least by the fact that zero interest subsequently causes zero inflation, and thus the currency is not only secure but also stable in value. With the proposal to introduce savings credits, even saving at 0% interest should still be attractive. The original meaning of saving is thus relaunched, you save, and another customer of the bank receives a loan with this money, you for it later in the credit phase, after half of the required money has been saved. Since taxation is an important element in the game of a currency with stable value, a tax reform is proposed here with cornerstones that should serve to avoid unnecessary taxes, because revenues that are better collected than levies are better collected than taxes. and revenues to be collected as rents or royalties, those should not be collected as taxes. On the other hand, the abolition of all substantial taxes and the reformulation of taxes on profits, which do not destroy substantial wealth, does not steer away anyone's basis of acquisition. Next, there is the question of control, whether socially, collectively or personally exercised. Community control is usually given little attention, although the many cooperatives in Germany are witnesses to a movement that combines ethical and social aspects in an excellent way. Communities are sometimes better at managing capital and pooling resources than private individuals can do, and better than state institutions can do. A special issue in this regard is the question of how to design a local market and how to integrate this market into global markets. Private property should in any case be protected by appropriate laws, and this should also be protected from the access of the state. To this end, the boundaries between private property and common property must be clearly delineated, more clearly than has been done so far; proposals are made to this end. The influences and effects of the various other factors that influence growth must also be clearly delineated. The interrelationships are only briefly touched on here, as they are to be shown in more detail in a later volume, and this will only be possible satisfactorily once all factors have been sufficiently described in their fields of action. Digitalisation makes many things easier through the simpler use of statistics, models and the results of AI research, which is pointed out but by no means discussed in detail. Subsequently, the chapter on sustainability shows how sustainability in finance is achievable and why it is also necessary in order to establish a stable economic zone and to keep the money used stable in the value allocations. In this way, proposals and approaches for new ways of thinking are presented that could lead to a new form of economic activity. The question arises as to how this modern society can be organised differently, this with a different currency, a different self-image of the market, a market in which unemployment becomes a foreign word and government debt only appears in historical contexts. All in all, personal responsibility should be strengthened, and co-responsibility promoted, which is sometimes better achievable through the introduction of a basic income for all citizens, but is rather prevented with the social legislation to da.

EPILOGUE

What can we do, and what will the future bring us, and what do we absolutely have to examine more closely in order not to miss, to overlook the parameters for a future worth living in? The energy available and the substantial resources are, along with the labour, the power to be expended and the information needed, the basic factorial conditions that are in no way to be neglected. The information that emerges from new knowledge may even be more important than money in the future. But let us first arrive at the present and talk about money!

So, we ask ourselves whether it is right for Brussels to issue the slogan that governments should save (austerity)? Shouldn't we follow Keynes and allow debt in countries with high unemployment in order to be able to finance government job creation measures? Currently, the interest rate on government securities is running towards zero, so the cost of further debt is close to zero, a clear invitation for the public sector to incur debt after all. Moreover, the ECB's key interest rate, which is quoted at zero, is also leading to falling interest rates in the immediate vicinity. In addition, the ECB is flooding the market with money from the QE programme. The goal is to achieve an inflation rate of 2%. Inflation is still below 2% (2021) but should actually be zero if the aim is to have a currency with stable value. At the end of 2018, you hear in the news that inflation is averaging 1.5%. The ECB's announcement to reduce the flooding of the markets with money from bond purchases seems crazy, not because they now no longer want to buy new bonds, but one wonders why bonds were and are bought at all? In America, the Fed has long since scaled back this measure (QE), and there has been no 0-interest rate from the central bank for some time now. Let's ask ourselves why the loose monetary policy in Europe cannot even keep inflation at a target level of 1% for the time being. Do we citizens then have to reckon with an ever-faster devaluation of money that suddenly sets in and can then no longer be stopped? The money from the ECB's asset purchases is still flowing into assets, being stashed away or ending up back in ECB accounts. It has not yet reached the everyday market, but for how much longer? Up to now, new purchases have been made for repaid bonds, the purchase programme has simply not been extended any further. Let's also ask ourselves why shares and insurance papers are not being bought up, since there would be no danger of creating stashed money. There is every reason to fear that the euro area will plunge into a recession in the next 10 to 15 years, which some economists believe is possible, but then quickly disappear. Money without interest and without inflation, released into the world by free banks in the hands of their customers, that would be a good way, perhaps the only way, to counteract a recession, because the activities of the FED are not really leading anywhere either. The fact that interest rate hikes by the FED will be rolled back again in America in 2019 points to a certain helplessness. But what about the tax system, which is currently upside down, it should finally be put on its feet, customs duties should be abolished completely as soon as possible. A profit tax that also includes iInternational cost control can dispense with customs duties and inspire fair free world trade. The demand for humane production conditions can thus also be effectively considered in developing countries through the deductible and non-deductible costs in the profit tax calculation. Can we expect in the next few years a tax harmonisation on a global scale? Perhaps, if the 129 states that are now negotiating tax laws in 2019 can come together for a positive outcome in the direction of profit tax.

In this context, the effects and consequences must be oriented towards the future. Fiscal policy and monetary policy must always be viewed from two directions, one from the perspective of the creditor and the other from that of the debtor. These perspectives also apply to mutual transactions and loans. However, money is not primarily a material asset due to the attribution of value in a debt relationship! Money only has the social value attributed to it within a social convention, whereas original tangible assets always have an intrinsic value, a value of their own for the owner as part of his or her life values, even if tangible assets can also have an exchange value. In the case of tangible assets, the claim to ownership is to be defended; in the case of debt relationships, the contractual agreement is to be defended.

If we now ask ourselves what constitutes our monetary system and what money really is, we come across different answers, starting with Adam Smith, via Keynes, Friedman, Gesell and Marx, just a few from history who have dealt with money, to more recent approaches such as that of Hayek at the beginning of the 20th century and that of Mayer towards the end of the 20th century. In weighing the different approaches presented by Mayer, the approach that assumes that money arose out of a debt relationship, insofar as it became necessary not only to hold credits and debts but also to make them convertible, seems to be the best-documented and, moreover, the most plausible approach. The ruler, king or prince, needed something to pay his servants for their services, first with land and in kind, eventually also with promissory notes. Gold coins then replaced the promissory note and bartering in kind. The likeness of the ruler on the coin guaranteed that the ruler would be the last creditor to pay the debt. This made it relatively easy for the ruler to pay for services rendered by his citizens, also in order to be able to pay the wages of the soldiers in his own army, for example. Debts were also recorded very early on, be it on stones, notched wood or in more detail in the bookkeeping that developed early on.

Even though the first coinage was used to pay debts, it was not credit money, but asset money, since it was issued without a credit agreement. It was only with the exchange offices and the banks and pawnshops that developed from them that the business of lending money on a larger scale emerged, and at interest. In an entanglement of religious institutions with secular claims to power, the first state securities were created, with which the Vatican initially paid its citizens 12% interest on the money they borrowed. In the course of time, less and less interest was then paid, until finally the interest ceased to be paid, after which no more government securities were offered. As a result, and with the growing private indebtedness of citizens, the influence of the state seemed to gradually diminish. With the founding of central banks, the states in the 18th and 19th centuries, above all Sweden and England, began to regain sovereignty over money. Subsequently, the national central bank granted loans to the commercial banks so that they could in turn pass on loans to private individuals and business people. The money thus put into circulation is central bank money. In the meantime, the money lent by the commercial banks is only marginally also central bank money; it is largely money generated solely by the commercial bank by means of credit, i.e., giro money.

Since the banks have not yet completely separated themselves from the central banks with the banks money, the most consistent demand is that this be done by completely detaching from central bank money as a separation to free lending with purely private money of a free bank. The Free Bank can create safe money with a purely legal safeguard, which is thus globally valid and usable as purely private money creation independent of the nation states. According to Mayer's terminology, this is a passive money order.

Mayer himself, on the other hand, calls for an active money order, which is of course also possible, but can only develop freely beyond a national framework to a limited extent. This problem also arises with free money, which Gesell introduced into the discussion and is widely known as "rusting money". A new attempt in the direction of a new asset money system was the Swiss initiative to create full money at the beginning of 2018. In contrast to full money, the free credit money of citizens (for example NIM) in the liability money system is no longer controlled by the state, it is subject to a privately bound contractual relationship. The state only checks that the contracts and statutes are correctly set up in accordance with the law. Savings credits and overdrafts can even reorganise savings behaviour and make it attractive again, if they are contractually stipulated. The guiding principle here is the motto: "Save without charging interest, so that afterwards you can also claim as much in interest-free credit as you have saved in advance." In addition, company law should also be changed, as it is not understandable that large companies in particular avoid responsibility through exclusion of liability, which is why liability should be distributed among more people and, in parallel, partially covered by insurance. This can be achieved if contracts are only concluded by natural persons and legal persons are prohibited from doing so. In order to challenge the responsibility of all citizens more than has been the case up to now, it can also be useful to build up the coercion of today's social security in the future with a basic salary on a basis that involves each citizen more strongly in the responsibility for himself and society. This will also avoid destabilising nonsensical spending of money. To reject this because it would encourage idleness is short-sighted, since the old social system already consumes more money and resources than a targeted basic salary would be able to do, and it would also avoid unnecessary, destabilising expenditure. In the passive money system, the basic income can also be introduced as a loan and misbehaviour can be better controlled than with prohibitions alone. Drug use and gambling addiction are to be acknowledged with cuts if necessary. The money that drugs addicts lack as a result should be credited to the drug dealers as debt and confiscated to be used as income to finance prevention programmes.

Since permanent growth is only conceivable if the recurring decay and destruction are not disregarded, the question arises as to how money is integrated into these cycles of new growth and recurring destruction. Money has been reclaimed from circulation via taxation for millennia. With asset money, one could thus create a cycle between taxation and new money creation. In the active money system, the adjustment of the money in circulation can be taken over by a state institution created separately for this purpose or by the central bank. In the passive money system, on the other hand, the citizen in the market, one could also say the market, determines the quantity in circulation through the swelling and ebbing quantity of loans taken out and repaid. In this system, the tax serves solely to cover state tasks, one could also say that the in this way, the citizen is put in a position to give to his state, to his community, only what he is able and willing to give to this community. Since in the secured private passive money system the state no longer has any debts, interest payments no longer must be financed through taxes and the balance sheets are likely to shrink. If, despite free trade, one wants to keep undesirable goods out of local markets, imports can be banned, and any proceeds can be subject to an additional tax (speculation taxes of up to 40%). In addition to import bans, customs duties are also conceivable to protect citizens quickly, but should be avoided if possible.

To prevent citizens from being lured into the credit trap by the state, taxes should no longer be levied on substantial assets. No one should be forced to sell his house, his company or his car in order to pay tax debts. This can be realised with a pure profit tax, since the profit made, even if taxed up to 60% and beyond, will not lead anyone to ruin and definitely not into debt. The profit tax should be offset against a basic salary when it is introduced, and exemption lump sums and social benefits should be dropped in return. Citizens, whether low-wage workers or millionaires, must be more involved in taking responsibility for their fellow citizens, their community, their city. Neither property nor any other asset should be able to exempt people from the demand to act responsibly towards themselves and society.

In the context of the 4th Industrial Revolution, work performance should also experience a new valuation. If productivity per employee is increased within the framework of digital automation and robotisation, this should not only be reflected in the profit for the financial capital brought in. Financial capital and human capital must be given equal consideration. In any case, it makes no sense to first tax the profits from capital assets at a lower rate in order to then try to recoup the missing money for old-age provision through, for example, a wealth tax. It is better to let everyone take responsibility for their own old-age provision, as long as the basic needs are covered, of course. To ensure that the necessary funds are available, employees should participate in company profits in the same way as capital owners. This could be achieved with a different view of the financing and profit-making intentions of a company, as well as the value attributions of financial capital and human capital. Every firm, every company, needs both human capital and financial capital. Only human beings working solely with natural means can still generate profits without financial capital, but because of the now highly labour-divided economy, this is only possible to a limited extent and with an effort that is hardly manageable and a disproportionately low profit, if not a loss, in comparison. Therefore, in modern economic systems we need both financial capital and human capital. Towards harmonisation, a change in company law could help. If the pre-tax profit is divided equally between financial capital and human capital, the profit should also reach the working population through increased productivity and, in addition, pensions should be secured. All this should largely work without a money system like Safe Money, but with Safe Money all the conditions are in place to optimally accompany sustainable growth with sustainable finance. The Safe Money offers a clear concept with which, above all, circulatory systems in a monetary economy are easy to set up. Only the exchange into other currencies requires special arrangements.

A link back to local structures is particularly important. The lack of ties back to local markets is also sometimes the reason why development aid does not always have the desired effect. Autonomous cities, on land provided free of charge, could bring better results to light as focal points, not only in developing countries but also in the old industrial nations.

Whether a common currency like the euro offers better conditions for a sustainable financial economy from the outset is a question that can hardly be answered adequately. However, due to its special construction with a still non-uniform currency area, the EU could certainly officially allow other currencies in addition to the euro throughout the currency area. Much would be easier if, in addition to the euro as the common currency, a national currency and an international private currency such as NIM were accepted as means of payment in all EU states. In practice, credit cards could be offered in three currencies each, with the card having to be loaded in advance in the individual currencies.

A lack of capital can be decisive for a lack of success and thus for a failure to grow, especially when a company is being founded. But also, in the case of short-term changes in the market, the lack of capital can prevent a necessary expansion of production capacities and thus stop growth. Debt can even slow down growth abruptly and thus cause subsequent disintegration. In order to avoid destructive effects caused by excessive debt, provision has been made for debt relief in the context of insolvency in the case of liquidation of a company after insolvency. In the meantime, there is also private insolvency, unfortunately not yet state insolvency, which should be part of the political inventory as a matter of course, especially within alliances of states such as the EU. Without community-accepted, i.e., legally regulated, debt relief at all levels, the accumulation of debt will sooner or later destroy not only individual livelihoods but also the democratic state. An insolvency procedure to get economically weak members back on track could also be more important for the EU than launching the European Finance Minister. However, one should not forget the creditors, so that they do not have to file for insolvency as a consequence. A necessary debt relief for banks should be sufficiently secured within the framework of the current insolvency law but should also be possible for states within a community of states in a kind of indulgence, as was done in biblical times in so-called indulgence years.

Money must not be allowed to degenerate into a speculative object, but must help in the real world to measure real values, to preserve them and thus to act safely and to be able to classify them, i.e. to be able to deal with them in a purposeful and respectful manner; this not as a precedent under natural law, but as a social obligation, integrated again and again in a code supported by all in agreements to be negotiated anew each time. These agreements also include interest and the remuneration for services legitimately demanded with interest, even the permissible speculation with money. Therefore, the Hayek triangle can be used to show correlations between interest as a slope angle and the variables time and value added quite obviously. However, this triangle is not suitable as proof of the necessity of an interest-based monetary economy. The interpretation of the hypotenuse as a succession of points of performance could certainly also put the angle of inclination in a different light; we must see the increased performance here, which in the money market also correlates with higher interest rates, insofar as an interest rate has been agreed upon for this purpose. A new view of the Hayek triangle could even justify the reform of the monetary system, even one without interest. This also includes a reform of company law with the abolition of all forms of exclusion of liability, as well as the transfer of liability to legal persons. In the case of companies, under the new company law, total liability would then be assumed on the one hand by the capital owners in the amount of the capital invested, and on the other hand by the managers for the main part of the remaining liability. Further liability claims are to be covered primarily by insurance. As a transitional measure, a new type of company could be legally established, a company with distributed liability. Distributed liability or also divided liability can, for example, set a liability of 30% for the capital and the same 30% for the management and then a further 30% cover by insurance. The remaining 10% can be assumed by the contractual partner, usually the buyer. This means that the liability risk, and thus also the risk of loss, of the buyer is a maximum of 10%. Specifically, if a car worth 30,000 euros is purchased new, the risk for the buyer is a maximum of 3,000 euros.

In order to put states in a state in which they can fulfil all their tasks with their current revenues without incurring debt, a debt cut is also unavoidable for over-indebted states; insolvency proceedings should always be provided for at the state level if a state is heavily over-indebted, for example with more than 150% of the annual GDP. The insolvency procedure for states should be seen as the possibility to get out of debt within 20 years. It will become clear that the state can meet all its obligations on its own even without taking on debt. Private debt should be sufficiently securely contained by limiting it to half of one's lifetime income, and private insolvency should only be the very last step. It should always be possible to cover the remaining liability risk.

Those who continue to allow debts to grow instead of recognising the natural limitations and socially agreeing to the associated restrictions on credit, as well as finally establishing them in a democratic manner, are encouraging social suicide.

From this follow 5 demands regarding the monetary economy, with the realisation of which we can make lasting growth very likely.

The abolition of interest on borrowed money as the first demand, no future borrowing by the states as the second demand and the admission of free banks with safe money as the third demand, in addition a land reform as the fourth demand. Of particular importance is the fifth demand, the demand for a paradigm shift in tax law! In a global economic order, we no longer need substantial taxes. The digital tax is a step in the right direction, as it is a tax on profits, but the isolated solution it represents should be rejected!

We need stable money without interest charges and a free economy in regional autonomy in the local market with state bodies that do not lay claim to ownership of local companies, but instead finance themselves from the rental income from land ownership and continue to levy only profit taxes, i.e., no more coffee tax or champagne tax. An economy organised in this way can confidently look forward to a future that will still make this world worth living in for our grandchildren. To It is also important to note the shift from a value-based to an action-based economy. Actions can always be clearly and precisely determined regarding the profits achieved, whereas the valuations in the value orientation sometimes even change extremely over time. In many cases, an evaluation can even only be carried out retrospectively based on the profits achieved.

With these demands and insights, not all problems can be solved, but the course can be set for a world with more justice and less social tension.

Unfortunately, contrary to all common sense, debt is being driven ever higher without seeing or even guessing the end of the line. Rainer Hank and Georg Meck explicitly point to the rapid increase in debt in recent decades and especially to the dangers of the rise in interest rates that will be necessary in the future. "One step towards the cliff is the interest rate, which the central banks will have to (…) raise again sooner or later." Now, however, in the summer of 2019, there can be no talk of this yet, as the ECB is discussing loosening monetary policy even further and buying up shares as well as bonds. The controversy on monetary policy is overlaid by that on fiscal policy, whether new debt should not be used to stimulate the economy, especially in southern Europe, in order to eliminate the extreme youth unemployment in these EU countries. The question of whether or not the economy can be restarted with borrowed money continues to be controversial.

All Berkley scholars cited by Bernauer agree that no debts, or only small debts, should be incurred in the good times, i.e., debts should only be accepted in bad times. There is, one could say, still a lack of reliable empirical data for clarification. The easily obtainable data on gross domestic product are not sufficient but are perhaps only used again and again because they are easy to obtain and not because of their relevance. An alternative approach is that of Samans, who includes not only money flows in his index, but also sensitivities and quality of life. However, the fact that many statistical variables are included in the index makes the whole thing very complex and complicated, and difficult to interpret. That is why I would like to propose here to develop a measure of efficiency that focuses on the effectiveness of work performance. Machines and robots are increasingly shortening the labour time that must be spent to produce a product, which means that productivity is increasing. Therefore, a measure of productivity should be found as productivity growth, which can replace GDP. If one understands economic growth as productivity growth in relation to the labour and capital employed with a fixed amount of information, then one could also make the productivity of individual firms, individual economic sectors, individual economies comparatively transparent in relation to each other with an appropriate formula.

An attempt to achieve this using GDP alone cannot really succeed, since GDP is defined purely in terms of money flows and money quantities. In principle, Ludwig Erhard already saw this correctly, which is why for him production in the various economic sectors was in the foreground as a measure, and indeed, this is perhaps how the unerring political control of the post-war economy can be understood, which then contributed to the German economic miracle. To understand Ludwig Erhard now also means to understand his ordoliberal approach, following the Freiburg school to understand. Even if times are not the same, even in the age of Industry 4, ordoliberal thinking could clarify economic actions and decisions and feeding them into a theoretical edifice. This can succeed with a new educational offensive that helps to meet the ever-increasing demands of everyday working life. Decision-makers and educators in the education and training system, are therefore challenged more than ever to increase the prosperity of all through their efforts.

Schools should be strengthened in the STEM subjects, but also provide a basic knowledge of the processes and social agreements in the economic sphere. Knowledge of monetary economics and finance should be part of the basic teaching content in our schools. To explain the educational canon in more detail would go beyond the scope of this book; the educational system will therefore be examined in more detail in a subsequent volume as part of an information network.

Since education with its educational institutions such as schools and universities, but also in state training centres and vocational schools, is part of an information network designed for education, it should be pointed out here that all networks facilitating coexistence must in principle be financed by the public sector. However, a re-financing of all money spent on networks through contributions and fees is certainly to be discussed and not excluded. Growth is not prevented by this, at most it is slowed down and integrated into the normality of growth and decay. Growth can also be represented in economic contexts with the familiar logistic growth curves, if we assume productivity increases in very specific areas of a very specific company, the familiar S-curves should also appear here.

A subdued initial phase is followed by an exponential growth phase, which then flattens out and runs out into an asymptote to the capacity limit. If the capacity limit is exceeded in the longer term, a discontinuation and then the transition to the phase of decay is to be expected. If the capacity limits change over a longer period, growth may well adapt to this.

Moreover, growth is not considered relationally enough in economic and social contexts. The GDP of an economy grows even without special innovations and without an increase in per capita growth if the population grows. If the population declines, a correspondingly lower GDP is to be expected. Conversely, a falling GDP value with a falling population will not necessarily indicate a poor economy with lower per capita growth. Such false conclusions become even more problematic if the GDP also declines because more and more companies are working with less and less financial capital, but even more with invisible intellectual capital.

In a future in which money no longer plays the role it did in the past, in such a world, the function of money and capital, which is important for growth, could become less and less important, but information, knowledge, could become the most important factor for further growth. The possession of material assets will probably also no longer be as important in the future as it is today, without therefore disappearing completely from the scene.

BIBLIOGRAPHY

Auerbach, A. J. (August 2017). Fiscal Stimulus and Fiscal Sustainability (manuscript for the monetary policy meeting *in Jackson Hole)*. https//www.kansascityfed.org/~/media/files/publicat/sympos/2017/auerbach-gorodnichenko-paper.pdf.

Baumgart, Michael (2009). Cradle to Cradle: Remaking the Way We Make Things. Vintage (ISBN 978-0-09-953547-8).

Beck, H. (2018). Geld verdirbt den Charakter. *FAZ (Frankfurter Allgemeine Zeitung)*, 39.

Beeger, B. (2018 [20.März]). Banden greifen HartzIV-Leistungen ab. *FAZ plus*, 1. Artikel unter Alles aus der Wirtschaft.

Bernau, P. (2017 [Oktober Nr. 42]). Lehren aus der Finanzkrise. *FAS (Frankfurter Allgemeine Sonntagszeitung)*, 24, Wirtschaft.

Bertalanffy, L.v. (1977). *Biophysik des Fließgleichgewichts*. Berlin: Akademieverlag.

Braun, B. (2018). Wie kommt das Geld in die Welt? *FAZ*, 35.

dc. Berlin, 25. Oktober (2017). Tricks und Tücken der Sozialstatistik. *FAZ*, 16.

de.m.wikipedia.org. (2017).

dmoh. (2017, 11. November). Gesetzlicher Rahmen für Green Bonds gefordert. *FAZ*, 31.

Emich, B. (2018 [23. Dezember]). Zinsen vom Papst. *FAS*, 34.

epd. (2018). Alternativen zu Hartz IV. *FAZ*, 2 (Politik, 27. März).

Erhard, L. (2009 [Originalausgabe 1957 im Econ Verlag]). *Wohlstand für Alle*. Köln: Anaconda Verlag GmbH.

Eucken, W. (1990). *Grundsätze der Wirtschaftspolitik*. Tübingen (Stuttgart: J.C.B. Mohr (Paul Siebeck) Herausgeber: Edith Eucken und K. Paul Hensel (UTB).

F.A. Hayek (1978). *Denationalisation of Money*. London.

F.A. Hayek (2001). *Freie Währungswahl: eine Methode, die Inflation zu stoppen*, in: *Aufsätze zur Wirtschaftspolitik*. Tübingen (London): Hayek, writings, A6, S. 146.

F.A. Hayek. (2011[1937]). *Monetärer Nationalismus und internationale Stabilität (Monetary Nationalism and International Stability)*,Tübingen (London, New York, Toronto): F.A

Hayek und das Walter Eucken Institute (Publications of the Graduate Institute of International Studies, Geneva, Nr. 18).

Feder, G. (2013 [1919, Heft 1]). *Das Manifest zur Brechung der Zinsknechtschaft*. Neustadt an der Orla: Arnshaugk Verlag.

fne Frankfurt, 11. Dezember (2017). Ein neues Zeitalter für Digitalwährungen. *Frankfurter Allgemeine*, 15 (Nr. 288).

Friedman, M. (11. Auflage, Dezember 2016 [1. Auflage 2004; c.1962, 1982]). *Kapitalismus und Freiheit (Capitalism and Freedom)*. München, Berlin: Piper (The University of Chicago).

Fukuyama, F. (2018). *Identity*. London: Profile Books.

Geldtheorie, O. I. (2017). *Wikipedia*. Von Seigniorage und Monetäre Seigniorage: www.de.m.wikipedia.örg abgerufen.

Gesell, S. (2015 [1919]). *Die Natürliche Wirtschaftsordnung durch Freiland und Freigeld*. London (Arnstadt i. Thür.): Dalton House Reprint (Forgotten Books).

Graeber, D. (2011). *Debt The first 5000 years*. New York: Goldmann.

Grazzini, E. (25. Juli 2018). *Social Europe*. socialeurope.eu.

Hank, R. (2017). GemeinWOHL. *Frankfurter Sonntagszeitung Wirtschaft*, 22.

Haskel, J. A. (2018). *Capitalism without capital*. Princeton & Oxford: Princeton University Press.

Hayek, F. (2011). Entnationalisierung des Geldes. In F.A. Hayek, *Entnationalisierung des Geldes*. Tübingen: Mohr Siebeck.

Hayek, F. (2011). *Entnationalisierung des Geldes*. Tübingen: Mohr Siebeck.

Hayek, F. A. (2011). *Entnationalisierung des Geldes –Gesammelte Schriften Volume 3*. Tübingen: Mohr Siebeck (Hrsg.: Alfred Bosch, Manfred E. Streit, Viktor Vanberg, Reinhold Veit).

hmk/tp. (2018). Turbulenzen in Griechenland – Bad Bank im Gespräch. *FAZ*, 17 (Nr. 231 vom 5. Oktober).

Höffe, O. (2017, 4. September). Der bestialische Ursprung des Geldes. *FAS,* 35.

hw/mas. (2018 [Mittwoch, 11. April]). Scholz: Keine Steuererhöhung für Mieter und Eigentümer. *FAZ,* 15.

hw/mas. (11. April 2018). Scholz verspricht Reform der Grundsteuer ohne Mehrbelastung. *FAZ*, Titelseite.

James C. Scott, a.m. (2019). *Die Mühlen der Zivilisation*. Berlin: Suhrkamp.

K. Schneider, E.S. (2018). Das Ende des Bargelds. *Handelsblatt*, 58 ff.

Kennedy, M. (2006 [9. Auflage]). *Geld ohne Zinsen und Inflation, Ein Tauschmittel, das jedem dient*. München: Goldmann.

Keynes, J. M. (1974, translation by Fritz Waeger). *Allgemeine Theorie der Beschäftigung, des Zinses und des Geldes*. Berlin: Duncker & Humboldt.

Kleber, Will (VEB, Berlin 1976) Einführung in die Kristallographie.

Klemm, T. (2018). Bewunderte Bankräuber. *FAS (Nr. 34)*,

Kloepfer, I. (2017). Inflation. 28, Wirtschaft.

Kloft, M. (28.19.2017). *FAZ NET,* Finanzen.

Kowalski, J. D. (2018). Entnationalisierung durch die Brieftasche? *FAZ*, 18.

Kremer, D. (2018). Geld regiert die Welt. *FAZ*, 37.

Mäkeler, J. H. (2018). Kleines Geld, große Probleme. *FAS*, 38.

Martin, F. (2015). *Money*. New York (London): Vintage Books. A division of Random House LLC.

Marx, K. (1872). *Das Kapital. Kritik der politischen Ökonomie*. Hamburg: Verlag von Otto Meissner.

Mayer, T. (2018 [1. April]). Geldexperimente von gestern. *FAS*, 36 (Wie geht es der Weltwirtschaft, Herr Mayer?).

Mayer, T. (2018). Das Versagen der Ökonomen. *FAS*, 39 (11. Mai, Nr. 19).

Mayer, T. (2019, 22 [2. Juni]). Facebooks neue Weltwährung. *FAS*, 29.

Mayer, T. (3. aktualisierte Auflage 2015 [2014]). *Die neue Ordnung des Geldes*. München: FBV (Finanzbuch Verlag).

McMillan, J. (2018). Digitalgeld. *FAS*, 34, Geld und Mehr.

Meck, R. H. (2018). Die Last der Schulden. *FAS*, 23 (Nr. 11 vom 18. März 2018).

Miller, M. (2017). *Die Welt vor dem Geldinfarkt*. München: FBV (Finanzbuch Verlag).

Möltgen, H. M. (2017). *Dauerhaftes Wachstum*. Bad Honnef: Eigenverlag (epubli).

Möltgen, H.M. Wert Faktor *Wissen, Bildung und das Bildungskapital.* Troisdorf – Bergheim, Bonn: noch nicht publiziertes Manuskript.

Möltgen, H.M. (1978). *Die soziale Lage der Studenten an der pädagogischen Fakultät in den 80er Jahren.* Köln: Universität Köln. Seminararbeit

NN. (2018 [Sa. 24. März]). "Der größte Vergütungsunfug passiert im Dunklen". *FAZ, Unternehmen.*

o. A. (2018 [20. März]). Suche nach Wegen aus dem Hartz-IV-System. *FAZ,* 7 (Nr. 67).

Oberhuber, N. (2018). Das Geld hat viele Namen. *FAZ,* 31.

Pernicka, E. (2019). Am Anfang stand der Steuereintreiber. *FAZ Nr. 178, Literatur und Sachbuch, 3. August),* 10.

Piketty, T. (2014). *Das Kapital im 21. Jahrhundert.* München: Beck.(Le Capital aux xxe siecle Seuil Septembre 2013, Les Livres de Nouveau Monde)

Reinhart, C.M. (May 2010). Growth in a Time of Debt. American Economic Review S. 573-578.

Rifkin, J. (2014). *Die dritte industrielle Revolution.* Frankfurt am Main: Fischer Verlag.

Rifkin, J. (2014). *Die Null-Grenzkosten-Gesellschaft: Das Internet der Dinge (The Zero Marginal Cost Society).* Frankfurt/New York: Campus.

Romer, C.D. (October 2017). Why some times are different: *Macroeconomic Policy and the Aftermath of Financial Crisis.* NBER Working Paper 23931.

Samans, R. (06.03.2018). A new way to measure growth and development: The Inclusive Development Index. VOX, CEPR Policy Portal, Schweiz.

Schäfers, M. (2019 (1. August)). Eine teure Rechnung für Finanzminister Scholz. *FAZ, Wirtschaft,* 19.

schio. (2006, 25.Dezember). Silvio Gesell und die Freiwirtschaftstheorie. tamtamvienna.com.

Schön, W. (2018). Der digitale Steuer-Irrweg. *FAZ,* 16 (Nr. 80, 6.April).

Sinn, H. W. (2018). Fast 1.000 Milliarden Euro. *FAZ,* 16.

Sinn, H.-W. (17. Juli 2018). *hanswernersinn.de 2018.*

Smith, A. (1776). *Wohlstand der Nationen Eine Untersuchung seiner Natur und seiner Ursachen (An Inquiry into the Nature and Causes of the Wealth of Nations).* München (London): IDION-Verlag.

Stiglitz, J.E. (13. Juni 2018). *PS Projekt Syndikat.* project-syndicate.org

Südekum, M.H. (14. April 2019). *Die Schuldenbremse ist nicht zeitgemäß.* Von http://sueddeutsche.de/wirtschaftsforum-die-schulden... abgerufen.

Thorwaldsson, K.P. (15. January 2018). Sweden's secret to keeping wages. Davos The World Economic Forum, Schweiz.

Varoufakis, Y. (2008). *Time for Change.* Herder; (audible).

Venezuelas Elend. (2018). *FAZ,* 28.

Wagenknecht, S. (2012). *Reichtum ohne Gier (Hörbuch* audible).

Wendorff, K. (2018). Rom sollte Italiener zur Solidarität verpflichten. *FAZ,* 24.

Weyerstrass, K. (2018). *How to Boost Productivity in the EU.* München: ifo Institute München: EconPol Policy.

Wiebe, F. (2018 [29.10.]). Gefährliches Urteil gegen die BafinBitcoin-Börsen dürfen ohne Genehmigung gegründet werden. *Handelsblatt,* 1 ff.

Wikipedia (11/2018). *htttps://de.wikipedia.org>wiki>mammon.* Von Mammon: https://de.wikipedia.org abgerufen.

The author

The author studied biology, chemistry, philosophy, psychology and sociology. In terms of academic degrees, he first obtained the state examination in biology and chemistry, then passed the pre-diploma examination in sociology and subsequently passed the viva voce examination for his dissertation in biology didactics with pedagogy and psychology as minor subjects.

After many years of work in the school service, he still ran a restaurant with wine trade and events in the cultural segment in his retirement. The contacts and conversations with artists, musicians and literary figures were a particular benefit during this time. Now that this phase is also over, there is time to take up sociological-ecological approaches from his student days again and expand them in the direction of a sociologically and psychologically underpinned economic theory in order to put them into writing for discourse.

novum PUBLISHER FOR NEW AUTHORS

The publisher

> *He who stops getting better stops being good.*

This is the motto of novum publishing, and our focus is on finding new manuscripts, publishing them and offering long-term support to the authors.
Our publishing house was founded in 1997, and since then it has become THE expert for new authors and has won numerous awards.

Our editorial team will peruse each manuscript within a few weeks free of charge and without obligation.

You will find more information about
novum publishing and our books on the internet:

www.novumpublishing.com